THE HISTORY OF ASSAM

THE HISTORY OF ASSAM
FROM YANDABO TO PARTITION
1826–1947

Priyam Goswami

Orient BlackSwan

For Ahan, Arav, Ayaan and Kabir

THE HISTORY OF ASSAM: FROM YANDABO TO PARTITION 1826–1947

ORIENT BLACKSWAN PRIVATE LIMITED

Registered Office
3-6-752 Himayatnagar, Hyderabad 500 029, Telangana, INDIA
e-mail: centraloffice@orientblackswan.com

Other Offices
Bengaluru, Chennai, Guwahati, Hyderabad, Kolkata,
Mumbai, New Delhi, Noida, Patna

First published 2012
Reprinted 2013, 2014, 2016, 2017, 2018, (twice), 2019, 2020, 2021, 2022, 2023, 2025

ISBN 978-81-250-4653-0

Laser typeset in Adobe Jenson Pro 11/13
by RECTO Graphics, Delhi

Maps cartographed by
The Agricultural Development Commercial Credit and Industrial Investment Company Private Limited, Hyderabad 500 029

Printed in India at
B.B. Press, Tronica City, Ghaziabad, U.P. 201 103

040899

Published by
Orient Blackswan Private Limited
3-6-752 Himayatnagar, Hyderabad 500 029, Telangana, INDIA
e-mail: info@orientblackswan.com

The following are applicable for the maps in this book:

The responsibility for the correctness of the internal details rests with the publisher.
The territorial waters of India extend into the sea to a distance of twelve nautical miles measured from the appropriate base line.
The external boundaries and coastlines of India agree with the Record/Master Copy certified by the Survey of India.
The spellings of names in the maps have been taken from various sources.

Contents

Maps, Figures and Tables

MAPS

FIGURES

TABLES

Preface

This book deals with the polity, society and economy of colonial Assam from 1826 to 1947. Although, it has been primarily written keeping students in mind, I hope this book, with its extensive bibliography, notes and references will prove to be an engaging read through the history of this period, for all those interested in its study.

Though there are innumerable studies on multiple aspects pertaining to this period, many of these are research oriented and detailed micro-studies. I have made an attempt in this text to present the history of colonial Assam in a comprehensive and lucid manner, so as to trigger the readers' interest and curiosity. I shall consider my purpose served if the book is able to generate new ideas and questions in their minds.

The book has evolved from my research on the society and economy of colonial Assam and from the discussions and interactions that I have had with my students, throughout my teaching career. I hope that I have succeeded, even if only partially, in providing a cohesive and critical analysis of this period. Post Independence, the names of certain places have changed, for instance Gauhati is now known as Guwahati, Sibsagar as Sivasagar and Nowgong as Nagaon. For the purpose of clarity, the earlier names have been used in this text.

I owe a great deal to my students who inspired me to write this book, several of my friends and colleagues for their valuable suggestions, and my family for their constant support. I am also grateful to Orient Blackswan for taking the initiative in publishing this work.

Guwahati **Priyam Goswami**
April 2012

Preface

[illegible]

Introduction

The annexation of Assam by the British bound her fate almost instantly with that of the other regions of the East India Company's domains in India. The transition from the old order to the new was swift and was characterised by a complete overhauling of the administrative machinery which brought about far reaching political, economic and social changes in Assam.

The Treaty of Yandabo (1826), which was signed at the end of the first Anglo-Burmese War (1824–6), marked the beginning of British colonial penetration into northeast India. Under the terms of the treaty, the King of Burma renounced his claim on Assam and the contiguous petty states of Cachar and Jayantia. The withdrawal of the Burmese provided the British with the opportunity to create spheres of influence in the region. In the decade before the war, the insecurity on the northeastern frontier had threatened the security of Bengal and it had, therefore, become imperative to ensure that the region did not relapse into further anarchy. Apprehensions of a renewed Burmese invasion loomed large and so, despite their earlier pledge that they would return once law and order had been restored, the British decided to stay on. Initial considerations of strategy, however, soon gave way to larger economic ones. Surveys and explorations conducted by a band of intrepid explorers and surveyors in the meantime had revealed the enormous economic potential of the region. This fitted in neatly with the British search for overseas markets. Nineteenth century England had seen a change from the phase of merchant capitalism to industrial capitalism, where emphasis shifted from revenue collection and trade to new forms of surplus appropriation. As European trade diminished, the vacuum was sought to be filled by the development of trade with China, Tibet and Burma. It was hoped that Assam would not only serve as a forwarding agency but also as a rich hinterland of Bengal as well. British commercial enterprises were enthusiastic at the prospect of getting thousands of new customers for their industrial products.

The annexation of Lower Assam in 1828 provided the British with a firm foothold that enabled them to extend their suzerainty in the region very quickly. Within a decade, the entire Brahmaputra Valley and the neighbouring principalities of Cachar and Jayantia and the Khasi Hills were subdued. The control of the routes to Bhutan, Tibet, China and Burma followed soon after. Meanwhile, R. B. Pemberton, in his lengthy *Report on the Eastern Frontier of British India* (1835), had given details of military and commercial routes that connected Bengal with Bhutan, Tibet, Sikkim, China and Burma through northeast India. The fond hope of extension of commerce to Tibet and China found expression in the words of Jenkins, Agent to the Governor-General, Northeast Frontier, when he wrote:

> There is every prospect of bringing all the races of hillmen bordering on this province under the same control as our Assamese subjects and at no distant period of opening out, through them, a direct route with the Tibetan and Chinese province from which we are divided by narrow ranges of hills but from which we are absolutely shut out by the intractable rudeness of intervening mountaineers.

With these high expectations, the Company embarked upon a determined process of penetration into a region that had remained practically isolated from the rest of the country for centuries. By the end of the nineteenth century, the Lushai Hills, the Naga Hills, the Garo Hills and the adjoining areas were also brought under British control. Colonial penetration into Assam and the neighbouring hill areas was accompanied by sweeping political, economic and social changes resulting in a spectacular transformation of the region within a very short time. Many of the changes were positive when seen in isolation, but when viewed in the overall colonial framework, it is apparent that they were part of the general process of underdevelopment. The former autonomy of the villages was eroded and indigenous crafts declined; the introduction of a monetary economy and systematic revenue maximisation led to escalating poverty while industrialisation resulted in dramatic demographic changes. Along with all these changes, came improvements in the transportation and communication network which broke down the isolation of the province, both physically and metaphorically, and opened her up to new forces, ideas and thoughts. The cumulative impact of all these was immense and far-reaching.

In any agricultural economy, progress in the agricultural sector must be concurrent with industrial growth if overall economic development is to happen. In Assam, industrial growth and development had no links with the agricultural sector. Many of the village industries had died out under pressure from new forces, and the organisation of those that survived still remained very primitive. The position of the artisan with respect to capital or the fact that he also cultivated some land underwent no change. The worst effect of this decline in traditional crafts and the failure of new industries to take their place was that the economy of the province came under foreign domination. The tea plantations, coal mines, oil refineries and railways all undoubtedly implied significant changes; but viewed in its full spectrum, the development transformed the province into a raw material producing and capital absorbing region. This lead to stagnation in agriculture, suppression of local industry and economic domination over the region by outsiders. The superimposition of the colonial economy on the traditional rural economy had its impact on the growth of urban centres as well. A distinct feature of industrialisation is the emergence of satellite towns in and around industrial areas. In Assam, industrialisation did not create links within the region. The tea, coal and oil industries procured all their requirements directly from Calcutta and had virtually no links with the surrounding areas, thereby sapping all possibilities of the growth of urban centres. In fact, even as late as 1941, the urban population of Assam was less than four percent of the total population of the province. Improved communication networks facilitated the active penetration of foreign consumer products in the local markets. Hence, the new townships that emerged were due more to the growth of commerce than that of industry and an important factor that determined the growth of an urban area was the construction of a road or a railway line in its vicinity. As the local economy was restructured and the control of the government on the land and resources solidly entrenched, Assam was systematically grafted into the scheme of colonial extraction and domination where enclaves of prosperity existed amidst a stagnant economy.

Colonial rule in Assam triggered a series of sweeping changes, not only in its polity and economy, but in society and culture as well. The British had brought along with them new institutions, knowledge, ideas, technology, beliefs and values. Within a few years of their occupation of Assam, they had laid the foundations of a modern state by surveying land, settling the revenue, creating a bureaucracy of officials, codifying the law and instituting law courts, introducing

Western education, establishing industries and a communication network, thereby opening her up to the outside world. In this setting, the activities of the American Baptist missionaries and the Bengal Renaissance had a profound impact on Assamese society. As the nineteenth century progressed, the changes became more and more perceptible. By the middle of the nineteenth century, they were distinctly visible. With improved means of communication and with hopes of greater employment opportunities, students began to leave for Calcutta for higher education. In Calcutta, they came into contact with the liberal ideas of the West which they enthusiastically grasped and brought back with them when they returned home. These youth, educated in English and imbued with 'modern' ideas, started the process of change in Assam. A wide variety of important issues were discussed and debated upon by the emerging intelligentsia and in the process, ideas and attitudes underwent a profound change. In course of time these ideas filtered down to the common man and although illiteracy was still rampant, the gradual infiltration of radical ideas instilled in the minds of the people a spirit of rational enquiry. There was a growing demand for social reforms and the eradication of certain social evils. A small section of the provincial population emerged to form the provincial elite, and it was this vocal group that took upon itself the task of organising public opinion. The emergence of the press and modern Assamese literature helped in the dissemination of ideas and information and this in turn resulted in the growth of a political awareness which found expression in the formation of a number of socio-political organisations.

Although there was a strong regional identity, no voice was raised for Assam's identity as wholly independent of the Indian one. Late nineteenth century Assamese literature had already created a framework alluding to the rightful place of Assam within India and *Sonar Asom* (Golden Assam) was never conceived as being outside *Bharat Varsha*. But the educated elite felt it necessary to infuse ideas of regional consciousness before they could begin thinking in terms of the larger Indian consciousness. Authors like Tillottoma Misra, (*Literature and Society in Assam*), Benudhar Rajkhowa (*Mor Jivan Dapon*), and Haliram Dhekiyal Phukan (*Assam Buranji*) etc., have written about it. Hence, the focal point of intellectual discussions of the time was the question of the existence of Assam as a distinct cultural, religious and linguistic entity, and until the beginning of the twentieth century, the predominant concerns of the people were those relating to regional issues The high rates of taxes, the question of immigration, the condition of the tea garden labourers and the language question were some of the major causes of apprehension.

The government's economic policies, in particular, had adversely affected the people and the peasantry had been reduced to penury. In course of time rural poverty became so acute that every assessment of land revenue raised a storm of protest. Attempts were made at the grassroots level to collectively resist the government's policy of upward revision of revenue. The *ryots* convened *mels* to give vent to their discontent. The mels, under the leadership of *gosains*, *dolois* or other influential people, were originally constituted as authorities on socio-religious matters. But gradually their base was broadened and was converted to *raijmels* or popular assemblies, for the redressal of all grievances. The popular raijmels were soon converted into more representative and more broad-based organisations. Known as *ryot sabhas*, they were formed with the active support of the Assamese intelligentsia. The emerging intelligentsia, however, was not in favour of the aggressive policy hitherto followed by the raijmels. Instead, it advocated constitutional agitation through prayers, petitions, memorials and public meetings and believed that only through such means could political awareness among the people be aroused. Thus, the ryot sabhas which followed were more leadership oriented unlike the raijmels where popular sentiment had dominated.

Newspapers and public associations also made their appearance simultaneously. These organisations advocated social reform, inspired the youth of the province to qualify themselves for higher positions, and worked for the all round progress of the society. The scope of their activities was broadened by the creation of the enlarged province of Assam in 1874 and soon after, began to develop political overtones. Jorhat emerged as the centre of activity. The *Jorhat Sarbajanik Sabha* was founded in 1884 under the initiative of Jagannath Barua. Like most other organisations of the time, the Sabha did not believe in direct confrontation with the government, but nevertheless espoused the cause of the people even at the risk of displeasing the government at times. The Sabha contributed significantly to social and political awakening in Assam and paved the way for democratic and popular movements in the province. Although its focus was on the particular needs of the province, it was able to establish strong links with pan-Indian aspirations. In fact, many of its members, including Debicharan Barua and Lakshminath Bezbaruah, attended the annual sessions of the Indian National Congress as delegates. However, after Jagannath Barua's death in April 1907, the differences of opinion between the members of the organisation widened and resulted in a virtual termination of its activities.

For some time the Assamese intelligentsia, led by Manik Chandra Baruah, had increasingly felt the necessity of a more broad based provincial organisation to articulate the wishes, grievances and aspirations of the Assamese people. The Assam Association was formed keeping these objectives in mind. The Association played a significant role in serving as the mouthpiece of the people of the Brahmaputra Valley during the first two decades of the twentieth century. Although the Association had been initially formed to focus on regional issues and to press for regional demands, it gradually merged into India's mainstream politics. Like the Brahmaputra Valley, the Surma Valley, comprising of the districts of Cachar and Sylhet, was also very active politically.

The end of the nineteenth century and the beginning of the next thus saw a new awakening in the province. The common bonds established by British rule, a uniform administrative set up, improved means of communication, the impact of Western thoughts and ideas and above all, shared discrimination and frustration at every step, induced the people of the region to look beyond the provincial boundaries and establish a commonality of purpose with mainstream India. The Indian National Congress provided the common forum. It was in this backdrop that Assamese nationalism merged with mainstream Indian nationalism while maintaining a distinct Assamese identity.

The *Swadeshi* agitation, the Home Rule Movement, revolutionary activities, contemporary world events and the stirring speeches of nationalist leaders like Gopal Krishna Gokhale, Bal Gangadhar Tilak and Bipin Chandra Pal, all combined to create a new awareness among the youth. Students in Assam translated this awareness into action by creating a platform for concerted action on matters of regional and national interest. The Assam Students' Conference, founded in 1916, though not a political organisation, helped to create a cadre of student leaders who actively participated in the national movement that followed.

The Assam Association had been following the political developments in the country avidly but for most people the concept of *swaraj* was still vague and incomprehensible. The seventeenth session of the Assam Association held at Tezpur in December 1920, endorsed the Indian National Congress' August 1920 resolution on non-cooperation and stated that the object of the Assam Association was to work for the attainment of swaraj. This was symbolically reflected in the merger of the Assam Association with the Assam Provincial Congress Committee in 1921. From then onwards, Assam identified itself completely with the national movement. As in other provinces, in Assam too popular response to the repressive measures was massive and ordinances were defied openly even at the cost of severe repression.

With a large number of men behind the bars, women came out in thousands defying prohibitory orders to demonstrate their solidarity with the freedom struggle. Women's power had been strengthened in the meantime by the organisational activities carried out during the preceding years of the movement and the formation of the *Mahila Samities*. The Government of India Act 1935 inaugurated electoral politics in Assam. In the elections of 1937, the Congress under the leadership of Gopinath Bardoloi emerged as the single largest party. But the Congress decision to not form a government led to the formation of a coalition government under Sir Syed Mohammed Saadullah, the leader of the Muslim group in the Brahmaputra Valley. The subsequent fall of the Saadullah ministry in September 1938 led to the formation of the first ministry of Gopinath Bardoloi. Briefly, the entire decade was one of political instability in the province.

Assam was profoundly affected by the Quit India Movement. It had a strong popular base and attempts were made at several places to form parallel governments. Jinnah's demand for the inclusion of Assam in Pakistan was strongly resisted by the people of Assam and it was in this backdrop that the Assam Provincial Congress emphatically protested against the Grouping Plan of the Cabinet Mission Plan (1946). With the acceptance of the Mountbatten Plan, the anti-grouping movement in Assam came to an end. The focus of political activity now shifted to Sylhet where the referendum was held on 6 and 7 July 1947. The creation of East Pakistan left Assam virtually isolated, being connected with the rest of India by the narrow Siliguri Corridor. With Independence, came new challenges of fighting the colonial legacy of under-development, facilitating economic development and bringing about social reform. In Assam, an additional problem has been that of immigration. Partition set in motion forces whose impact is felt even today. The northeastern region of India is home to a large number of tribal communities.

Table 1 shows the major geographical areas under discussion in the book and their position in modern India. It also gives the names of the major tribes that inhabit these areas.

Table 1: Major Geographical Areas and Tribes

Area	Names of major Tribes
Khasi Hills (Now in Meghalaya)	Khasi-Bhoi, Lynngam, War
Jayantia Hills (Now in Meghalaya)	Pnar, Bhoi, Khynriam, War
Garo Hills (Now in Meghalaya)	Awe, Chisak, Matchi, Dual, Metabeng, Atong, Chibok, Ruga, Ganching, Megham, Dussani, Cheani, Rabhas, Koch, Rajbongsi, Dalu, Mech, Hajong
Lushai Hills (Now Mizoram)	Chakma, Pawi, Ralte, Kuki, Dulien, Ralte, Poi, Jahao, Pankhup, Lakher, Paite, Falam, Tangur, Khuangli, Dalang, Sukte, Fanai, Leillul, Mar
Naga Hills (Now Nagaland)	Angami, Ao, Chakhesang, Chang, Khemungan, Konyak, Lotha, Phom, Pochury, Rengma, Sangtam, Sema, Yimchunger, Zeliang
North East Frontier Tracts (Now Arunachal Pradesh)	Abors(Adis), Apatani, Bugun,, Galo, Daflas (Nyishis), Akas (Hrusso), Jingpho, Koro, Memba Meyor, Mishmis, Monpa, Nocte, Sherdukpen, Sajolang, Sartang, Tagin, Tai Khampti, Yobin
Assam	Bodo, Dimasa, Kachari, Karbi, Khamti, Khelma, Kuki, Hajong, Santal, Khamyang, Mising, Rabha, Singpho, Tiwa, Deori, Mech, Phake

1

Decline of the Ahoms and the Emergence of the British

Chapter Highlights

- Early British interest in Assam
- First Anglo-Burmese War (1824–6)
- Treaty of Yandabo
- Britain's colonial policy

THE AHOM RULE

Prior to British occupation and annexation in the early nineteenth century, the medieval kingdom of Assam had been under the Ahom kings for nearly six centuries. Under the leadership of Sukapha, a Tai prince, Ahom migrants from Upper Burma had crossed the Patkai Range and established a kingdom in the neighbourhood of modern Sivasagar (earlier called Sibsagar) in the early thirteenth century. By the end of the seventeenth century, they were the unchallenged masters of the entire Brahmaputra Valley, with many tributary chiefs and princes owing allegiance to them. During this period, the Ahoms had to fight and subdue many tribes. The Moran and Barahi tribes, whom they easily subdued, were assimilated with the Ahoms through marriage. During the following three centuries, the Ahoms brought under their effective control the more powerful Chutiyas and Kacharis and by 1536, they were supreme in Assam. The emergence of the Koches to the west of their territory checked the expansionist policy of the Ahoms to a considerable extent, but their most formidable adversaries in later centuries were the Mughals.

The monarchy's territorial limits extended from the Patkai hills in the east to the Manas river in the west, an area approximately 800 kilometres in length. It covered both the north and south banks of the Brahmaputra. On the north, it touched the territories of the Bhutia, Aka, Dafla, Miri, Mishmi and Singpho tribes whose habitat covered the area up to the foothills of the Himalayas, bordering Tibet. To the south of the Brahmaputra, the monarchy extended to the foot of the hills inhabited by the Nagas, beyond which lay the kingdoms of Manipur and Burma. Westward, on the southern border, were the principalities of the Khasis and Garos and the kingdoms of Cachar and Jayantia. While direct Ahom rule was confined to the Brahmaputra Valley, the monarchy's supremacy in the entire region was recognised in one form or another.

Assam remained virtually cut off from the rest of the world for a long time partly because of its geographical location, separated as it

Map 1.1: The Ahom Kingdom

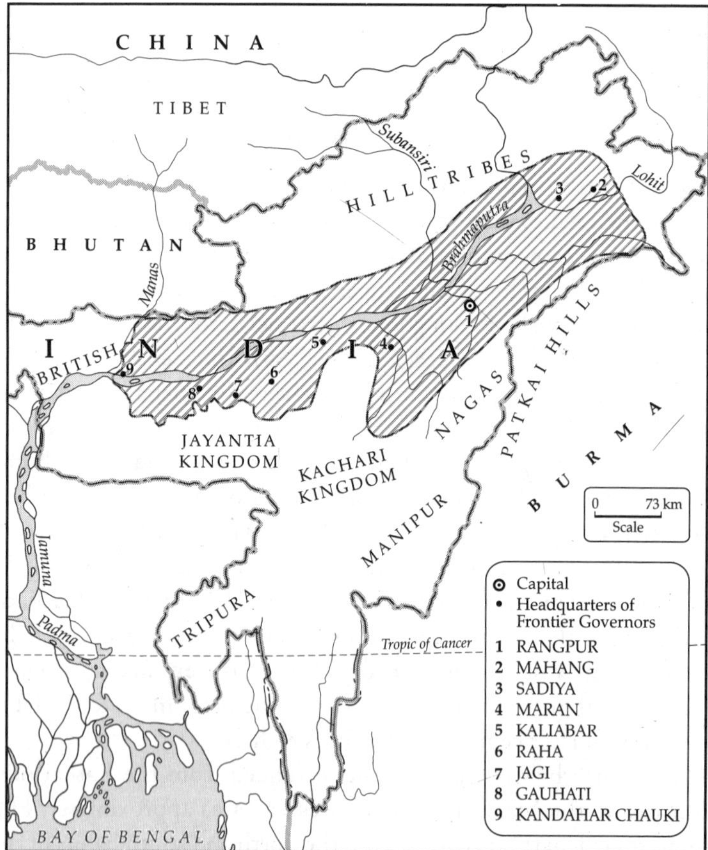

Source: Adapted from Dr I. S. Mumtaza, *The External Relations of the Ahom Rulers with Special Reference to the Diplomatic Exchanges*, Unpublished Ph.d thesis, Gauhati University.

was by numerous hills and rivers interspersed by deep valleys, and partly because of the deliberate Ahom policy of isolation. Most of the inhabitants settled along the fertile banks of the Brahmaputra or on the banks of its tributaries. These alluvial plains were bordered by a wilderness of tall grass beyond which lay the inhospitable and impenetrable jungles. The mode of transport was primitive, the only means of communication being by country boat, elephants or *palki*. Wheeled traffic was unknown and even the bullock car made its appearance only after the advent of the British. Under the circumstances, the Brahmaputra was the only highway that connected Assam to the rest of India. The journey to and from Assam was extremely long and tedious. The adverse climatic conditions were an additional problem.[1]

Ahom-Mughal Conflicts and Advent of the British

The history of seventeenth-century Assam is the history of Ahom-Mughal conflict. In 1662, during an invasion, Nawab Mir Jumla, the Mughal *subahdar* of Bengal, advanced as far as Garhgaon, the Ahom capital, and compelled the ruling king, Jayadhaj Singha, to cede the western part of the Ahom territory to the Mughals. However, in 1682, Gadadhar Singha (1681–95) recovered the lost territory and from then on Goalpara remained the frontier outpost of the Mughal dominion. Ahom power reached its zenith during the reign of Rudra Singha (1695–1714). In the years following his rule, the monarchy showed signs of decay. Weak and unscrupulous rulers occupied the throne and each succession became a scramble for power. Taking advantage of the situation, and provoked as they were by the Ahom rulers, the Moamarias, a socio-religious sect, rebelled in 1788. The *burgandazes*, marauders from Bengal, who ravaged and pillaged the adjoining villages of Kamrup, aggravated the situation. The royalists were overpowered and Gaurinath Singha, the reigning monarch, was deposed. Gaurinath was forced to flee from his capital to take shelter in Guwahati from where he sent frantic appeals to the British for help.

BRITISH INTEREST IN ASSAM

East India Company and Trade with the Ahom Kingdom

The acquisition of the *Diwani* of Bengal in 1765 brought the East India Company into direct contact with the Ahom kingdom. Prior to that, Major James Rennell, an official of the Company, had surveyed the frontier of Assam and collected information about the region.[2] He identified the Brahmaputra with the Tsangpo River. However, his efforts at gathering more information were cut short by the refusal of the Ahom government to grant him permission to enter the kingdom.[3] Subsequently, several Europeans had tried their luck in trade in Assam with varying fortunes. Interestingly, the majority of the early European merchants trading in Assam were army men. For instance, Colonel James Mill of the Ostend East India Company, Jean Baptiste Chevalier, Commander-in-Chief of the French settlements in Bengal, Paul Richard Pearkes, an officer in charge of the English settlements in Patna, were all actively involved in the Assam trade. Several others followed these officers and soon, many of the Company's employees in Bengal were engaged in the highly profitable trade. Matters came to a head when Mir Kasim, the Nawab of Bengal, complained to Vansittart, the Governor of Bengal, of losses amounting to over 40,000 rupees in the trade with Assam, Rangamati and Karaibari because of the monopoly that the Company's employees had over the whole of the trade.

Alarmed at the notorious corruption of the English officials in Bengal, the Court of Directors sent Robert Clive as Governor of Bengal for the second time with full powers to reform the abuses in the Company's administration. In 1765 Clive set up a Society of Trade to compensate the civil officers for the losses they sustained because of the restrictions he had imposed on the practice of private trade and the acceptance of presents. The Society was granted the monopoly of trade in salt, betel nut and tobacco. The profits were to be shared in predetermined proportions. It was suggested that the Committee of Trade should appoint certain European agents to transact business in different parts of the country. Of the 11 agents appointed in 1765, three were to reside in the district of Rangpur: Hugh Ballie in Goalpara, Tom Lewis in Rangpur town and Hargreave in Chilmari. It was soon apparent that there was no demand for betel nuts and tobacco from Bengal as these were locally grown in Assam. Hence, in 1767, the Society relinquished its trade in these two items and confined itself to salt which soon became the most important item of inland trade. Meanwhile, the overbearing attitude and the mode of functioning of the Society of Trade attracted the attention of the Court of Directors. Realising that the lucrative trade with Assam would eventually open up new markets for European commodities in the hills of northeast India, they decided to abolish the monopoly and open the trade to all persons. Thus, trade with Assam now acquired a new dimension and was viewed with renewed interest.

Increasing British Interest in the Region

In the initial years, the importance of Assam and the eastern Himalayan region was for its strategic location, as the region shared its border with Tibet and Burma. The British search for overseas markets has to be seen in the context of the economic condition of Europe in general and Britain in particular. Britain sought to encourage trade with Tibet and Burma. Of the two, trade with Tibet had added importance as it imported more than it exported, and the balance was made up in gold and silver. As long as the chiefs of the Newar dynasty ruled over the petty kingdoms of Kathmandu, Patan and Bhatgaon, trade flourished between India and Tibet. The conquest of the Newar state by the Gurkha ruler King Prithvi Narayan Shah in the second half of the eighteenth century disrupted the traditional trade between India and Tibet. He adopted a 'closed-door policy' with regard to the British. The East India Company desperately needed the gold from Tibet to finance its growing China trade. Hence, an alternative route to Tibet became an urgent necessity. They believed that such a route might be possible via Assam.

Political instability in Assam, however, was not at all conducive to economic activities. When Gaurinath Singha appealed to the British for help in 1788, Lord Cornwallis, the Governor-General, was not inclined to involve the Company in the internal affairs of a frontier kingdom especially at a time when Mysore was engaging his attention. Moreover, he felt morally bound by the directives of the Pitt's India Act that had been passed in 1784.[4] The collector of Rangpur and the commissioner of Cooch Behar, however, emphatically pointed out the adverse effects that the disturbances had on the prosperous Assam-Bengal trade and the strong possibility of the anarchy in Assam spilling over to Bengal if such a situation was allowed to continue. Since the Raja had asked for aid and had agreed to pay for the troops, it was felt that there was no reason why the Company's government should not comply with the request. In the meantime, the Second Anglo-Mysore War had come to an end and this left the English relatively free to turn their attention to Assam. Thus, prompted by 'motives of humanity' as well as a desire 'to be better informed of the interior of the state of Assam, its commerce etc.,' Cornwallis decided to despatch a small contingent of troops under the command of Captain Thomas Welsh.

Captain Welsh and the Restoration of the Ahom Monarchy

Captain Welsh's expedition was sent into Assam in September 1792.[5] Lord Cornwallis specifically instructed Welsh to enquire into the economic potential of the region and, in spite of his military pre-occupations, Welsh did not overlook the commercial object of his deputation to Assam. He had written to the Governor-General of his confidence that with restoration of peace and order in Assam, 'a new source of wealth and riches must flow to the Company' and that the Company would then be able to sell at least 100,000 lbs of salt in Assam alone. Gaurinath was reinstated on the throne shortly after Welsh's arrival in Assam. Kamrup was cleared of the burgandazes, the resistance of the Moamarias in Upper Assam was broken and some semblance of law and order was restored in the territory. However, a radical change in policy occurred following the appointment of John Shore, the new Governor-General. Shore was not prepared to take on any avoidable political commitment, especially in a region that lay outside the sphere of the Company's domain. Therefore, Welsh was recalled despite Gaurinath's repeated pleas for the retention of the British troops. As a result, Assam lapsed into the former state of anarchy and internal strife. The burgandazes reappeared and renewed their depredations in Kamrup and Darrang, while the Moamarias, the Singphos and the Khamtis, all raised the standard of revolt.

BURMESE INTERVENTION IN ASSAM

The situation deteriorated further when even the Ahom court was divided following the premature death of Gaurinath Singha. His successors, Kamaleswar Singha (1795–1811) and Chandrakanta Singha, (1811–18), were mere puppets in the hands of Purnananda Buragohain, the prime minister, who became the virtual *de facto* ruler of Upper Assam. Badan Chandra Barphukan, the king's Viceroy in Lower Assam, was bitterly opposed to this personal rule of the *buragohain*. Their enimity went so deep that the buragohain sent a senior officer with an adequate force to arrest the *barphukan* and bring him to the capital. Having got scent of this, the barphukan fled to Calcutta to seek British aid. Being unable to successfully convince the British, Badan Chandra went to the Burmese court at Amarapura for help. The Burmese, who were ever anxious to extend their dominion westwards, made their appearance on the scene in 1817.

A Burmese army crossed the Patkai, reinstated Chandrakanta to his rightful position and returned with a huge indemnity and an Ahom princess for the Burmese monarch. However, shortly after their withdrawal, Chandrakanta was deposed and mutilated in order to disqualify him from claiming the throne.[6] Purandar Singha, another scion of the royal family, was enthroned in his place. Chandrakanta once again appealed to the Burmese who returned with a larger force in 1819 under the command of Ala Mingi. After putting up a feeble resistance, Purandar fled to Gauhati and thereafter, took refuge in Chilmari in Bengal. Chandrakanta was reinstated on the throne by the Burmese.

Chandrakanta, however, soon realised that Burmese attitude towards Assam had undergone a change. In 1817, the Burmese had retreated from Assam content with a large indemnity, a princess and a vague acknowledgement of their suzerainty by the Ahom king. But the second time around, they appeared to have territorial designs. The new Burmese king, Ba-gyi-daw, was determined to make Assam a part of the Burmese kingdom. In the circumstances, Chandrakanta found himself being increasingly sidelined and a mere puppet in the hands of the Burmese. Without any hope of aid from any quarter, Chandrakanta was left with no option but to flee to British territory from where he made abortive attempts to recover his lost position. The Burmese king viewed these developments with serious concern and in 1822 sent one of his greatest generals, Mingimaha Bandula, with an army of 30,000 men, to cow Chandrakanta into submission. This virtually marked the end of Ahom rule in Assam.

Assam thus came under the control of the Burmese. Jogeswar Singha, another member of the Ahom royal family, was installed as the new puppet ruler but the *de facto* ruler was Mingimaha. They unleashed a reign of terror in Assam. They plundered and burnt villages and committed terrible atrocities while the helpless people suffered untold misery. David Scott, the Civil Commissioner of Rangpur, had highlighted the significance of these developments in his correspondences with the Company. As early as July 1822, he had reported that, 'the Burmese, having obtained complete mastery of Assam and a person of that nation having been appointed to the supreme authority, the country may now be considered as a province of the Burman Empire'.[7] Meanwhile, the relations between the Burmese and the British had become strained. The Burmese had not only plundered villages in Habraghat in Rangpur but had also encroached upon British possessions in Goalpara. It was also rumoured that Mingimaha was contemplating a full-scale attack on Goalpara. In 1823 the Burmese occupied the island of Shahpuri on the Chittagong frontier. They had forced Gambhir Singh, the Raja of Manipur, to abdicate and expelled Govinda Chandra, the Raja of Cachar. Burmese preparations for an impending three-pronged attack on Bengal made the situation all the more alarming for the government.[8]

Apart from being a security threat, Burmese activities on the frontier also hindered British commercial interests in the region. In such circumstances, the East India Company's government was compelled to review its prevailing policy of non-intervention.

FIRST ANGLO-BURMESE WAR 1824–6

In November 1823, David Scott was appointed as Agent to the Governor-General of the North Eastern Frontier in addition to his duties as Commissioner of Rangpur. Scott's continued reports of the alarming situation on the frontier convinced the Governor-General-in-Council of the necessity of adopting strong measures to punish and humble the Burmese.[9] Reviewing the encroachments of the Burmese in Arakan, Assam and Cachar, the Council adopted a Resolution concluding that the activities of the Burmese, 'must be regarded as having placed the two countries in a state of actual war'.[10] The British declared war against the Burmese in1824.

Some of the British forces were led by Lieutenant Colonel Richards who advanced up the Brahmaputra and occupied Rangpur. Soon after, the Burmese were also expelled from Cachar and Manipur. Meanwhile, simultaneous campaigns in Arakan, Tenasserim, Pegu and Upper Burma had taken a heavy toll on the Burmese. The death of Mingimaha Bandula in April 1825 compounded their problems and by the beginning of 1826 the Burmese were no longer capable of offering any resistance to the British. When the main British army under General Archibald Campbell reached Yandabo, a village in the neighbourhood of Ava, the Burmese capital, Bai-gyi-daw, the Burmese king, was prepared to accept any terms the British imposed on him. Thus, Bai-gyi-daw and the British signed a peace treaty on 24 February 1826 at Yandabo.

THE TREATY OF YANDABO

The Burmese and Assam, Cachar, Jayantia and Manipur

The Treaty of Yandabo contained several clauses but the only article in the Treaty that vaguely referred to the disposal of the Burmese conquests in the northeastern frontier of British India, was Article II.[11] It is generally assumed that under the terms of this Treaty, 'Assam was ceded' to the East India Company. But this concept of Assam being 'ceded' was a loose interpretation of the Treaty of Yandabo by the authorities of the Company. Article II merely stated that, 'His Majesty, the King of Ava, renounces all claims upon, and will abstain from all future interference with the principality of Assam and its dependencies, and also the contiguous petty states of Cachar and Jyntea' (Jayantia).

With regard to Manipur, it was stipulated that, 'should Gambhir Singh desire to return to that country, he shall be recognised by the king of Ava as Rajah thereof'. There is no mention of Assam, Cachar, Jayantia and Manipur in any other Article of the Treaty. The Burmese version of the Treaty is similar in substance although there is a slight difference in the wording. It states that the 'the King of Burma shall no more have dominion over, or in the direction of, the towns and country of Assam, the country of Ak-ka-bat (Cachar) and the country of W-tha-li (Jayantia)'. With regard to Manipur, it states that if, 'Gam-bee-ra Sing desires to return to his country and remain ruler, the king of Burma shall not prevent or molest him, but let him remain'.[12]

From the clauses stated above, it is clear that neither version contains even an indirect recognition of the East India Company's right to establish political control over any of the above-mentioned territories. In the case of Assam, Cachar and Jayantia, the Burmese simply formalised their withdrawal leaving a political vacuum while committing themselves, 'to abstain from all future interference' in these territories. In the case of Manipur, they recognised Gambhir Singh's right to the throne but remained silent about his future relationship with the Burmese monarchy. Significantly, there was no assurance that they would abstain from future interference in Manipur. The renouncement of claims over these territories by the King of Ava cannot be construed to mean that that they were ceded to the British. This is further clear from Article III which provided that, 'to prevent all disputes respecting the boundary line between the two great nations, the British government will retain the conquered provinces of Aracan, Ramree, Cheduba and Sandung; and His Majesty, the King of Ava, cedes all rights thereto'.[13] If Assam was also to be automatically retained by the British by virtue of the Treaty of Yandabo, a provision of this nature would have been inserted. Moreover, Article II of the Treaty treated Assam, Cachar and Jayantia equally. These three principalities, therefore, stood on the same footing at the close of the war in relation to Burma and the peace treaty. It was now left to the British government to settle its terms with the legitimate rulers.

The British and Cachar, Jayantia, Manipur and Assam

It was here that the British discriminated between the neighbouring kingdoms. While the right of Raja Govinda Chandra and Raja Ram Singh to their respective thrones of Cachar and Jayantia was recognised, this right was not conceded to the Ahom raja. As a matter of fact, this discrimination started before the declaration of the war against Burma. In 1824, on the eve of the war, separate treaties[14] were signed by David Scott, on behalf of the Company's government, with the rajas of Cachar and Jayantia, whereby the rulers of these kingdoms placed their territories under the protection of the British against external aggression.

Cachar: Govinda Chandra of Cachar agreed to pay an annual tribute of 10,000 rupees and to allow British interference in the internal administration of his country.

Jayantia: No tribute was demanded of Raja Ram Singh, but he was required to 'assist [the British government] with all forces and to afford every facility in his power in furtherance of ... (its) military operations'. Like Govinda Chandra, he too agreed to accept the 'advice of the Governor-General-in-Council' in matters relating to the internal administration of his kingdom.

It appears that the inclusion of these two petty principalities adjoining the British district of Sylhet was part of the government's general policy on the defence of the frontier. Therefore, when the war ended, the protected rulers were left undisturbed in their respective kingdoms.

Manipur: The case was slightly different with regard to Manipur. Although the loyalty of Gambhir Singh towards the British during the war was open to suspicion, it was generally recognised that he had played an important role in expelling the Burmese from Cachar and Manipur. Moreover, the Treaty of Yandabo explicitly recognised his claims to the Manipuri throne. Therefore, it was logical for the British to accept him as the ruler of Manipur. But the Treaty had remained silent on the status of Gambhir Singh in relation to the Burmese monarchy and this posed a problem. The British considered it unsafe to allow Burmese influence in Manipur to continue for they believed that it would expose the Sylhet frontier to renewed Burmese incursions. Major Burney, the British Resident at Ava was, therefore, asked to make enquiries and report back on this delicate matter. To their relief, the government was informed that the Burmese no longer demanded the allegiance of the Manipuris, but Burney was quick to point out that they insisted on the restoration of the Kabaw Valley, a hilly tract to the east of Manipur, which Gambhir Singh had occupied during the war. The British readily accepted this claim for they were confident that they would be able to persuade Gambhir Singh to hand over the territory to the Burmese.

Assam: The position of Assam at the end of the war was quite different from that of Cachar, Jayantia and Manipur. Although she had been clubbed along with Cachar and Jayantia in the Treaty of Yandabo, the British were not bound to her by any treaty obligation. Hence, once the Burmese renounced their claim on Assam, the British felt free to decide her future. One does question why a treaty along the line of those with Cachar and Jayantia had not been signed with Assam in 1824. In fact, as early as 1823, while recommending intervention in the affairs of Assam for the expulsion of the Burmese, David Scott had presumed that the Company's government would place a prince of the Ahom royal family who had the best claim on the vacant throne. He also felt that if Ahom rule was to be restored in Assam, the British should reserve the right to interfere in its internal administration because, 'in view of the peculiar conditions prevailing in the Ahom kingdom, this departure from the general principle followed by the Company in its relations with friendly states was not only justified but essential for the maintenance of order'.[15] The Company had then informed Scott that it indeed favoured the restoration of Ahom rule in the near future.

Even prior to the commencement of hostilities, the government had realised that any military advance into Assam would involve a long-term commitment to protect the inhabitants against the Burmese. Yet, they still did not contemplate an alliance with an Ahom prince. This was probably because they were unable to identify a suitable claimant to the throne. In any case, Scott was opposed to any immediate declaration on the installation of an Ahom prince. He was convinced that the people had lost all confidence in their princes on account of their, 'imbecility, cowardice and treacherous principles'. Accordingly, in a Proclamation addressed to the people of Assam in February 1824, the government observed, 'We are not led into your country by the thirst of conquest, but are forced in our own defence, to deprive our enemy of the means of annoying us. You may, therefore, rest assured that we will ... re-establish ... a Government adapted to your wants and calculated to promote the happiness of all classes.'[16] It is clear that the government had no intention at this stage to extend their dominion but only wanted to ensure the protection of their eastern frontier.

However, with the defeat of the Burmese, other factors emerged that forced the British to revise their earlier position in relation to the Brahmaputra Valley. These factors were:

- Fears of a renewed Burmese invasion. It was also strategically important for them to ensure that the region did not relapse into anarchy.
- The newly discovered economic potential of the region. The East India Company was primarily a commercial concern and was, therefore, motivated by economic considerations while taking major decisions.

Hence, when the war came to an end, the Company's government informed David Scott that they did not consider themselves pledged by any engagement or declaration to restore an Ahom prince to the throne of Assam. Justifying this changed policy of the government, Edward Gait wrote:

> Not only had the Burmese been in possession (of the Brahmaputra Valley) for several years in course of which they had overthrown most of the old administrative landmarks, but the people were also split up into many conflicting parties, and the elevation of any particular pretender to the throne would have resulted, as soon as the British troops were withdrawn, in a renewal of the fatal dissensions and civil wars which had prevailed for many years before the Burmese occupation.[17]

The decision not to reinstate an Ahom monarch was indeed a departure from the government's earlier stand. Pending arrangements for its future administration, the renouncement of the claims by the Burmese made the East India Company the *de facto* ruler of Assam.

BRITAIN'S COLONIAL POLICY

Background

Britain's activities in the northeastern region of India must be viewed in the overall context of her colonial policy. It is important to remember that from the outset, the colonial system of England envisaged two types of possessions:

1. The first consisted of sparsely populated regions, usually in the temperate zone, where white men could settle, and make a home.
2. The other consisted of densely populated tropical or semi-tropical areas which were forced to adopt a policy of free trade and which were governed almost autocratically to promote her commercial interests.

Of the two, the latter was considered by far the more important. One can see two broad phases in Britain's economic relations with her colonies, viz., the old economic order pursued prior to the Industrial Revolution and the new economic system that evolved after it. The rise of British power in India was the result of the development of that phase of capitalism that came about post the Industrial Revolution. This occurred in the nineteenth century.

The Old Order

The old economic system prevalent in Europe in the sixteenth and seventeenth centuries had been largely national in character in which one nation could benefit only at the cost of another. Consequently, imports were checked by heavy protective tariffs while exports were stimulated by bounties on production or export and by retaining the exclusive possession of colonies as markets. The navigation laws of Britain, for example, laid down that it's trade must be carried in its own ships,[18] while trading companies were encouraged by the grant of monopolies for trading with specific areas. It was also believed that it was essential for the government to control the economic activities of the nation. Colonies were regarded, above all, as estates to be worked solely for the benefit of the metropolis.

The New Order

As the nineteenth century dawned and progressed, several factors combined to create a new impetus among the European powers for colonial expansion. This imperialism, largely the result of the new economic order produced by the Industrial Revolution, initially took place in Britain and soon spread to the rest of Europe. It was indeed a period of momentous economic change. There was growing demand for raw materials and food while new markets were developed to cater to the increased production. Thus, by the end of the century, the whole world was knit in a globally interdependent economy. As a result, colonies began to acquire new value and a fresh scramble occurred among the great powers for the unoccupied territories of the world. The general belief gained ground that the acquisition of colonies was a prerequisite towards recognition as a great power. Nationalism became very aggressive and patriotism developed from the love of one's own country into the expansion of its territorial limits.

The Hunt for Colonies

The European powers began to actively look for colonies. Their technique of incursion was almost identical throughout the world. The arrival of traders or missionaries heralded the beginning. Their activities often led to trouble which made official protection necessary. From there it developed gradually to a sphere of influence, then to a protectorate and finally, to full economic and political control of the country. Of all the European powers, Britain took the lead in colonial expansion. During the nineteenth century she built an empire that was the largest under a single ruler. It comprised one-fourth of the world's habitable area with one-fourth of the world's human population.

Factors that Helped Britain's Colonial Expansion

Britain's rapid colonial expansion was helped by many factors like:

- The rapid mechanisation of her modes of production due to the Industrial Revolution. This was possible because it had an accumulation of capital amassed from it's trade with colonies like India. England had made large profits out of the products brought from India and it's other colonies and was the foremost distributor of these goods in Europe. She, therefore, was in a position to invest in industries and wait for returns.
- It's banking sector was highly organised and made this capital easily obtainable.
- Wealthy individuals who were also eager to enter into partnerships with inventors.[19]

Britain thus became an active participant in the new imperialism. In India, the East India Company had already laid the groundwork by establishing trading posts in coastal areas. Trade gradually led to economic control, and finally to political control.[20] The general result was that large areas were acquired and opened up rapidly and new markets and sources of raw materials exploited at very little cost to the Imperial government. This lucrative hinterland of Britain increased her appetite for more and more territories and she looked around for expansion in the direction of virgin land. It was in this context that British interest in Assam developed.

The Burmese invasions changed the whole character of the Company's relations with Assam. The hitherto primarily commercial motive gradually began to develop political overtones. This became all the more pronounced during the Burmese War and the years following the Treaty of Yandabo. Indeed, the year 1826 is a very important landmark in the history of Assam. It witnessed the final collapse of the Ahom monarchy that had ruled Assam for over six centuries and marked the entry of the British who stepped in to fill the political void in the region. In a sense it was a beginning: the beginning of the transition from the medieval to the modern age.

NOTES AND REFERENCES

1. M'cosh, wrote that a large boat took between six and seven weeks to reach Gauhati from Calcutta though the post, which was conveyed in small canoes, rowed by two men (who were relieved every fifteen or twenty miles), reached Gauhati in ten days. J. N. M'cosh, *Topography of Assam*, Calcutta, 1837, p. 82.
2. J. Rennell, *Journals 1764–67*, cited in S. K. Bhuyan, *Anglo-Assamese Relations 1771–1826*, Guwahati 1949, (Reprint), 1974, p. 62.
3. The Ahoms were wary of foreigners and looked upon them with suspicion. They apparently feared, that these 'intruders' might conspire to create disruption in the kingdom.
4. The Pitts India Act had explicitly declared that 'to pursue schemes of conquest and extension of dominion in India are measures repugnant to the wish, honour and policy of this Nation.'
5. Foreign Department, Miscellaneous Records No. 8, Memoranda i, No. 7. Welsh was accompanied, among others, by Lietenant Robert MacGregor as Adjutant, Ensign Thomas Wood as Surveyor and John Peter Wade as Assistant Surgeon.
6. According to Ahom tradition, it was essential for an aspirant to the throne to be free from any physical scar.
7. H. K. Barpujari ed., *An Account of Assam and Her Administration*, Guwahati, 1988, pp. 54–5.
8. H. K. Barpujari ed., *The Comprehensive History of Assam*, Vol. II, Guwahati, 1993, pp. 258–9.
9. H. H. Wilson, *Documents Illustrative of the Burmese War*, No. 25, Calcutta, 1827.
10. Ibid., No. 22 (d).
11. For full text of the Treaty see C. U. Aitchison, *A Collection of Treaties, Engagements, and Sanads*, Vol. XII, (Reprint), Delhi, 1983, pp. 230–3.
12. Ibid., pp. 405, 408.
13. Ibid., Appendix B.
14. For full texts of treaties see C. U. Aitchison, *A Collection of Treaties, Engagements, and Sanads.*
15. A. C. Banerjee, *The Eastern Frontier of British India*, (Third edition), Calcutta , 1964, p. 355.
16. Wilson, *Documents Illustrative of the Burmese War*, No. 32.
17. E. Gait, *A History of Assam*,(Third edition) Calcutta,1963, p. 342.
18. If foreign ships could not frequent her colonies, and if colonial ships could not trade with foreign countries, then the manufactured goods were bound to come through England; and tobacco, spices and sugar actually came to England.
19. L. C. A. Knowles, *The Industrial and Commercial Revolutions in Great Britain during the Nineteenth Century*, London, 1927, Chapter 2.

20. The English had come as traders and later became armed traders. Soon they needed soldiers to defend their settlements, and, as the Mughal Empire disintegrated, spheres of influence became necessary if the Company was to survive. Slowly, the aim of empire building was imposed on the initial quest for trade.

SUGGESTED READINGS

Banerjee, A. C., *The Eastern Frontier of British India*, (Third edition), Calcutta, 1964.

Bhuyan, S. K., *Early British Relations with Assam*, Shillong, 1928.

Lahiri, R. M., *The Annexation of Assam*, Calcutta, 1954.

2

Foundation of the Company's Rule

Chapter Highlights

- Appointment of David Scott as agent to the governor-general
- Revenue measures
- Judicial measures
- Police administration
- Estimate of David Scott as an administrator

The state of the Brahmaputra Valley at the time of Burmese expulsion was deplorable. Thousands of people had been taken away as slaves and those that had survived the loot and plunder had been reduced to destitution. Harassed and oppressed by long years of internal strife and chaos, people had been compelled to give up a settled life and flee to the jungles where they were prey to famine and pestilence. The economy was in shambles, the social structure had collapsed and even a semblance of administration was non-existent. The royalty itself was divided into several factions with many claimants to the throne. In the circumstances, when the British appeared on the scene, they were heralded by the Assamese as saviours and were welcomed with open arms. Even Maniram Barbahandar Barua, a diehard rival of the British in later years, expressed his loyalty and gratitude to the *Company Bahadur* in no uncertain terms and prayed to the almighty for its continued glory and greatness.[1] Haliram Dhekial Phukan not only acclaimed the new order, but also prepared, on behalf of David Scott, seven *slokas* in Sanskrit interspersed with English words, appealing to the *sants* and *mahants* of Assam to cooperate with the British.[2]

Encouraged by the enthusiastic response of a large section of the Assamese, the British decided to hold on to the territory under military occupation for the time being. The management of this newly acquired territory was entrusted to David Scott, who was specially selected for the assignment by the Company for his, 'invaluable local experience' and 'on account of his high general character, his eminent and varied talents and his urbane and conciliatory conduct to the natives'.[3]

DAVID SCOTT IN ASSAM

Born in 1786, David Scott started his official career in India as assistant to the collector of Gorakhpur in 1807. He subsequently became registrar of the *zilla* court and assistant to the magistrate of Gorakhpur and later, officiating judge and magistrate of Purnea and Rungpore. In 1823, David Scott was appointed Agent to the Governor-General for the whole of the northeastern frontier of Bengal. He was at the same time special civil commissioner of North East Rungpore (Goalpara and Garo Hills) and judge of the Court of Circuit and Appeal of Sylhet. As agent to the governor-general, he was also entrusted with the additional responsibility of maintaining political relations with the hill tribes of the region for which he was vested with overriding powers. Scott's competence was well known in official circles. Commenting on his selection, Major Adam White wrote:

> To exercise power beneficially, it was required that a master mind should appear, which throwing aside all the technicalities of the Regulations, should grasp, at once, the spirit of the new system, that it might mould it to its purposes, and engraft upon it those improvements which a more enlightened system of rule demanded; at the same time, combining this with a proper attention to the peculiar customs and prejudices of Assam.[4]

The government was confident that Scott would be able to meet these expectations successfully.

Scott was aware of the tremendous responsibilities that he had been saddled with and was prepared to take up the challenge. Nevertheless, he did have certain reservations about the future of Assam. In fact the immediate problem confronting Scott was the necessity of filling up the vacuum that had been created by the flight of the erstwhile raja's of Assam in the years immediately preceding the Burmese war. Of the fugitive Ahom kings, Jogeswar Singha had settled at Jogighopa, in the north of Goalpara, where he died in 1825; Chandrakanta Singha was deported to Kaliabar, in Central Assam, on an annual pension of 200 rupees, a hundred *paiks* and some rent-free land grants; Purandar

Singha was allowed to return to Gauhati. The Company's government was not morally bound to restore any of them for no such commitment had been made earlier. Yet, keeping in mind the assurance given by the government in February 1824 that, 'the Governor-General-in-Council does not contemplate the permanent annexation of any part of it (Assam) to the British dominion',[5] Scott put forth two recommendations for solving the political vacuum in Assam.

1. The restoration of the Ahom monarchy, as a tributary of the Company's government under its protection.[6] Though he was aware of the weakness and instability of the Ahom monarchy, he felt that these could be counteracted by the provision of constitutional checks and the right of interference by the Company's government.
2. Alternatively, Scott suggested that the British could retain Lower Assam as far as Bishwanath, and hand over Upper Assam, with the exception of the territories occupied by the Moamarias, Khamptis and Singphos, to an Ahom prince.

He further recommended the occupation of an area near Sadiya for the maintenance of a body of irregular troops which were to be supplied by the neighbouring chiefs. Sadiya could also serve as the permanent station of a European officer appointed to supervise the conduct of these tribes.

The Company's government found Scott's proposals unacceptable. The Burmese war had put a heavy strain on the exchequer. The surplus revenue of 743,139 pounds in 1822–3 had turned into a huge deficit of nearly ten million pounds by the end of the war. They believed that Scott's proposals saw the extension of British protectorate over large areas, the resources of which had not yet been calculated. Moreover, from the strategic point of view it was considered inexpedient to install a weak government on the frontier. Hence, he was asked to review his proposals and submit fresh recommendations.

Scott's Agreements with the Singphos, Moamarias and Khamtis

Meanwhile, Captain Neufville, an officer of the 42nd Native Infantry, had been successful in restoring tranquillity on the frontier. He had even succeeded in emancipating over six thousand Assamese from the captivity of the Singpho tribe. In May 1826, Scott visited Sadiya and entered into formal agreements with 16 of the 28 Singpho chiefs. These chiefs promised their allegiance to the British and agreed to refrain from all connections with the Burmese or any other foreign power. They also undertook to supply provisions to the British troops and help out in whatever manner possible in the case of outbreak of hostilities. In return, Scott exempted them from all taxes. He also granted them the freedom to administer their territory according to their former customs on condition that they referred serious disputes among villages to the British authorities for a decision.

Matibar Bar Senapati was recognised as the chief of the Moamarias. He was required to supply 300 paiks to the British and to supply provisions on payment if required. The position of the Sadiya Khowa Gohain as the Khamti chief was recognised on condition that he contributed a contingent of 200 paiks to be trained and equipped by the British. Scott wanted to retain the independence of these tribal chiefs and exercise an indirect control over them. Having thus settled the immediate problems on the frontier, Scott turned his attention to the equally pressing demands of internal reform and the challenges facing him.

Scott's Reforms

Scott's foremost difficulty lay in the wide range and multiplicity of his duties. The territory under him, moreover, was too large to be administered by one person and that too, without any infrastructural support. Recognising these constraints, the government instituted the office of a joint commissioner for the areas east of Bishwanath, commonly known as Upper Assam. Lieutenant Colonel Richards was appointed to this office in 1825 with the civil charge of the area in addition to his military duties. His headquarters was at Rangpur. Scott remained at Gauhati in charge of the western division or Lower Assam. Captain White, an officer of the 49th Regiment, assisted him. Each commissioner was to exercise civil duties independently although they were expected to maintain, as far as practicable, a uniform system of administration.

Revenue Measures

The revenue possibilities of the area had attracted Scott's attention as early as 1824. He realised that if the future defence of the country was to be provided for, income had to be generated locally. He also realised that in Upper Assam, which was the stronghold of the Ahom nobility, the introduction of any measures affecting their interests would be strongly resented. In Lower Assam, on the other hand, the social and political institutions were more or less akin to those of the neighbouring Bengal and the introduction of a new system was, therefore, less likely to be resisted. In any case, Scott was convinced of the utmost necessity of adapting new measures that would fulfil the wants and needs of the people. He also realised the necessity of employing local people in the administration as far as possible subject to the supervision of European officers.

The Ahom Revenue System: Scott based his revenue measures on the earlier *khel* system[7] and altered the existing institutions only when he considered it absolutely necessary. The following points talk about the economic structure under Ahom rule.

- Within the Ahom social framework, one's position in society was largely determined by birth. The king, the nobility, the priests and other vassal chiefs, all had agricultural lands cultivated by paiks.
- The paiks themselves were primarily peasant cultivators whose hereditary private proprietary rights existed only in the case of homesteads and gardens but not in the case of paddy lands. Each paik received two *puras* of wet paddy land as *ga mati* (land attached to the person) in lieu of which he had to render three or four months of service to the state. In addition to his ancestral homestead lands, a paik could obtain inferior land if he desired. Additional wet paddy lands were also allotted in certain cases, but only if surplus land (*opar mati*) was available.[8]
- Normally, everyone had free access to the unoccupied dry lands for the collection of fuel wood and building materials or for grazing their livestock.
- Certain sections were exempted from manual service. For instance, people belonging to high castes or those with special skills were allowed to make payments in kind or to contribute in terms of their specialised services. They were awarded *chamua* status. In some areas of Kamrup, the rent was paid in cash. Here the ga mati was referred to as *jumma mati*. The king, as the representative of the community, owned all communal wet

paddy lands and waste lands. The Ahoms did introduce nominal taxation on additional holdings but only during the later part of their rule. The whole of the taxed portion of land or a portion of ga mati could be taken back by the crown, i.e., the community, if necessary.[9]

- Since the cultivable lands by their very nature were common territory, they were also protected from floods by dykes constructed through collective efforts. After the crop was harvested, the land served as a common grazing ground. Thus, the basic pattern of the land system and distribution rested on the concept of communal ownership of land and land revenue consisted of the personal labour service of the peasant-paik.[10]
- The Ahom rulers considered their subjects as alienable property. Hence, when land grants were awarded[11] it usually also meant the donation of the people settled in those areas. This was perhaps reasonable because, in a sparsely populated land with an agriculture based economy, the donation of cultivable land without cultivators would have been meaningless. The donated paiks were freed from the obligation of personal service to the state and were attached permanently to the donated lands. However, both the donee and the donated people continued to remain within the purview of the state judiciary.[12]
- The population was divided into khels or units each under a gradation of officers. The fact that many khels were named locality-wise, such as Jokaichukia, Abhaypuria, Charingia, suggests that the first khels 'were presumably organised into localised kin groups, jointly in control of the adjacent fields, pastures and jungles'.[13] Even the later khels that were formed on a functional basis (eg., Sonowal, Kakaty), were more or less similarly organised groups.

Scott's Revenue Reforms: Scott did not wish to make any drastic changes and his reforms were based on the system that existed under the Ahoms. The following points describe the measures he introduced.

- He retained the khel system in Upper Assam, but in lieu of personal service and produce, revenue was now demanded in the form of a poll tax of three rupees per paik. No other tax was levied here. Apparently, Scott was so convinced of the propriety of restoring an Ahom prince on the throne of Upper Assam that he 'considered the realisation of any substantial revenue from that territory as a matter of secondary importance'.[14] In order to ensure some form of continuity and in accordance with his policy of employing suitable local people, Janardan Barbarua, a former officer of rank and influence, was placed in charge of the revenue department. He was assisted by a number of *kheldars*.

- In Lower Assam, Scott introduced a revenue system similar *to* that of Bengal as he believed that its institutions were, in any case, akin to those prevailing in the neighbouring territories. The revenue department was now placed under the supervision of a *sheristadar*, instead of the barphukan, the Ahom king's viceroy who had been in charge of the revenue affairs of Lower Assam.[15] Since the family of the Duaria Barua had been particularly helpful to Scott ever since his arrival in Assam, he appointed one of their members, Haliram Dhekial Phukan, to this office. The sheristadar was aided in his work by a number of subordinate officials like the *rubakars*, *navis* and *peshkars*, usually recruited from Bengal.
- The settlement in the twenty-six *parganas* of Kamrup was made with the hereditary *choudhurys* who were on the same footing as the choudhurys of Bengal before the introduction of the decennial system. They were not the owners of the land and were liable to be removed at the pleasure of the government. When in office, they were entitled to *man mati* or rent-free grants and the services of a specified number of paiks. *Patwaris* or accountants and *thakurias* or subordinate collectors assisted the choudhurys in their work. These officials also received rent-free grants as remuneration.

Scott attempted to make the initial settlements on the basis of certain records available in the *perakagaz*, a register of a survey undertaken by the former government, which he obtained from Majumdar Barua, the head *qanungo* of Kamrup. But these documents were so outdated that he found them of no relevance and had to act on information that was immediately obtainable.

- Scott decided to impose a tax of two rupees known as *ga dhan*, on every paik for which he was entitled to three puras of arable land. This land was not hereditary and it was not transferable by sale, gift or bequest.

- In addition, the *kharikatana*, or poll tax was levied in various forms. In Darrang it was in the form of a hearth tax, known as *charukar*, calculated on the number of *saroos* or mess-pots in each household and varied from eight *annas* to one rupee; in Nowgong, a tax of a rupee per head was collected, while in Kamrup, the tax was fixed at a rupee per plough.
- In order to widen the tax base, Scott imposed a tax on the vast areas of *lakhiraj* lands.[16] A provisional survey had shown that of the 1,600,000 *bighas* of cultivable land in Lower Assam, 480,000 bighas were rent-free holdings. These lands were now assessed at half the rate of the arable land. However, in order to prevent distress among the poorer brahmins and other holders of such lands, he directed that no tax be collected from holdings which were smaller than two acres.
- Apart from the above, he levied a professional tax on braziers, silk-weavers, gold washers, (Under the Ahom monarchs, individuals who washed gold were required to pay one *tola* (11.66 gms) per head per annum to the royal exchequer), fishermen, blacksmiths and others along with duties on *haats*, ghats and ferries.

These taxes were also applicable to the area around Darrang, Raha and Nowgong, commonly referred to by the British as Central Assam. A settlement was arrived at with Raja Balinarayan of Darrang, a former vassal of the Ahom monarch, whereby he committed himself to collecting an amount of 42,000 rupees annually besides supplying 1,500 paiks to the Company's government. Nowgong and Raha were made into a separate fiscal unit under the collector of Gauhati and placed in charge of two *sezwals* or farmers of revenue, Aradhan Ray and Lata Pani Phukan. With the chiefs of Beltola, Rani, Demorua and Naduar, all former vassals of the Ahom king, settlements were made on what they 'voluntarily offered to pay' since there was no accurate account of their estates. In any case, their good behaviour was felt to be of greater importance than any financial gain.[17]

The revenue system in the hill districts was not uniform. Virtually no land revenue was imposed except in a few specific areas of the Jayantia Hills and the sub-montane regions of the Garo Hills. Assessments were generally done on the houses and not on the land. This was primarily because most of the people were shifting cultivators and it was not feasible to assess the land under cultivation.[18] Although Scott had levied a variety of taxes, the initial receipts of revenue fell far below his estimated calculations. At a time when the paying capacity of the people was minimal, his assessments were higher compared to that of the Ahom rulers. That apart, the revenue was fixed as cash payment, which itself was a strain on the peasant cultivators at a time when the economy was in transition and had not been fully monetised. Hence, even though the Company desperately needed the money, Scott could not contemplate raising the land revenue further. Instead, he had to explore other possibilities for raising revenue.

Scott's Proposals for Increasing Revenue: Scott put forth several proposals to increase the revenue:

- One possible source that attracted the attention of Scott was the large tracts of cultivable land lying fallow in Assam. The general land survey that had been conducted in 1825–6 had revealed that of the cultivable land in Lower Assam, two-thirds remained fallow. Scott believed that if this source could be tapped, the Company's revenue would increase considerably. Keeping this in mind, Scott decided to allot each paik three puras as *juma mati* in addition to the ga mati, at the rate of seven annas (*jumadhan*) per pura. He further directed that whatever remained after this double allotment be allocated to the choudhurys to be disposed off by another assessment.
- The poll tax or kharikatana was extended to include even slaves who were required to pay eight annas each. To cover the expenses of the administration, a *barangani* of between 12.5 per cent and 37.5 per cent on the gross collection was levied. On top of all this, the people also had to pay half per cent commission for the exchange of the *narayani* rupee.[19]
- Scott proposed the withdrawal of the narayani currency from circulation and its replacement by the Company's *sicca* rupee. He calculated that this measure was likely to result in an initial loss to the government of around 150,000 sicca rupees. On the other hand, an annual profit of 50,000 sicca rupees would be derived from the second year onwards if the revenue was henceforth collected in sicca rupees and would make up for the loss. He

also pointed out that a common currency would facilitate trade and commerce in the region which in turn would increase the paying capacity of the people.[20]

- Another measure that Scott thought of was to levy a tax on opium cultivation. He estimated that roughly two thousand puras of land was under poppy cultivation, the most important cash crop in the region. He realised that if it was suppressed completely, shortage of money would become more acute. Many cultivators would lose their only source of cash income, while those addicted to opium would require additional money to buy *abkari* opium (opium on which excise duty was levied). At the same time he also realised that by allowing local cultivation of opium to continue, the government was losing out not only on a considerable amount of excise revenue but also on land revenue because the *chapari* and *basti* lands in which poppy was generally cultivated, was assessed at lower rates than the rice lands. Scott, therefore, proposed a tax of 20 rupees on every pura of land under poppy cultivation. He calculated an estimated collection of at least 25,000 rupees from this source.[21]

In spite of Scott's best efforts, the revenue of Lower Assam did not improve substantially. He was now convinced that the only way to rectify the situation was to improve the general economy of the region. In a detailed report to the authorities he pointed out that the constant drain of currency to the Presidency had adversely affected the commerce of the region. That apart, shortage of cash had even compelled the administration to revert to the old system of accepting revenue in kind in many places. In the face of acute hardship, many defaulting paiks had even left their homes and taken shelter in the adjoining hills.[22] In the circumstances, Scott believed that the only solution lay in the production of commodities for export with technical and financial aid from the government. As early as 1826, he had identified silk as one such commodity. The subsequent discovery of coal encouraged him to urge the government to introduce steamers on the Brahmaputra. He was convinced that unless communication between Assam and the rest of the country improved, the region could never prosper. A proposal for the introduction of a steamer service on the Brahmaputra had received the concurrence of the government as early as 1831, but the project was shelved by the Marine Department of the Government of Bengal. Unfortunately, Scott did not live long enough to see the successful implementation of his proposal.

Judicial Measures

Scott made an effort to make justice accessible to all people without wholly upsetting the old institutions. He made the following reforms in the judiciary.

- To ensure unlimited freedom of petitioning without any expense to the complainant, a large box was placed in the *kutchery* into which petitions could be dropped. The only restriction was the length of the petition which was limited to thirty lines. The entire proceedings of the court as well as the petitions were either in Assamese or Bengali.[23]
- In Upper Assam, Lambodar Barphukan, brother-in-law of Chandrakanta Singha, was appointed co-adjutor with Janardan Barbarua of the revenue department for the trial of civil cases. Minor cases were referred to the *surasree* panchayats comprising former *pundits*. Criminal cases were usually disposed off by the junior commissioner but in certain cases they were referred to the barphukan who was empowered to pass sentences of thirty lashes, imprisonment for six months or a fine of upto 50 rupees. Serious offences were tried by a jury presided over by the barphukan although the verdict was subject to revision by the commissioners.
- In Lower Assam, the senior commissioner occupied the position held by the former viceroy of Gauhati and tried civil cases without any limit, and criminal cases not involving death sentences. He set up a tribunal under Colonel Richards to try the more serious offences.

In spite of Scott's best intentions, the system was not entirely successful because of the very large number of petitions that were presented and the inadequate infrastructure available to deal with them. The tribunal that was constituted could not assemble even once because of certain difficulties, as a result of which a large number of criminals had to be confined in the Gauhati jail. By the end of 1826, Scott found 1,500 cases awaiting judgment. In order to ease the situation, he was left with no other alternative but to institute native courts to dispose off certain civil suits.

Keeping in mind the set-up of the Ahom judiciary, Scott instituted three such courts, each of which was presided over by an Assamese judge with judicial experience under the old regime. Scott also decided to appoint three assessors to each court with the idea of instituting a system of checks and balances.

1. The first court, presided over by a *rajkhowa*, tried civil cases up to 150 rupees.
2. The second, under a barphukan, tried civil cases up to 1,000 rupees and heard appeals from lower courts.
3. The third, also under a barphukan, tried criminal cases of minor importance and heard appeals from the tributary rajas and revenue officials.

In order to reduce the congestion of the courts at the headquarters, Scott set up *moffusil* panchayats, in certain areas of Nowgong, Kaliabar and Charduar. These panchayats, comprising of members elected by the people of the locality, were allotted a number of paiks as remuneration. These courts were successful in clearing the accumulated backlog of the civil and petty criminal cases to a large extent. But the increasing capital offences convinced Scott of the urgent necessity of instituting suitable machinery to deal with major crimes. He, therefore, urged the authorities at Calcutta to extend the jurisdiction of the *Nizamat Adalat* in Calcutta to Lower Assam. But when there was an inordinate delay in arriving at a decision on such an urgent issue, Scott requested permission to constitute a *bar* panchayat comprising three Assamese judges of experience who were to be assisted by two pundits and six assessors. Eventually, the authorities at Calcutta came to the conclusion that in the existing circumstances, it would be 'premature and inexpedient' to introduce the authority of the Nizamat Adalat in Lower Assam. They favoured Scott's second proposal considering the fact that he had very effectively and 'judiciously revived and put in action' the indigenous tribunals and institutions for the dispensation of civil suits and petty criminal cases.[24] Thus in 1828, the government accorded its approval to the proposal of the bar panchayat as a temporary measure on condition that its proceedings were subject to the supervision of the Political Agent,

Upper Assam and Assistant to the Commissioner, Lower Assam. In the case of very serious crimes, it was made mandatory to transfer the proceedings to the Commissioner who was empowered to impose the death penalty if necessary.

Scott's judicial reforms were based on western ideas adapted to indigenous institutions. They were far from perfect. But in the prevailing situation and in the absence of better infrastructure, more could hardly be expected.

Police Administration

British occupation of the region had aroused hopes for an end to the chaotic law and order problem that had followed the Burmese invasion. The situation, however, had not improved as expected and Scott was constrained to admit that the number of violent crimes had in fact increased. He attributed this partly to the discontinuation of the traditional methods of physical torture resorted to by the Ahom rulers [25] but more to the absence of an effective police force. A small police force comprising one *daroga*, a *jamadar* and a few constables was maintained at the headquarters, but *moffusil* police was the responsibility of the various revenue officers. Thus, for all practical purposes, security provided by the police was confined to a limited area around the police station at the headquarters. In the rest of the territory, the maintenance of law and order was considered to be the responsibility not of the state, but of the people. Hence, if a particular area required the services of a regular police force, the expenses for the same had to be raised by a collective tax on the inhabitants of that area. The darogas and revenue officers were expected to maintain peace and security, suppress crimes, apprehend offenders, prevent frays, and conduct preliminary trials of all crimes. With such varied responsibilities and without any supporting infrastructure, the officers could hardly be expected to carry out the work entrusted to them effectively. Had they received some support from the army, their problems would have been eased to a certain extent. That was, however, unavailable.

On the eve of the Burmese war, the defence of the northeast frontier had been entrusted to the Rangpur Local Corps and regiments of the Bengal Native Infantry besides several detachments of irregulars. With the conclusion of the war, as internal troubles subsided and apprehensions of a renewed Burmese invasion gradually receded, the government decided to recall the regular troops from Assam and to entrust the defence of the frontier to a local militia. The government believed that an armed and disciplined local militia would be more effective than the Hindustani soldiers who appeared to have difficulty in adjusting to the terrain and climate of the region. Drawing his idea from the Ahom paik system, Lieutenant Bedingfield suggested that as most of the militia men would be peasants, they might be allowed leave for specified periods in rotation to enable them to look after their crops. He also suggested that, to keep them active and alert, they be employed in activities like building stockades, digging trenches and making canoes during peacetime. While accepting the ideas of Bedingfield, Scott felt that a local militia alone was inadequate to protect the frontier and that a garrison of regular troops in addition was necessary. Besides, it was felt that it would 'also be productive of the best impression by convincing the people of the country in the permanence of our protective influence'.[26] The Gurkhas, known for their bravery and capacity to endure fatigue, were considered to be the most suitable for the purpose. Hence, the Assam Light Infantry Battalion, comprising of the Rangpur Corps and augmented by two Companies of the Gurkhas, was constituted. They established a permanent cantonment at Bishwanath while a garrison was stationed at Sadiya. But contrary to expectations, this force was not adequate to even protect the troublesome frontier, let alone supplement the duties of the police, and as a result crimes continued to multiply.

Anandaram Dhekial Phukan, in his *Observations on the Province of Assam*,[27] commented that the police system was 'wholly inefficient to preserve the lives and property of the people'. He mentioned that corruption was rampant at every level and that more often than not, justice was sold for money. The investigations and trials were often, 'mercenary and biased' and were, in many cases, held in such a way as 'to convict the innocent and exculpate the guilty'. He further stated that 'the unlawful means practised by them (darogas) to extort confessions are notorious: and the number of cases that are allowed to escape from punishment through the connivance of the police, exceeds all belief.

The severe criticism meted out by Anandaram Dhekial Phukan reflects the poor state of law and order in Assam in the years immediately following British occupation. David Scott was no doubt also aware of the situation; but he had to deal with many problems simultaneously that it was impossible for him to solve all of them effectively within his brief tenure.

Scott's Relations with Neighbouring Hill Tribes

An overview of David Scott's administration will be incomplete without a reference to his relations with the Khasis, Jayantias and Garos.[28] He realised the importance of a friendly relationship with the Khasis during the Burmese war itself when the need to establish a postal link from Sylhet to Assam was greatly felt. After the war, when Assam was brought under the military occupation of the British, a road connecting Sylhet to Gauhati through the Jayantia and the Khasi Hills became an urgent necessity. Meanwhile, the deteriorating administrative conditions in the Garo Hills, created serious law and order problems in that area. The need for political stability and British dominance in the region resulted in military interventions on all fronts. This subsequently led to a vision of European colonies in the entire northeastern frontier which would assure British dominance not only in India but also perhaps in Burma, making Assam the centre of a fourth presidency.[29] With this imperial concept also went that of trade through Assam into Burma and China for the Industrial Revolution had given a new dimension to imperialism. Scott's relations with the Khasis, Jayantias and Garos were thus determined by these considerations. A detailed account of his dealings with these hill tribes is given in Chapter 4.

Estimate of David Scott

David Scott died on 20 August 1831 at the age of 43. He was buried at Cherrapunji where a monument was erected in his memory.[30] This monument bears ample testimony to the high esteem in which Scott was held not only by the government but by the local people as well. An able, enthusiastic and extremely hardworking officer, Scott had tremendous respect for the people whom he governed and often lamented 'the general attitude of Europeans who evinced so little regard for the feelings of Natives with whom they had occasion to associate'.[31] He sincerely believed that the traditional local institutions had their own strengths and that, with proper supervision, they could be very effective. Perhaps it was this inherent desire in him to learn more that made him the linguist that he was.[32] He was also convinced that the only way to elevate the people in their own estimation was to have them participate in their administration. Hence, sharing of power and authority with them was a prominent feature of his administrative setup. He further realised that laws should be simple and in order to be effective, the procedures for their implementation should also be equally simple. Scott knew that a successful administration depended largely on the easy accessibility of his officers and in order to ensure this, he himself religiously practised what he preached. White's *Memoir* bears ample testimony to this.

Scott's concern for the local population was reflected in his keen interest in all issues that were connected to their welfare. He was quick to realise the immense economic potential of the indigenous silk. With a view towards increasing its production, he brought experienced workers in silk from Rangpur to instruct the Assamese on improved methods of spinning and reeling. He set up agricultural farms, distributed vegetable seeds among the people for cultivation and laboured hard to improve the breed of cattle. Prisoners in jails were encouraged to develop interest in agricultural pursuits and were taught certain crafts so as to prepare them for meaningful employment. Scott supported missionary activity in the Valley but he believed that religious instruction alone was not adequate and that it must be combined with basic education along with instructions in agriculture and basic technical knowledge if society at large was to be uplifted.

When Scott took over the administration, formal systems of education in Assam was nearly non-existent. Long years of turmoil had practically eroded whatever little had remained of the infrastructure for education under the Ahoms. He realised that if the Government was to find capable persons to work for it, then serious effort had to be made to revive the educational set up in the province. With this end in view he requested the government, soon after taking charge, to sanction land grants to the *pundits*. He proposed that between 20 and 50 puras of land be allotted to individual pundits who would then be required to teach a specified number of pupils. The government showed considerable interest in his plans for payment in land rather than in cash which was 'much less onerous to the Government'. It was also arranged to send an intelligent Assamese to Serampore in order to get him acquainted with the latest mode of instruction. Scott also sought the help of missionaries in this regard. In fact it was with their assistance that a school for girls was established at Gauhati.

Despite his good intentions, Scott was unable to achieve what he desired and however well meaning his measures might have been, they failed to ameliorate the condition of the people at large. Initially, his policy had been to employ the erstwhile nobility in the Company's service, but he soon realised that they were totally unfit for the task. Their indolence and incapacity had resulted in large-scale extortion and corruption. Scott had cherished hopes of a large collection of revenue, but when this was not forthcoming he had to resort to imposing new taxes. This, coupled with over-assessments, made life extremely difficult for the ryots. Moreover, the revenue administration was itself defective. In Lower Assam, tracts of territories were allotted to individuals and taxed without taking into account the fertility of the area. No effective measures were taken to protect the ryots from the choudhurys who were invested with considerable policing powers as well. In Central and Upper Assam the situation was equally deplorable. Cases of embezzlement of funds, extortion and oppression were rampant.

It is, however, important to remember that the officials were required to work within a system with which they were totally unfamiliar. They were simply unable to cope with the voluminous writings and minute details which were involved even in day to day administration. Further, although the khel system was retained, it could not be expected to work successfully because during the Burmese invasions many members of the khels had died, and those that had survived had been scattered across the region. As such, the collection of revenue became very difficult and the amounts that were eventually paid into the treasury were ridiculously small. Matters were made worse by the introduction of money as a medium of exchange when little trade existed and a market economy was practically unknown to Assam. There was, moreover, a shortage of coins and many ryots, unable to pay the requisite taxes, migrated to neighbouring areas where taxes were either low or non-existent.

David Scott had too much to do on his hands; time and resources were limited, infrastructural support was minimal and his area of operation too vast. While just one of these would have been a severe constraint by itself, the combination of all these was indeed insurmountable. In spite of such adverse circumstances, Scott's achievements were many and he can be credited with laying the foundations of the Company's dominion in the northeast. Alexander Mackenzie has very aptly commented:

> David Scott was one of the most remarkable men who have from time to time been the ornament of our Indian services. Had the scene of his

life's labours been in North West or Central India, where the great problem of Empire was then being worked out, instead of amid the obscure jungles of Assam, he would occupy a place in history by the side of Malcolm, Elphinstone and Metcalfe.[33]

NOTES AND REFERENCES

1. In a letter to *Samachar Darpan*, 21 September 1839. Text included in *Benudhar Sharma Rachnavali*, Vol. IV, 'Tokora Bahor Koota', Guwahati, 1987, pp. 144–5.
2. Ibid., p. 143.
3. Adam White, *A Memoir of the Late David Scott*, DHAS, 1988, p. IV.
4. Ibid., p. 1.
5. *Bengal Secret and Political Consultations*, (henceforth BSPC), 20 February 1824, No. 15.
6. Scott proposed that the ruler would have to agree to the following: (i) Pay an annual tribute of two lakh rupees; (ii) provide men and money for works connected with the defence of the frontier; (iii) abolition of the former practices of mutilating and torturing criminals; (iv) trial of offenders before regular courts of law; (v) revival with modifications of the time-honoured council of patra mantri.
7. Under the Ahom government, the entire adult male population was divided into guilds or khels according to their occupations. Each individual was known as a paik and three or four paiks formed a *gote*. Every paik was required to serve the state for a specific period or to supply a certain quantity of his produce in lieu of which he received two puras (approximately three acres) of arable land. The paiks were supervised by a gradation of kheldars such as Borahs, Saikias, Hazarikas, Baruahs, Rajkhowas and Phukans. The kheldars were remunerated with the services of paiks and grants of rent-free land.
8. In view of the limitations of a family's working capacity, two puras was considered a reasonable amount as anything above that would mean stretching the resources with difficulty.
9. Revenue Department, Jenkins to Secretary, Revenue Department, Government of India, 3 February 1836, Transcript of file at DHAS.
10. Shihabuddin Talish who accompanied Mir Jumla to Assam during his expedition in 1662–3 wrote: 'It is not the custom here to take any land tax from the cultivators, but in every house one man out of three has to render service to the Raja.' Talish, *Fathiya-i- ibria*, tr. J. N. Sarkar, Journal of the Bihar and Orissa Research Society, Vol.1, p. 179.
11. For instance, *devottar*, *brahmottar* and *dharmottar* land grants as well as secular grants made to officers and nobility for distinguished services.
12. For details, refer to Amalendu Guha, *Medieval and Early Colonial Assam: Society, Polity, Economy*, New Delhi, 1991, pp. 44–51.
13. Ibid.
14. H. K. Barpujari, *Assam in the Days of the Company*, 1980, p. 28.
15. The barphukan was transferred to Upper Assam on a judicial post with a salary of 300 rupees per month.

16. These were rent-free grants which had been allotted by the former government and were classified as *debottar*—lands granted for the maintenance of temples; *brahmottar*—lands granted for the maintenance of the brahmins; *dharmottar*—lands granted for religious and charitable purposes.
17. *BSPC*, 5 April 1825, No. 27.
18. S. Goswami, *Aspects of Revenue Administration in Assam*, Delhi, 1987, pp. 24–31.
19. This coin was originally introduced by Maharaja Nara Narayan (1540–84) in Cooch Behar. The rate of exchange was: 100 sicca rupees = 126-7-4 narayani rupees.
20. *BSPC*, 9 March 1827, No.18.
21. Ibid.
22. H. K. Barpujari, *Assam in the Days of the Company*, p. 44.
23. Adam White, *A Memoir of the Late David Scott*, p. 2.
24. For details, refer to N. K. Barooah, *David Scott in North East India*. Delhi, 1970, pp. 234–6.
25. Commenting on the punishments meted out by the Ahom government, Hamilton wrote: 'The capital offences are treason, murder, rape, arson and voluntary abortion. Rebels are never excused; for other offences, pardon may be purchased. Capital punishment extends to the whole family of a rebel—parents, brothers, sisters, wives and children. Offenders are put to death in various manners—by cutting their throats, by impaling them, by grinding them between two wooden cylinders, by sawing them asunder between two planks, by beating them with hammers, and by applying burning hoes to different parts until they die. ... There are few robbers and atrocious housebreakers or pirates. Such persons are punished in summary manner by thrusting out their eyes or cutting off the knee-pans.... Petty thefts are very common and are punished by whipping or by cutting off the nose and ears.' Francis Hamilton, pp. 51–2.
26. *BSPC*, 10 November 1826, No. 22.
27. A. J. M. Mills, *Report on the Province of Assam*, Appendix J.
28. Detailed discussion in Chapter 4.
29. *Bengal Political Consultations*, 13 August 1930, No. 72.
30. This monument stands near the government dak bungalow at Cherapunjee. The epigraph on the monument reads thus: 'This monument is erected by the order of the Supreme Government , as a public and lasting record of its consideration for the personal character of the deceased, and of its estimation of the eminent services rendered by him in the administration of the extensive territory committed to his charge. By his demise, the Government has been deprived of a most zealous, able and intelligent servant, whose loss it deeply laments: while his name will be held in grateful remembrance and veneration by the native population, to whom he was justly endeared by his impartial dispensation of justice, his kind and conciliatory manners, and his constant and unwearied endeavours to promote their happiness and welfare.'
31. Adam White, *A Memoir of the Late David Scott*, p. 6.
32. David Scott was well versed in Persian, Hindi, Bengali and several local languages of Assam. But it was the diversity of his pursuits that characterised his mind.

He was interested in almost everything—philosophy, chemistry, geology, natural history, medicine and sociology.

33. A. Mackenzie, *A History of the Relations of the Government with the Hill Tribes of the North East Frontier of Bengal*, Calcutta, 1884, p. 5.

SUGGESTED READINGS

Barooah, N. K., *David Scott in North East India*, Delhi, 1970.

Barpujari, H. K., *Assam in the Days of the Company, 1826–58*, Guwahati, 1963.

White, A., *A Memoir of the Late David Scott*, Calcutta, 1831, (Reprint), Guwahati, 1988.

3

The Company's Expansion in the Brahmaputra Valley

Chapter Highlights

- Annexation of Lower Assam
- Anti-British uprisings
- Reorganisation under Robertson, the political agent
- Restoration of the Ahom monarchy
- Treaty of Gauhati
- Administration of Purandar Singha, the Ahom ruler
- Annexation of Upper Assam
- Annexation of Sadiya and Muttock

The political settlement in Assam following the Treaty of Yandabo was initially meant to be a transitional arrangement. It was essential that the British remain in the region for the security of the frontier, but the extension of British protectorate over an extensive area of doubtful value was not thought of as a wise move. Apart from the possibility of the area being subjected to frequent raids by the predatory tribes, it was assumed that the amount of revenue that was likely to be obtained would not be commensurate with the risks and responsibilities involved. Scott, therefore, examined the problem with three objectives in mind.

1. First, the necessity of collecting adequate revenue for the defence of the territory;
2. second, the restoration of an Ahom prince with limited power in at least one portion of the Brahmaputra valley; and
3. third, ensuring the security of the eastern frontier which had for long been in a state of chaos.

ANNEXATION OF LOWER ASSAM

We have already observed[1] that Scott's initial proposal for the restoration of the Ahom monarchy in Assam under the protection of the Company had been turned down. He was asked to review the issue and submit fresh recommendations. After much deliberation Scott submitted a fresh proposal in 1828. He was convinced that the only solution acceptable to all lay in the retention of Lower Assam by the British. He calculated that Lower Assam would yield revenue of over three lakh rupees which was expected to cover the expenditure resulting from the military occupation of the region. Moreover, since the region had been administered almost independently by the barphukan, the Ahom king's viceroy at Gauhati for a long time, it was assumed that the inhabitants did not have any strong allegiance to the monarchy and would, therefore, not resent the transfer of power to the British. Scott also pointed out that the revenue of Lower Assam was likely to increase under strict supervision. Besides, with the restoration of peace, military expenditure would decrease as the local corps alone would suffice for the internal defence of the region.

Scott, however, emphasised the importance of appeasing the Ahom nobility who had held positions of power for nearly six centuries. He understood that the acquisition of Upper Assam, which had been the stronghold of the Ahom nobility would be a political mistake. This was because the alienation of the nobility would have resulted in adverse repercussions on the consolidation of British administration. Scott feared that it would provoke bitter resentment within Assam which in turn was likely to trigger off restlessness in the neighbouring kingdoms of Cachar, Jayantia and Manipur. Moreover, he pointed out that the acquisition of Upper Assam would be of little financial benefit to the Company. He reiterated his earlier suggestion of handing over Upper Assam to an Ahom prince. In order to maintain tranquillity on the frontier, he suggested that the territory in the extreme east, inhabited by the Moamarias, Khamtis and Singphos be placed under the control of a European officer stationed at Bishwanath.

Scott's report was the subject of prolonged discussion at Fort William. While agreeing with the first part of the report, the government was not prepared to accept the recommendation regarding Upper Assam. Scott was informed that since none of the aspirants to the

Ahom throne had rendered any aid to the British during the war, the Company's government was not obliged to restore a native prince to the throne of Assam. Moreover, in view of the large number of claimants, it would be difficult to select a prince who would be able to command the support of the majority of the people. Referring to the economic potential of the region, the authorities argued that since the revenues of Upper Assam were fluctuating, there was every possibility of its yielding a surplus under better management even after making adequate provisions for the royalty. While admitting the possibility of troubles on the frontier, the authorities pointed out that frontier defence would in any case be the responsibility of the British. Taking all these aspects into consideration, they strongly felt that 'extreme poverty, limited resources and entire dependence on the support of a foreign government'[2] were not conducive to the restoration of a native monarchy in Upper Assam. Scott was, therefore, asked to review the matter once again and submit another report.

These were indeed strong arguments. No Ahom prince had played a role similar to that of Raja Gambhir Singh in the expulsion of the Burmese. It was also true that neither had any Ahom prince entered into a treaty with the British prior to the Burmese war nor was the right of any claimant explicitly recognised by the Treaty of Yandabo. But it was equally true that Lord Amherst's government had made a public commitment to re-establish a government adapted to the wants of Assamese society; and the reversal of this policy to one based on expediency was not consistent with the British declaration in 1824 that they were not motivated by the thirst of conquest. It was thus obvious that unless forced by circumstances or by definite proof that the retention of the region was economically not viable, the British were not prepared to relinquish the territory at this stage. The idea was to advance into the territory step by step.

On 7 March 1828, the President-in-Council communicated to Scott its decision to permanently annex Lower Assam to its dominions. One of the main grounds for the decision was the expectation of large revenue, though the other arguments put forward by Scott also held weight. Captain Neufville, was appointed Political Agent, Upper Assam, in addition to his military duties on a salary of 600 rupees and headquarters at Bishwanath.

ANTI-BRITISH UPRISINGS

The Assamese people had initially welcomed British rule because it had ensured peace and security. Years of turmoil and suffering had taken its toll. The assurance of the British, moreover, that they would re-establish 'a Government adapted to your wants and calculated to promote the happiness of all classes' had kindled hopes of the restoration of the Ahom monarchy in the minds of the nobility. Yet it soon became apparent that this was not to be. The annexation of Lower Assam merely confirmed their fears. The erstwhile nobility that had held positions of power for centuries suddenly found itself edged out by 'interlopers from below'. The establishment of a hierarchy of new officials operating through new legal and administrative machinery, and that too through a new language, opened the way for widespread corruption and extortions. This inevitably produced a deep sense of resentment; and this resentment manifested itself in a series of attempts by the nobility to overthrow the government.

There were three major uprisings to unseat the British after they continued to stay on in the valley.

First Uprising

The first attempt was made towards the close of 1828 when a group of nobles under the leadership of Dhanjoy, a former borgohain, took up the cause of Gomdhar Konwar, a member of the Ahom royal family, to install him as the ruler of Assam. Strengthened by the support of several influential nobles and priests, Gomdhar Konwar proceeded towards Jorhat. The timing seemed opportune because the major part of the Company's troops had been withdrawn from Upper Assam[3] and the Singphos and Bhutias were carrying out depredations in the north. Gomdhar was formally enthroned at Bassa in the south-west corner of Jorhat. The *bailungs* (royal priests) performed the rituals and invested him with a *hengdang*, white shoes and an umbrella, the symbols of royalty. An armed force was hurriedly collected, contributions raised and plans made for the seizure of Rangpur. As the insurgents marched towards Jorhat, they were intercepted by Lieutenant Rutherford at Mariani. Gomdhar and his followers put up a feeble resistance but in the confusion that followed most of his followers abandoned him, compelling Gomdhar to flee as well. Deserted by all, Gomdhar had no alternative but to surrender. Dhanjoy and his son were subsequently apprehended. Gomdhar was tried by the bar panchayat at Jorhat, found guilty of rebellion and sentenced to death. However, considering his age and the fact that he had been a mere tool in the hands of others, the sentence was commuted by Captain Neufville to an imprisonment without labour for seven years. Dhanjoy was awarded capital punishment but he managed to escape to the Naga Hills.

Captain Neufville did not take this uprising very seriously. But Scott was able to gauge its real implications. He observed that unless steps were taken, the discontented elements were likely to engage in similar schemes again. Subsequent events proved that he was right.

Second Uprising

A second attempt to overthrow British rule was made about a year later by Eyang Goomendao alias Gadadhar Singha. His attempt to enlist the support of the sepoys at Sadiya ended prematurely when he fell into a trap laid by Zalim Khan, the *subedar* of the regiment stationed there. Gadadhar was handed over to the authorities at Gauhati.

This abortive attempt, though fairly insignificant in itself, brought to light an important development. In his statement, Gadadhar Singha stated that Atan Meengh Burukuwari, the Assamese princess whom Raja Chandrakanta Singha had earlier presented to the Burmese king, had acquired considerable influence in the Burmese Court. She had apparently pressurised the king to make an attempt to place her brother, Dhanjoy, on the throne of Assam. Although the Burmese Court promptly denied having any hand in the activities of Gadadhar, the British were convinced of Burmese involvement in the matter. Major Burney, the British Resident at Ava, the Burmese capital, was instructed to look into the matter. Meanwhile, as immediate precautionary measures, the existing forts at Sadiya and Borhat were strengthened and a new fort was proposed to be built near Jorhat.

Third Uprising

The last rebellion of this kind was led again by Dhanjoy. Towards the close of 1829, Dhanjoy, who had been implicated in the earlier uprisings, eluded police vigilance and entered Legee, a Moamaria village. Actively aided by his two sons, Harakanta and Haranath, and his son-in-law, Jeuram Dulia Barua, Dhanjoy made preparations for yet another grand uprising. He was able to enlist the support of several influential nobles like Peali Phukan, Deuram Dihingia Barua and Krishnanath. He even sought aid from the Singphos, Khasis, Garos, Nagas and Moamarias to expel the British from the region. Although this was not forthcoming, the protracted engagements of the political agent in the neighbourhood of Sadiya and inadequate defence measures in Upper Assam emboldened Dhanjoy and his associates to defy British authority. Projecting Rupchand Konwar as the future raja of Assam, the rebels marched towards Rangpur which was at that time defended by a small contingent of around thirty sepoys under a jamadar. Dhanjoy's ragtag army of around 400 men made a desperate attempt to occupy Rangpur but was quickly repulsed by the British troops. Dhanjoy and Harakanta escaped to the hills.

Meanwhile, Captain Neufville reached Jorhat with a detachment of the Assam Light Infantry. By the middle of 1830 the rebellion was crushed and the principal leaders arrested. Rupchand Konwar, Jeuram Dulia Barua, Haranath, Peali Phukan, Dihingia Barua and Boom Singpho were tried by the bar panchayat at Jorhat, found guilty of treason and sentenced to death. The proceedings were forwarded to Scott for approval. Scott confirmed the verdict on Peali and Jeuram since he was convinced that such a punishment would act as a deterrent against further insurrections. For the others, capital punishment was commuted to banishment to Bengal and confinement in the Dacca Jail for 14 years and confiscation of all their property.

This was the last attempt of the nobility to expel the British from Assam. These ill-organised rebellions did not reflect a concerted movement on the part of the erstwhile Ahom nobility. Some of the nobles were indifferent while others even betrayed the cause of the rebels. Maniram Barua, for instance, took no interest in these rebellions at all, while Madhabram Borgohain, a member of the bar panchayat co-operated with the sepoys in apprehending the rebels. Moreover, these rebellions were led by people with no political acumen or any military or financial resources worth mentioning. They were unable to harness the support of the common people because they still harboured bitter memories of the injustices and oppressions they had suffered during the anarchical conditions in the recent past under weak Ahom rulers. Thus, in the absence of a common programme of action, a common objective, adequate financial and military resources, and a suitable leader, the rebellions were doomed to fail. Yet, the rebels succeeded, as Captain Neufville wrote, 'in unsettling the minds of the natives throughout Assam'.

These anti-British movements represented the early stage of the resistance of the Assamese nobility to the imposition of British rule. Although Captain Neufville had not given them much importance, Scott was able to grasp the political implications of such attempts. He was convinced that unless an early political settlement in Assam was arrived at, the region would continue to be a virtual tinderbox. Hence, he once again tried to impress upon the authorities at Fort William the immediate necessity of placing Upper Assam under the rule of an Ahom prince.

REORGANISATION UNDER ROBERTSON

Scott died before any settlement could be arrived at. Captain Neufville also passed away prematurely at Jorhat in 1830. Reports of mounting discontent convinced the government that Assam had not been governed well and that remedial measures had to be implemented urgently and effectively. Pending a permanent arrangement, W. Cracroft was temporarily deputed in 1831 to officiate as agent to the governor-general, northeast frontier, and commissioner of Rangpur. Captain Adam White was directed to assume charge of political agent, Upper Assam, a vacancy created by the demise of Neufville, while Lieutenant Matthie continued as magistrate and collector of Gauhati.

Cracroft soon realised that rampant maladministration prevailed in Lower Assam, especially in the revenue and judicial departments. He attributed this primarily to the large volume of business and insufficient manpower. Hence, in order to lessen the burden of administering such an extensive division, he procured permission to transfer six western parganas of Kamrup, viz., Bouse, Chake Bouse, Barnagar, Barpeta, Bagaribari and Nagarbera, to the jurisdiction of the officer in charge of northeast Rangpur. In pursuance of Scott's general policy of associating local people in the administration, he appointed Haliram Dhekial Phukan, a respected Assamese noble, as the assistant magistrate at Gauhati to deal with minor criminal cases. These were, however, only interim measures. Cracroft realised that in order to solve the problem he had to find out the root causes. He, therefore, deputed Lieutenant Rutherford to Darrang and Lieutenant Bogle to the transferred parganas to make a thorough assessment of the prevailing situation and to report back with recommendations.

Meanwhile, Cracroft was relieved of his temporary assignment and replaced by T. C. Robertson, an able civil servant who had served with distinction in Bengal and Arakan.[4] Rutherford and Bogle both toured their respective areas extensively and submitted their reports to Robertson. These reports revealed alarming facts. It was pointed out that:

> ... that there had been a direct tendency to reduce the *ryots* to a state of poverty and dejection of the most distressing nature, to cause a great decrease in population, to impede cultivation, to ruin those resources whence the Government might have somehow derived a handsome revenue, to create constant distrust and anxiety in the minds of the people, to eradicate every feeling of gratitude towards their rulers and to enrich a few worthless beings at the expense of the whole population of the country.[5]

Robertson realised the immensity of his task. He identified three major problem areas, viz., revenue reform, administrative reorganisation and restoration of the Ahom monarchy, and decided to tackle them one at a time.

Robertson's Reforms in Revenue Administration

Robertson's primary concern was reform in the revenue administration. Bogle's Report had highlighted certain serious lapses and he was determined to rectify the situation. Both Rutherford and Bogle attributed the existing conditions to the paucity of European officers and the ignorance and inefficiency of those working under them. They pointed out that the demands of the government were not based on any proper survey and that a system of irregular and undefined additional assessments existed. The choudhurys were empowered with extensive judicial authority which, along with their loosely defined fiscal powers, left the ryots completely at their mercy. The situation was further aggravated by the corrupt practices and intrigues of the *omlahs*. The multiplicity of taxes, the diversity in the methods of assessments and collection, and the system of payment in 'inferior coins of capricious value' added to the confusion. Moreover, the practice of 'underletting', i.e., assignment of lands of a deceased choudhury by his legal heir to another person for a stipulated amount, had crept in although it was prohibited by the *sanad* of appointment. This threw the parganas into the hands of unscrupulous persons with obvious dire consequences.

Certain important suggestions for the reform of the revenue administration were made by Bogle and Rutherford. In view of the large arrears in revenue[6] and the limited paying capacity of the people, it was felt that rehabilitation was the foremost need of the hour. They, therefore suggested, the remission of all irrecoverable balances. It was also recommended that in order to encourage those who had migrated to neighbouring areas to return to their lands, incentives had to be provided in the form of rent-free grants for a few years with an assurance of moderate assessments subsequently. It was also proposed that settlements be made for fixed periods so as to ensure some form of continuity. To rectify the maladministration in the parganas, it was recommended that smaller administrative units be created and placed under the supervision of respectable men residing in or possessing influence in the area. It was stressed that assessments were to be determined only after extensive enquiries. On the whole it was emphasised that the entire revenue system should be simple and effective.

Robertson's Measures for Revenue Reforms

Commenting on the above Report, Robertson remarked that the picture drawn by Bogle and Rutherford was 'melancholy in the extreme' and without waiting for approval of the authorities at Fort William, he acted upon most of the recommendations put forth in the report. He enacted the following measures to relieve the ryots of their burden.

- The collection of arrears in several parganas was held in abeyance. He also abolished the collection of irregular taxes in Darrang, Nowgong and some areas of Kamrup.
- He ensured that there was strict vigil against any form of extortion. Each revenue officer was required to submit a detailed statement regarding the assessed area. Copies of all the relevant records were kept in the collector's office for future reference in case of extortions or complaints.
- He replaced the khel system, which was found to have become totally irrelevant, with direct settlements with the ryots.
- The duties of the revenue official were confined to assessments and the collection of revenue. Except in minor cases, they were not empowered to exercise any judicial authority without referring the matter to the collector. In return for their services, they were entitled to remuneration in the form of a commission.

- The district of Kamrup was divided into a number of parganas, each under a choudhury. The choudhurys were required to reside within their respective jurisdictions so as to be readily available. They were to be assisted by accountants, designated as patwaris, and were to receive a commission of seven per cent of the gross collection by way of remuneration.
- Each pargana was divided into a number of *talukas* and further subdivided into *mouzas* for easy revenue collection.

Robertson believed that these measures would help in streamlining the revenue administration and go a long way in rectifying the earlier defects.

The government approved of the new arrangement in the beginning of 1833. Many ryots who had migrated to the neighbouring areas returned to their old homes. The benefits became apparent from the very next year when the revenue receipts of Lower Assam increased from 183,196 in 1832–3 to 227,128 rupees in 1833–4.[7] As the new settlements were made with individual ryots and not with the entire village, there was better distribution of liabilities. Moreover, the abolition of all the additional taxes reduced the burden on the ryot and helped create a more conducive atmosphere. Some semblance of normalcy seemed to return to the countryside.

Administrative Reorganisation

Robertson then turned his attention to the general administration. He was convinced that without effective European supervision no improvement could be expected. Scott's policy of involving local people in the administration had not been successful in spite of his best intentions. In a communication to the government, he wrote: 'The system of native agency had the fairest possible trial and its failure proves conclusively that Assam is not sufficiently advanced for its reception.'[8] Robertson judged the administrative requirement from a broad political view. He realised that the cost of employing Europeans would be out of proportion to the amount of revenue received, yet he felt that in view of the political and strategic importance of the territory, this was an urgent necessity.

He was extremely critical of the attitude of the government towards the affairs of Assam and pointed out in the strongest terms that grave injustice had been done by entrusting all responsibilities on a single official, viz., the agent to the governor-general, northeast frontier. He was successful in convincing the government that unless immediate administrative reforms were initiated, the situation was likely to deteriorate. In March 1833, the government issued orders for the reorganisation of the administrative structure in Assam. The order was based on Lord Bentinck's Minute which had taken into account Robertson's proposals. The changes that were subsequently introduced laid the foundation of the district administration in Assam.

Administrative Changes

- The province was divided into four districts—Goalpara, Kamrup, Darrang and Nowgong.
- Each district was placed in charge of a European officer designated as principal assistant to the commissioner on a consolidated salary of 1,000 rupees a month.
- He was to officiate as judge, magistrate and collector. He was aided in his duties by a junior assistant who was paid 500 rupees a month.
- All district officers were taken from the army but owing to the paucity of qualified officers certain adjustments had to be made from time to time.

Having modified the administrative structure, Robertson turned his attention to the civil and criminal administration. He based his new system on lines similar to the Regulations in Bengal (The Bengal Regulations, around forty in number, were a code of laws for the administration of the Bengal Presidency enacted by Lord Cornwallis as the East India Company was transforming itself from a trading concern to a territorial power), but with certain modifications to suit local conditions.

Judicial Reforms

- In the administration of civil justice, Robertson abolished the *mofussil* panchayats, surasree panchayats and the powers that had been vested earlier on the choudhurys.
- The principal assistant was empowered to decide suits between 500 to 1,000 rupees and to hear appeals from lower courts. All suits exceeding this amount were to be referred to the Commissioner.

- Each district was to have two courts, viz., a *sadar munsif*'s court which was empowered to try all civil suits between 100 and 500 rupees and to hear appeals from panchayats; and a munsif's panchayat which investigated all petty cases up to 100 rupees. All the civil courts were located at Gauhati.
- In criminal cases, the commissioner exercised the functions of the Nizamat Adalat in dispensing justice. The principal assistant was theoretically on the same footing as the Magistrate of Bengal but he was vested with greater powers.
- Since the revenue officers were deprived of police duties, the *thana* establishment, which had hitherto been confined to the headquarters, had to be extended to other areas as well. The village officials were expected to help the administration and the police in the maintenance of law and order.
- The *sadar amin*, munsifs and omlahs were recruited as far as possible from the local gentry; but owing to the dearth of qualified Assamese persons, the authorities had no option but to recruit people from Bengal to fill the vacancies. As a result, the proceedings in the courts were conducted in Bengali although Assamese, Persian and English were also occasionally used.

The essence of Robertson's measures was European supervision and control over what he termed the 'native agency'. Although he was largely successful in rectifying the earlier defects, certain anomalies remained. Anandaram Dhekial Phukan later commented that the entire judicial procedure was 'defective, tedious, dilatory and expensive'. In his memorandum to Mills twenty years later he wrote: 'All classes (of Assamese) are unanimous in declaring that the mode in which justice is at present administered by the British Government is ill adapted to the simple habits of the people and the impoverished state of the country.'[9] It has, however, to be admitted that Robertson had to work in rather adverse conditions. The paucity of qualified officers, both European and Indian, and the government's concern for economy in the administration, resulted in a paucity of courts. Those that existed were often too far away from the interior areas, causing undue delay in the dispensation of justice. Moreover, the corruption in the courts, inefficiency of the police and expenditure incurred in litigation all added to the harassment of the people who were indeed not used to this form of judicial administration. Yet, in spite of many shortcomings, Robertson was able to streamline the administration in Assam to a large extent and it cannot be denied that it was during his tenure that the foundation of British administration in Lower Assam was firmly laid.

RESTORATION OF THE AHOM MONARCHY

The fate of Upper Assam had remained undecided (See Figure 3.1 for the timeline). We have seen that the British were neither prepared to annex the territory immediately nor hand it over to an Ahom prince. Lord William Bentinck, however, had been convinced by Scott's arguments. He favoured the restoration of the Ahom monarchy for he believed that a monarchy that had lasted for six centuries must be 'intrinsically good' and that 'under the support and advice of a British officer' might in fact provide the right solution to a vexed problem. But the interim measures following the sudden demise of David Scott had delayed matters. Robertson pointed out the advantages of both native and European administrations, but he strongly recommended the retention of Upper Assam as an integral part of the British dominion provided the government was prepared to spare an adequate number of European officers and was willing to provide compensation to the

Figure 3.1: Annexation of Upper Assam

Year	Event	Consequence
1833	Treaty of Gauhati	Restoration of Ahom monarchy as vassals of the British. Purandar Singha crowned ruler of Upper Assam
1833–8	Purandar Singha's reign	Deterioration in relations with the British
1834	Appointment of Francis Jenkins as commissioner and agent to the governor-general	Directs Adam White to survey Purandar Singha's territory and submit a report
1835	Adam White submits report	Recommends reduction in the tribute to be paid to the British
1838	Jenkins goes on a three month tour of the territory	Recommends annexation of a part of Upper Assam
1838	White announces takeover of Upper Assam by the British	End of Ahom rule in Assam and establishment of British rule over the territory

ruling families. If this was not possible, Robertson believed that the only solution lay in handing over the territory to an Ahom prince but with certain conditions laid down. Robertson proposed that that the headquarters of the political agent, Upper Assam, and the main wing of the Assam Light Infantry be located at Jorhat. He further suggested that an area of four square miles within the Raja's territory be retained by the British authorities for the purpose of setting up a cantonment. In order to ensure the defence of the frontier, Robertson proposed that a frontier outpost be maintained at Sadiya under a European officer. The expenses of this station, which was estimated at around 50,000 rupees annually, would be borne by the Bar Senapati, the Moamaria chief.

The Court of Directors concurred with most of the views of Robertson but entertained grave doubts about the success of the restored monarchy in Upper Assam. On the other hand, the prevailing administrative confusion and the defiant attitude of certain sections of the nobility convinced the authorities that it would not be easy for the British to govern the territory effectively either. In the circumstances, Lord William Bentinck again wondered if the restoration of an Ahom prince in Upper Assam would be a good idea. While agreeing in principle to the restoration of the monarchy, the Vice President-in-Council expressed its doubts about stationing British troops within a foreign state. It was, therefore, decided that Bishwanath would be retained as the headquarters of the regiment. The question of imposing the financial liability of the Sadiya post on the bar senapati was deferred. It was further resolved that the restored prince would be required to pay a moderate tribute and to modify criminal law in consonance with British jurisprudence. The power of deposing him in the event of maladministration was to rest explicitly with the British government.

Eventually, in October1832 it was decided to assign Upper Assam to a member of the Ahom royal family who was considered capable of effectively administering the territory. But this was to be on an experimental basis. The immediate question that cropped up related to the choice of the candidate. Two were short listed for consideration from among the many claimants: Chandrakanta Singha and Purandar Singha. Although Chandrakanta's claim to the throne was stronger, both Cracroft and Robertson had recommended Purandar in preference to him. According to Robertson, Chandrakanta was considered 'degraded both in mind and feeling' and as such totally unfit to rule.[10]

Even Scott was not in his favour because of his earlier connections with the Burmese and his 'aptitude to be easily misled by others'. Moreover, it was also pointed out that as Chandrakanta was more closely related than Purandar to the last Ahom monarch, he might consider himself deprived of half the kingdom. Purandar, on the other hand would have no such grievance and would accept even a part of the Ahom kingdom with gratitude.

The governor-general felt that the choice should be determined not by 'proximity of relationship to the last head of state' but rather by 'superiority of qualifications'. Purandar was young and likely to be amenable to new ideas. Hence, taking all factors into consideration and after much debate and discussion, the choice ultimately fell on Purandar Singha. Chandrakanta submitted an appeal but it was summarily rejected.

Treaty of Gauhati, 1833[11]

On 2 March 1833, Robertson, on behalf of the East India Company, concluded a treaty with Purandar Singha at Gauhati. The main terms of the treaty were as follows:

1. The East India Company handed over the portion of Assam lying to the east of the Dhansiri river on the south bank of the Brahmaputra river and the territory lying to the east of the small river near Bishwanth on the north bank to Raja Purandar Singha.
2. The Raja promised to pay the Company's government an annual tribute of 50,000 rupees out of an estimated revenue of 120,000 rupees.
3. The Raja bound himself to abide by the principles of British jurisprudence and to abstain from the practices of the former Ahom rulers with regard to the physical torture of criminals.
4. He also agreed to abide by the advice of the Political Agent, Upper Assam and the Agent to the Governor-General, North East Frontier.
5. He further promised to release, on demand from British officials, any fugitive from justice who might take refuge in his territory.
6. The Raja would have no power over the Moamaria country of the Bar Senapati or over the territory of the Sadiya Khowa Gohain.

7. The Raja was assured of British protection so long as he remained loyal; but if he was found to be unfaithful or guilty of oppressing his subjects, the Company's government reserved the right to either hand over the territory to another ruler or to annex it to the British dominions.
8. Purandar Singha agreed to cooperate with the British in matters relating to the cultivation and sale of opium within his territory.
9. He also agreed to ban *sati* within his territory.

Purandar Singha was formally installed as Raja of Upper Assam in April 1833 with his headquarters at Jorhat. As he was not happy with the title of raja, it was decided that he would be officially addressed as Shree Shree Maharaja Purandar Singh Narendra.

Within a few days of the above agreement however, the British began to have doubts about the wisdom of the restoration of the Ahom monarchy. Reports of the survey of the northeastern frontier conducted by Pemberton and Jenkins had come in the meantime. These reports dwelt at length on the economic potential of the region and stated in no uncertain terms that the area was indeed 'worth having'. It further reaffirmed that in view of the doubtful fidelity of the neighbouring chiefs, it was not advisable to abandon the Sadiya frontier completely.

The governor-general even thought of reopening the issue of restoration. After all, one of the main considerations of the Company had been financial gain. But since headway had already been made, it was decided to modify the terms of the treaty for the time being. In order to strengthen its hold on Purandar Singha, the government decided to impose certain restrictions on the new Raja. Accordingly, in June 1833, the treaty was recast in the form of an agreement whereby Purandar Singha was recognised as the ruler of Jorhat region. This virtually reduced the status of the king to that of a *jagirdar*.

The entire episode of the restoration, which was marked by indecision and vacillation from the beginning, was subjected to severe criticism by the Court of Directors. They expressed their misgivings on two main counts. Firstly, they doubted whether Purandar would be able to pay the stipulated tribute which amounted to almost half his estimated collection. Secondly, they felt that by reserving to itself the 'discretionary right of interference', the government had actually taken upon itself the obligation of interfering whenever the province was mismanaged. In a dispatch to Fort William, the Court of Directors wrote:

> In carrying into effect a measure of so much importance, of such a questionable policy and of no urgency whatever, without a previous reference to us, you have incurred our disapprobation ... we are only prevented from annulling the whole transaction by our reluctance to do anything which might weaken your authority.[12]

Since Purandar Singha had already ascended the throne, the Court of Directors had no option but to accept the situation. Nonetheless, they issued a strict injunction to the effect that in future, 'no portion of the public revenue and still less the government of any portion of our territories be permanently alienated without a previous reference to us for our authority and sanction'.[13]

The restored Ahom monarchy, therefore, rested on shaky foundations.

PURANDAR SINGHA'S ADMINISTRATION

When Purandar Singha ascended the throne, he was about twenty-five years old. He had spent most of his youth in Calcutta and it was expected that his general education and exposure would make him amenable to new ideas. But Purandar had no political experience and could not have anticipated the numerous difficulties that would confront him when he accepted the treaty that had been imposed on him. He was willing to learn, but the problems that he had to face were so formidable that tackling them was not easy by any standard.

When he took over the administration, Purandar Singha found Upper Assam in a state of chaos. The old Ahom system of government had broken down and the half-hearted measures that had been introduced by the British during the period of occupation had resulted in utter confusion. Corruption and anarchy were rampant in every sphere. The khel system was in ruins, agriculture had declined and trade and commerce had practically collapsed. The judicial system, too, was in complete disarray. In such circumstances, the condition of the ryots, who were subjected to constant abuse, was deplorable. For Purandar Singha rehabilitating the country was indeed a formidable task. And, to top it all, his very position was being questioned. Purandar did not command universal support. In fact, a section of the nobility actively supported the cause of Chandrakanta Singha who not only reiterated his claim to the throne but also offered to pay a tribute of 70,000 rupees yearly to the Company's government. Although Chandrakanta was eventually deported to Kaliabar on a monthly pension of 500 rupees, his supporters continued to be a source of constant trouble.

Despite these difficulties, Purandar Singha tried his best to rectify the situation. He realised that in order to win his subjects' confidence, he had to assure them that their traditional customs and institutions would be respected. The erstwhile nobility who had lost all their earlier positions of power and wealth would also need to be conciliated. And perhaps, most important of all, he would have to ensure adequate protection to the ryots. Keeping these objectives in mind against the backdrop of his commitments to the British under the Treaty of Gauhati, Purandar Singha enacted certain Regulations.

Regulations

At the outset, Purandar revived the old *patra mantri* (cabinet of ministers) comprising the buragohain, *bargohain, and barpatra gohain* and retained the subordinate officials like *phukans*, rajkhowas, *hazarikas*, *boras* and *saikias*. Taking them into confidence and after consultation with the political agent, Upper Assam, he issued a series of regulations relating to revenue and judicial matters. These measures are commonly referred to as the Regulations of Purandar.

Revenue Reforms

- Purandar revived the khel system in order to try and implement a successful revenue system. The entire territory was divided into regular khels with well defined boundaries. Each khel was under the supervision of a kheldar who was responsible for the collection of revenue within his jurisdiction.
- Each paik was numbered and allotted two puras of arable land in lieu of a capitation tax of three rupees. Initially, White favoured ten year settlements with the kheldars, but the term was eventually fixed at four years because it was pointed out that this would provide opportunities for frequent revisions.
- The kheldars did not receive a salary as such but were remunerated by the services of paiks and received, in addition, a commission on the total collection. It was made mandatory for

the kheldars to reside within their respective areas. They were allowed to go on leave only with prior permission and after a substitute had been appointed. A kheldar could hold office as long as he paid his dues to the government regularly and could not be dismissed without being tried by the court of the patra mantri.

- As a measure of protection to the ryots, the kheldars were instructed to issue receipts against all collections. No consideration in the form of remission in revenue was made for deserting ryots. It was hoped that such a regulation would compel the kheldars to maintain conditions which would prevent emigration of ryots to other areas. It was further stipulated that after three years, only those who could read, write and maintain accounts would qualify as revenue officials. If such persons were not available among the nobility, then the vacancies would be filled up by literate persons irrespective of class.

Judicial Reforms

Changes were also made in the judicial administration. Under British occupation, justice had become complicated, slow and expensive. The procedure involving written petitions and depositions were new to a people most of whom were completely illiterate. Moreover, the courts were located only in the principal towns and were unable to cope with the large volume of litigations. Purandar realised that the first step towards the solution of the problem lay in decentralising immediately. He, therefore, introduced several new measures.

- The kheldars were vested with judicial powers. In criminal cases, they were empowered to inflict penalties not exceeding imprisonment for six months, to punish with 15 lashes and impose fines up to 20 rupees. In civil matters, they exercised jurisdiction over civil suits to the extent of ten rupees and investigated complaints of irregularities against omlahs.
- He set up four courts of *gram adhikars* at Rangpur, Majuli, Uttarpar and Bassa Doyang which exercised appellate jurisdiction over the kheldar courts. They were empowered to investigate into cases of extortion and oppression by kheldars and also to try civil cases up to 100 rupees. In an effort to blend both the Ahom and British systems, it was decided that no written

pleadings or depositions would be required in these courts though the judges were required to regularly submit abstracts of the cases tried by them. The district judges could be dismissed only after a regular trial.

- In the capital, petty cases were heard by two panchayats. The barbaruah's court was empowered to award sentences of imprisonment up to three years and to try civil cases upon written depositions, up to 1,000 rupees.
- At the apex was the *sadar* (supreme) court presided over by the king and consisting of three judges. It was to decide civil cases over 1,000 rupees and try all grave criminal cases. The judges were expected to visit and assess the functioning of the district courts and kheldar courts. All judges were to be remunerated in cash because it was felt that the earlier system of payments in kind encouraged corruption.

Socio-Economic Reforms

Purandar did not confine his reforms to administration alone. He believed that a state could prosper only if there was all round development in society. Having spent a considerable part of his life in Bengal, he had been exposed to new ideas. He now tried to translate these ideas into action.

Social Reforms: The young Raja realised that the state could function as it should only if corruption was rooted out and other measures introduced to make the life of the people easier and administration, more efficient.

- He decided to raise the salaries of the omlahs as one of the main causes of corruption among them was inadequate remuneration.
- He was also convinced that much of the prevailing chaos and confusion in the administration would automatically disappear if the officers were literate. With a view to training prospective personnel for the administration, he issued instructions to the kheldars to set up and supervise schools within their jurisdiction.
- He was determined to put an end to slavery and as a first step, he decided to impose a penalty of imprisonment for 14 years if anyone was caught enslaving a *paik*.

Economic Reforms: The economy of Upper Assam was practically in ruins when Purandar Singha took over. He needed to pay immediate attention to agriculture and industry. He undertook certain measures to ensure that the life of the ryots and other industries.

- During the troubled times that followed the Burmese invasion, much of the cultivable land had gone back to being jungles. As an incentive to cultivators to bring back these lands under tillage, Purandar allotted them free of rent for a period of two years after which an assessment was to be made at nominal rates.
- To stimulate industry, kheldars were instructed to take their dues in kind in lieu of cash in remote areas.
- Keeping these interior places in mind, the Raja abolished the custom *chowkies* on the Brahmaputra so as to facilitate the free flow of goods.

Factors Constraining Purandar

Resentment among the Nobility

It is evident that Purandar Singha earnestly tried to bring about overall development in Upper Assam. But he had to work under severe constraints and many of his measures provoked adverse reactions among the nobility who had expected that the restoration of Ahom monarchy would mean the return of their lost power, prestige and privileges. Purandar's regime belied their expectations. The requirement of educational qualifications for the post of kheldar, for instance, closed the door for many who had earlier enjoyed the coveted post. The resettlement of lands on the basis of an accurate survey also deprived many of the income from large tracts which they had held illegally. These, together with other grievances, created bitterness and frustration among sections of the nobility. Despite Purandar's efforts to conciliate them and to take them into confidence, they remained a constant source of trouble throughout his reign.

Purandar faced other problems as well. Having spent a considerable part of his life in Bengal, he was regarded more as a Bengali than an Assamese. This perception was reinforced when Purandar inducted Bengali omlahs in the administration. He was unable to employ the Assamese as they were not familiar with the British methods of administration which he was bound by the treaty to implement. This naturally created much ill-feeling among the erstwhile aristocracy who felt that they had been denied their rightful place in the administrative setup.

Purandar's Financial Constraints

Purandar may have been able to overcome these difficulties had he been financially secure. But this was not so. He had pledged to pay a huge annual tribute of 50,000 rupees although his source of income was limited to taxation on paik lands, duties on haats, ghats and fisheries and taxes on professions and castes. He soon realised that the estimated revenue of 120,000 rupees was indeed too high.[14] In November 1833, he submitted a petition to the British asking for the restoration of the remaining portion of Upper Assam. The following year he renewed his petition with an offer of an additional annual tribute of 100,000 rupees for that area; but the petition was summarily rejected.

Migration woes: The financial problem was aggravated by the very serious issue of migration. Adjacent to Purandar's territory was the relatively prosperous area ruled over by Matibar Bar Senapati, the Moamaria chief. The Muttocks, who were the original inhabitants of the region, were exempted from all taxes but immigrants from other areas were subjected to a nominal tax. In order to encourage cultivation, the Bar Senapati often waived this tax and even granted subsidies in times of need. He encouraged the production of cash crops and adopted a free trade policy which added to the prosperity of the region. The security of life and property in turn encouraged merchants to set up trading establishments in the Maomaria territory. Such favourable conditions saw large-scale migration from Purandar's territory where taxation was much higher. As a large number of people migrated to the Muttock area, Purandar Singha was left with a dwindling income. He repeatedly appealed to the British for a remission in tribute on account of this constant exodus but to no avail. White attempted to partially remove the anomaly by proposing that the services of the contingent furnished by the Bar Senapati be commuted for an annual payment of 10,000 rupees in cash. In return, he was to be invested with the title of Raja and the succession of his heirs was guaranteed. White believed that under this arrangement, the Bar Senapati would be compelled to levy taxes on his subjects in order to raise the money. Initially, the Moamaria chief opposed the proposal outright: he would rather abdicate his position than tax his subjects. But after prolonged negotiations he agreed to a modified proposal requiring him to pay 1,800 rupees in lieu of the paiks. The new arrangement, however, made little difference to Purandar's financial position.

Apart from migration into the Muttock territory, there was a flow of migrants into the neighbouring British territory as well. In this case, the migrants consisted of *doms* (fishermen) and *mariyas* (artisans in brass). In Nowgong and Darrang districts, these two classes of people were exempted from all taxation unless they held land. This naturally induced migration from Purandar's territory and the Raja was constrained to lower taxes on these classes in order to check the exodus. This adversely affected his already depleting resources. As a remedial measure, Purandar put forth two proposals to the Political Agent: to either make a suitable remission in his tribute or to arrange for the collection of taxes due to him from his subjects who had migrated to Nowgong and Darrang. White considered the case sympathetically but it did not evoke a similar response from Jenkins, Agent to the Governor-General. Instead, he instructed White to make an enquiry and submit a detailed report on the condition of the Raja's territory.

Shortage of Coins

There was another serious problem that persisted throughout Purandar's reign. This was the shortage of coins. The economy of the region had been monetised only recently, and there was no great accumulation of cash. Besides, there was no mint either in Lower or Central Assam for minting the *Rajamohri* or narayani coins that were in circulation. White had recommended the establishment of a mint in Upper Assam but the proposal was turned down in view of certain objections raised by the Superintendent of Mint. There was, moreover, hardly any trade or commerce which might attract coins from other regions. As a result, most of the ryots were constrained to pay their taxes in kind. Even Jenkins admitted that it was impossible, even for the most willing ryot, to pay his dues in cash. But Purandar was bound by agreement to pay his tribute in cash. He was, therefore, compelled to devise various means of collecting the stipulated amount. White gives an account of one way in which this was done.

> The king has various devices for extorting the payment of revenue from his subjects, and though not so barbarous as the tortures practiced by

> his ancestors, they are sufficiently painful and humiliating ... he has them promptly conveyed to the edge of a large pit, dug on purpose and filled with mud, cow dung and bars, and into this, delinquents, whatever their rank might be, are driven waist deep and compelled to stand under a boiling sun until they make payment; as if in mockery, a bamboo rail is carried through the middle of the pond to divide the nobles from the lower classes. A threat of this punishment to the gentry usually induces a speedy adjustment of dues, and when the parties have not the means of satisfying the demand, they fly from the country.[15]

Purandar Singha had committed to the British that he would refrain from indulging in physical torture. He was constrained to break his commitment in order to meet his obligations. It is indeed surprising that the British authorities conveniently overlooked these acts.

Despite overwhelming odds, Purandar remitted the full sum of his tribute for the first two years. Robertson had commented in 1833 that he was 'happy to speak well of Raja Purandar Singha' and that although sections of the nobility were discontented, the people at large were happy with a 'mild and beneficent master'.[16] In the following years, however, the situation changed. The outbreak of a cholera epidemic and subsequent famine in his territory, adversely affected Purandar's revenue collections which dropped to 42,216 rupees in 1837–8. The Raja found himself in a precarious condition. He was left with no option but to default on his payment.

THE ANNEXATION OF UPPER ASSAM

Meanwhile, major administrative changes had taken place in the northeastern frontier. In January1834, the government abolished the office of the political agent to the northeast frontier of Bengal and commissioner of Rangpur and instead created the post of commissioner and agent to the governor-general for Assam and northeast Rangpur. Captain Francis Jenkins[17] was appointed to this new post under the supervision and control of the *Sadar Diwani Adalat* and the *Sadar* Board of Revenue. It was for the first time that a military officer was placed at the head of the civil administration in Assam.

Captain Jenkins and Purandar Singha

Jenkins realised that the manifold problems of Purandar Singha were genuine and indeed very serious. Initially, therefore, his sympathies lay with the helpless Raja. He believed that in light of the treaty between Purandar and the British, the Company's government was morally bound to support him in his troubled times because it could not be denied that Purandar had tried hard to meet his treaty obligations. In course of time, however, Jenkins' attitude towards the Raja underwent a change. Constant bickering among different sections of the people, numerous allegations against the Raja and a large number of anonymous letters that he received poisoned his mind against Purandar. He now began to doubt the Raja's integrity and capability. In an effort to gather authentic information so as to form an independent opinion, he directed Adam White, the Political Agent, to personally survey the Raja's territory and report to him.

In the meanwhile, under pressure from the nobility, Jenkins had requested the Government of Bengal for permission to place a magistrate at Jorhat to look into the alleged oppressions of Purandar Singha, and call for explanations from the king. Considering this an outright insult to his dignity, Purandar promptly wrote to the commisioner, 'If it be your intention to hear appeals and continue to question me in all my actions in such petty cases, you ought to have in the first place instead of making me a *Raja* have made me a Judge or a Magistrate.'[18] Jenkins replied that he believed that some sort of check was essential.

Adam White's Report on Assam

Under instructions from Jenkins, Adam White began his extensive tour of Upper Assam towards the end of 1835. He was impressed with the extent of cultivation, especially considering the fact that this had been the most adversely affected area during the troubled times following the Burmese invasion. He found certain instances of corruption and mismanagement in the judicial and revenue departments, but he attributed many of the irregularities to the inability of the king to pay reasonable salaries to the omlahs in cash. Commenting on the functioning of the police department, he stated that he found the police 'tolerably efficient' and observed that the punishment inflicted by the Raja was very mild compared to the 'barbarous mutilations' to which criminals had been subjected to under the earlier regimes. White also reported the financial difficulties of Purandar and confirmed that the large-scale exodus of his subjects had contributed greatly to the sorry state of affairs. He pointed out that in the prevailing circumstances the demand of 50,000 rupees was an unreasonable amount and recommended a reduction of the tribute by 15,000 rupees. He concluded by observing that, 'it cannot be considered that his [Purandar's] Government has had a fair trial but making due allowances for them, I am of the opinion that it has worked as well as it could have been expected'.[19]

Jenkins, unfortunately, did not agree with White. He insisted that the inefficiency of Purandar Singha was responsible for the grave situation and that since he had not fulfilled his obligations, he should be asked to relinquish his office. The conflicting views of the commissioner and the political agent confused the authorities at Calcutta. In the circumstances, they directed Jenkins to immediately proceed to Upper Assam to undertake a personal survey. At the same time he was informed that the authorities at Calcutta would consider lowering the amount of tribute if it was likely to promote the prosperity of the region.

Jenkin's Report on Assam

Jenkins set off on a three-month tour of Upper Assam in January 1838. The *Journal of Upper Assam,* his meticulously maintained tour diary, is a document of unique historical importance containing detailed geographical, economic and statistical information about the region. In April 1838, Jenkins submitted his final report to the authorities. He dwelt at length on the deteriorating economic, social and political condition of Upper Assam and attributed this primarily to the Raja's inefficient and corrupt administration though he admitted that, 'the misrule of the Raja was not entirely without excuse'. He pointed out that since Purandar had defaulted on his payments, he had technically forfeited his claim to the territory. But in light of his investigations, he recommended that a part of Upper Assam[20] be taken over by the British leaving Purandar with the rest of Upper Assam. No tribute would be demanded of him but he would be expected to clear his dues within a period of five years. Even while forwarding these proposals, Jenkins had serious doubts about Purandar Singha actually agreeing to the proposition. As an afterthought, perhaps, and within a few hours of sending this proposal, Jenkins sent a letter to H. T. Prinsep, Secretary, the Government of India, describing Purandar as, 'one of the worst characters', a 'rapacious miser' and one totally unfit to rule. He even hinted at the existence of an organised conspiracy to get rid of him. As such, he recommended the immediate annexation of the whole of Upper Assam.

The Company's Takeover of Upper Assam

When they received the report, the Vice-President-in-Council, after a detailed discussion, decided that the experiment of the restored monarchy had failed miserably and that it would not be expedient to leave the territory in the hands of Purandar any longer. Lord Auckland, the Governor-General, endorsed this recommendation, though with some reluctance. The implementation of the decision was, however, delayed for a few weeks by the arrival of a dispatch from the Court of Directors prohibiting the annexation of any territory under a native prince without their prior approval.[21] The governor-general referred the matter to the vice-president-in-council who came to the conclusion that in view of the urgency of the situation the above directive could be overruled. The political agent of Upper Assam was instructed to assume the charge of the territory and to place two principal assistants, Lieutenant Brodie and Lieutanant Vetch, with headquarters at Jorhat and Lakhimpur respectively. Accordingly, on 16 October 1838, White announced the changes at Jorhat by a Proclamation on behalf of the Company's government. Purandar Singha registered a mild protest that he had not been given an opportunity to defend himself against the charges levelled against him but the petition was summarily dismissed. He was offered a monthly pension of 1,000 rupees which he rejected in the hope of regaining his lost territory one day.[22]

Thus, the Ahom monarchy which had ruled over Assam for almost six centuries came to an inglorious end. The entire episode demonstrates very clearly that responsibility without adequate financial resources is bound to have adverse repercussions. At the root of all the problems of Purandar Singha was financial stringency. The Company had sealed the Raja's fate at the very beginning by demanding a tribute which at the best of times exceeded more than half his total revenue collection. Dwindling resources accompanied by internal opposition and massive depopulation complicated matters beyond repair. The situation would not have deteriorated had Purandar been give a fair chance. He had been elevated to the throne on strong recommendations of his capabilities and after prolonged discussions by the authorities at Fort William. Both Robertson and White had been sympathetic toward him and had even suggested measures to alleviate his problems. But Jenkins was not convinced and had remained sceptical. His adverse report and the hurried manner in which Purandar was deposed, therefore, raise serious questions as to the real motive behind the annexation.

Political instability appears to have been merely an excuse for annexation. After all, Upper Assam had been politically unstable since the end of Rudra Singha's reign (1696-1714), and the British could have annexed the region much earlier had they so desired. The actual reason, therefore, must be sought elsewhere. Captain Welsh's expedition into Assam in 1792 had opened up new economic vistas for the British and for the first time they had received authentic information about the economic potential of the region. Welsh had painted pictures of great possibilities. It now appeared that these possibilities could be converted into reality. The discovery of the indigenous tea plant in Upper Assam and the definite proof that tea could be successfully cultivated as a commercial crop in the region convinced the authorities both in Calcutta and London of its economic prospects. This conviction was reinforced when the tea plant was discovered in Cachar as well in 1831.[23] Cachar was promptly annexed thereafter. It is therefore likely that similar considerations worked behind the resumption of the administration of Upper Assam. H. L. Gupta suggests that the single factor responsible for influencing the annexation of Upper Assam was the discovery of the tea plant in the area.[24] It must be remembered that the East India Company was primarily a commercial enterprise and as such was bound to be motivated by economic considerations while taking decisions. The authorities were persuaded to believe that since British rule would ensure peace and security, it would create conditions that would facilitate the acquisition of 'tea grounds' and the subsequent establishment of a profitable tea industry in Upper Assam. It is quite possible that the intention of the British at this point of time was to convert 'Assam into an agricultural estate of the tea drinking Britons'.[25] The inefficiency, corruption and maladministration of Purandar Singha were merely an excuse for it.

ANNEXATION OF SADIYA AND MUTTOCK

The military occupation of Upper Assam in 1826 had brought the British into direct contact with the Moamaria, Khamti and Singpho tribes inhabiting the area known as the Sadiya country. The Moamarias

Figure 3.2 Annexation of Sadiya and Muttock

Year	Event	Consequence
1826	David Scott concludes treaties with the Singphos, Khamtis and Moamarias of Muttock	The chiefs of these tribes accept British overlordship
1830	Singphos rebel	Khamtis under the Sadiya Khowa Gohain help the British in quelling the rebellion
1834	Dispute between the Sadiya Khowa Gohain and Matibar Bar Senapati of Muttock	Sadiya Khowa Gohain removed from office by the British. Khamtis on the whole are not punished
1839	Khamtis rebel	Adam White killed by the rebels; British cantonment shifted to Saikhowaghat; Last of the rebels surrenders in 1843
1839	Matibar Bar Senapati, chief of the Moamarias, dies	Maju Gohain succeeds him but the British want him to sign a fresh treaty that enhances the tribute
1839	Internal strife in Muttock led by the brahmin *gossain* of Muttock and Bhaktananda of Tiphook	British decide to annex the whole of Muttock

inhabited the tract lying between the Brahmaputra and the Buridihing rivers known as Muttock and were ruled over by their chief, Matibar Bar Senapati. During the Burmese invasion, the Bar Senapati was able to successfully resist the invaders and protect his subjects. This had resulted in a considerable influx of people from the neighbouring areas into his territory.[26] On the other hand, the Singphos, inhabiting the areas to southeast of Muttock, had identified their interests with the Burmese and had ravaged the land as far as Jorhat. In the process they had broken up into a number of independent groups, each under a chieftain, and were divided into two hostile camps under the Beesa and Duffa *gaums* (both Singpho chiefs). Their plundering raids necessitated continued British operations in this region even after the Burmese evacuation of Rangpur. The Khamtis settled in the area south of the Na Dihing river merging into the Hukang Valley in Upper Burma. Under the leadership of the Sadiya Khowa Gohain, the Khamtis had acted in collusion with the Singphos and had carried out widespread incursions into the Brahmaputra Valley. (See Figure 3.2 for timeline)

Scott's Treaties with the Moamarias, Khamtis and Singphos

The British needed to guard the frontier to protect the territory that had been brought under British occupation following the Treaty of Yandabo. It was also essential to neutralise the opposition of the frontier tribes in the event of another Burmese invasion. David Scott realised that the best possible way to do this was to bring these tribes under the British sphere of influence. With this in mind, he entered into agreements with the chiefs of the Moamarias and Khamtis on 13 May 1826.

Matibar Bar Senapati, the chief of the Moamarias, acknowledged the suzerainty of the British government. He was not required to pay any tribute to the British but he promised to furnish a contingent of 150 militiamen and an equal number of labourers. He further agreed to supply provisions to the British on demand.[27]

The Khamtis[28] also acknowledged British suzerainty. No tribute was demanded of them either. The chiefs, however, agreed to supply 40 militiamen, 20 paiks and ten boatmen. They were also required to maintain a contingent of 200 men who were to be provided with arms and ammunition by the British.[29]

At an impressive durbar at Sadiya on 5 May 1826, 16 Singpho chiefs concluded an agreement with the British government acknowledging its supremacy, agreeing to give up captives, referring disputes to arbitration and promising cooperation in times of war and disturbances.[30] In the same durbar, the Beesa gaum was made the 'paramount chief' and the channel of communication between the Singphos and the British.

The Company decided to post a British officer at Sadiya in order to ensure a 'dominating military and political presence' in the area. Captain Neufville emphasised that the British must be guided by the fundamental principle of guaranteeing the chiefs their time honoured rights and privileges while at the same time ensuring their subservience when maintaining their ties with the latter. After taking this into consideration, the chiefs were allowed to decide upon civil cases and minor criminal cases within their respective jurisdictions. Serious criminal cases were, however, to be referred to the political agent, Upper Assam. The government approved of these measures. Sadiya, though not under direct administrative control, was under its indirect control. It was hoped that these measures would help in creating conditions necessary for the maintenance of peace in the region.

Deterioration in Ties and Annexation

Singphos and Khamtis

Subsequent events belied this optimism. The Singphos rebelled in 1830. During this rebellion, the Khamtis rendered some assistance to the British but the loyalty of their chief, the Sadiya Khowa Gohain was questioned because of his alleged anti-British connections. He was alleged to have brought the Burmese invaders into Assam as he had given his daughter in marriage to the Burmese king. He was also suspected of aiding the anti-British Singpho rebellion in 1830. An ambitious chief, he aimed at becoming an independent king instead of a mere zamindar under the British. Moreover, his disputes with the Bar Senapati of Muttock were a source of constant trouble to the government. Towards the end of 1834 both the chiefs were engaged in hostilities over rival claims upon migrants who had deserted Purandar Singha's territory and had settled at Saikhowaghat. Lieutenant Charlton, Officer-in-Charge posted at Sadiya, asked both the parties to submit their claims to the political agent for arbitration. In an outright defiance of British authority, the Sadiya Khowa Gohain not only refused to comply with the request but went a step further by assaulting the settlers and forcibly taking possession of Saikhowaghat. Enraged by his defiance, the commissioner ordered the removal of the Sadiya Khowa Gohain from office and British administration in the area which had been under his control.[31] The Khamtis in general were left undisturbed under their respective chiefs but the Assamese paiks, who constituted around two-thirds of the population and lived as bondsmen and slaves, were freed and brought under regular assessment. The Khamtis, unable to reconcile themselves to this loss, rebelled in 1839. Around 600 armed men attacked the cantonment, seized the magazine and set fire to the military lines killing many, including the political agent, Adam White. Despite the initial setback, the Khamtis were repulsed.

Jenkins later commented that this attack of the Khamtis was the 'boldest attempt' made by the hill tribes on the northeastern frontier. The incident demonstrated the vulnerability of Sadiya. Hence, the cantonment was shifted to Saikhowaghat so that it would be nearer to the sources of supply and less exposed to sudden raids of the tribes. As a further defence measure, stockades were built at Tazee, Koojoo, Ningroo, Beesa, and Jaipur.

The Moamarias

The conduct of the Bar Senapati too was questionable. An independent-minded person with an overbearing personality, he regarded the non-payment of tributes to the British as a symbol of his special status. He was widely believed to be an accomplice in the anti-British uprisings in Upper Assam and it was suspected that he had allowed his territory to be used by the rebels. He had also consistently refused to enhance his tribute but had agreed to compensate in cash for the paiks who had migrated from Purandar Singha's territory.[32] He had allotted each of his sons different tracts of territory to administer under his general supervision. But he was getting old and the question of succession along with the possibility of internal dissensions following his death cropped up from time to time. Anticipating such a situation, he nominated his second son, Maju Gohain, as his successor.

The discovery of the tea plant in the area meant that British speculators had begun to take special interest in Muttock. Jenkins had already highlighted this discovery to the government with the suggestion that the territory be brought under more effective control. He reiterated his views in 1838. The Bar Senapati died the following year and in accordance with his wishes, was succeeded by Maju Gohain. Although the question of annexation loomed large in the background, the government was apprehensive of taking such a drastic step immediately. The possibility of a renewed Burmese invasion still existed and in the case of such an eventuality, the neutrality, if not active assistance, of the Moamarias would be of immense help. Moreover, they also realised that as far as revenue was concerned, the acquisition of the principality was unlikely to be profitable. Nevertheless, pending a final decision, the political agent announced that Maju Gohain's succession would be recognised only if he entered into a new agreement[33] with the British on the following terms:

- Payment of an enhanced tribute of 10,000 rupees per annum.
- Setting aside of wastelands for the cultivation of tea.
- Appointment of a British officer to adjudicate disputes arising between the Moamarias and the European tea planters.

The exorbitant tribute was considered an outrageous demand; there was no question of Maju Gohain agreeing to it. The two other conditions were more or less acceptable.

Internal Strife in Muttock and Annexation

Meanwhile, Captain White had been succeeded by Captain Vetch. The new political agent realised that it would be futile to insist on the tribute because it would only lead to disaffection. At the same time, foregoing the demand completely would be taken as a sign of weakness. Opting for a middle course, Vetch decided to fix the amount of tribute payable on the basis of a new census. Before any action could be taken in this regard, the principality was rocked by internal dissensions that changed the course of events. The people were divided into two sectarian groups each under a gossain or a spiritual head. The upper areas of Muttock were inhabited by the Morans who formed the bulk of the population. They were the followers of the brahmin gossain of Tiphook. The lower region was inhabited by non-Morans, mostly immigrant Assamese paiks, who were followers of Bhaktananda, the head of the Moamaria sect. The Morans had opposed the accession of Maju Gohain because they believed that he was completely under the influence of Bhaktananda and had sent several representations to the British to that effect. Jenkins once again pointed out to the government that such unstable conditions on the frontier were detrimental to the safety and security of the British territories. In fact, he saw in this internal conflict of the Moamarias an unexpected opportunity to annex their territory.

After long deliberations, the government resolved to acknowledge the rights of Maju Gohain subject to certain conditions.[34] He had to part with a considerable portion of his revenue to the British and agree to place the unoccupied jungle lands under the control of a British officer. Further, his authority would not extend to the tea plantations or any other British establishment within his territory. Upper Muttock was to be excluded from the purview of this arrangement. This meant dividing the Muttock territory which had been ruled as a single unit by the late Bar Senapati. Maju Gohain and his brothers strongly objected to the separation of the Morans and refused to even consider the other terms if the integrity of the territory was not maintained. Failing to come to an agreement, Captain Vetch issued a general Proclamation on behalf of the Company's government in December 1839, assuming charge of the entire Muttock territory.

With the annexation of Sadiya and Mutttock, the entire Brahmaputra valley was practically under the British.

NOTES AND REFERENCES

1. See Chapter 2.
2. *BSPC*, March 1828, No. 8.
3. The defense of the northeast frontier following the British occupation of Assam had been entrusted to the Rangpur Local Corps reinforced by seven Companies of the Bengal Native Infantry and several detachments of irregulars. However, it soon became apparent that the climate of the region was totally unsuitable for up-country sepoys. Therefore, as the danger of further hostilities with Burma receded, the government resolved in 1828 to withdraw the regular troops from Assam and leave the defense of the province to the Rangpur Corps augmented by two companies of the Gurkhas.
4. Robertson served in Assam for two years (1832–4) and later, after a brief term as judge of the *Sadar* Court, eventually became a member of the Governor- General's Council.
5. *Bengal Political Consultations*, May 1833, No. 89, Bogle to Robertson.
6. Accumulated arrears in the revenue between 1828 and 1832 had exceeded five lakh rupees.
7. A. J. M. Mills, *Report on the Province of Assam*, Calcutta, 1854; (Reprint), Guwahati,1984, para 22.
8. Cited in H. K. Barpujari (ed.), *The Comprehensive History of Assam*, Vol. IV, Guwahati, 1992, p. 53.
9. Mills, *Report on the Province of Assam*, Appendix 3.
10. *Foreign Political Consultations*, 14 May 1831, No. 124.
11. For details, refer to C. U. Aitchison, *A Collection of Treaties, Engagements and Sanads*, Vol. XII, New Delhi, (Reprint), 1983, pp. 135–7.
12. Letter from Court, No. 14 of 1834, Cited in Barpujari (ed.), *The Comprehensive History of Assam*, p. 84.
13. Ibid.
14. In fact White's survey later revealed that the highest collection of revenue was 70,150 rupees in 1833–4.
15. A.White, *A Memoir of the Late David Scott*, Calcutta, 1831, (Reprint), Guwahati 1988, p. 151.
16. H. K. Barpujari, *Assam: In the Days of the Company*, NEHU, first edition, 1996, p. 120.
17. Francis Jenkins was born in 1793 at Cornwall in England. After the completion of his military training, he joined the Indian Army in 1811 and served in various capacities including that of Assistant Secretary to the Military Board. Along with Pemberton, Jenkins conducted a survey of Assam, Cachar and Manipur for the British Government in 1831. This provided him with invaluable insight into the various aspects of the region. He was, therefore, considered the most suitable person to succeed Robertson in 1834. Jenkins subsequently became a member of the Supreme Council. He died at Gauhati in August 1866.
18. Cited in Barpujari, *Assam: In the Days of the Company* , p. 122.
19. Barpujari (ed.), *The Comprehensive History of Assam*, p. 97.

20. The whole of the north bank, yielding an estimated revenue of 23,000 rupees; Majuli island, a revenue of 5,000 rupees; and the tract between the Rivers Buridihing and Disang on the south, a revenue of 6,000 rupees.
21. In connection with the annexation of the kingdom of Jayantia, the Court of Directors had issued a dispatch on 28 March 1838, directing the Governor-General not to annex any territory under a native prince without their prior approval in future.
22. In 1845, circumstances compelled Purandar to appeal to the Governor-General for the zamindari of Jorhat along with a stipend of 1,500 rupees a month, with retrospective effect, so as to enable him to pay off his accumulating debts. While forwarding his application, the Commissioner recommended that in view of his financial difficulties he may be paid the amount of pension that had been originally granted to him. Several years elapsed before a decision was arrived at and ultimately in 1856 when the pension was sanctioned in his favour, he was on his deathbed.
23. J. B. Bhattacharjee, *Cachar under British Rule in North East India*, Delhi, 1977, p. 189.
24. H. L. Gupta, 'An Unknown Factor in the Annexation of Assam', *Proceedings of the Indian Historical Records Commission*, 1959.
25. A. Guha, *Planter-Raj to Swaraj: Freedom Struggle and Electoral Politics in Assam 1826–1947*, New Delhi, 1977, p. 2.
26. H. K. Barpujari, *Problem of the Hill Tribes North East Frontier*, Vol. I, NEHU, (Reprint), 1998, p. 28.
27. Aitchison, *A Collection of Treaties, Engagements and Sanads*, p. 121.
28. Of the four Khamti chiefs, Sadiya Khowa Gohain, Captain Gohain, Tawa Gohain and Ranua Gohain, the last three were well disposed towards the British. The loyalty of the Sadiya Khowa Gohain , who reportedly gave away one of his daughters in marriage to the Burmese king, was open to question.
29. Aitchison, *A Collection of Treaties, Engagements and Sanads*, p. 122.
30. Ibid., pp. 119–20.
31. By an Agreement on 23 January, 1835, Matibar Barsenapati renounced his claims on Saikhowa. Ibid. pp. 141–2.
32. Ibid.
33. The British sought to justify the new agreement on the ground that the earlier settlement had been made with the late *bar senapati* and was therefore no longer valid.
34. For details, refer to H. K. Barpujari (ed.), *The Comprehensive History of Assam*, pp. 119–20.

SUGGESTED READINGS

Barpujari, H. K., Assam in the Days of the Company 1826–58, Guwahati, 1963.

——— (ed.), *The Comprehensive History of Assam Vol. IV*, Guwahati, 1992.

Mills, J. M., *Report on the Province of Assam*, Calcutta, 1854, (Reprint), Guwahati, 1984.

4

Consolidation of Power

Chapter Highlights

- Problems faced by Jenkins, commissioner and agent for Assam
- Administrative reorganisation under Jenkins
- *Mills' Report on Assam*
- Repercussions of the Revolt of 1857 on Assam
- Assam under the chief commissioner

The annexation of Upper Assam, Sadiya and Muttock was undoubtedly of great importance to the British. Francis Jenkins, commissioner and agent to the governor-general for Assam and northeast Rangpur, was elated for he was convinced that the rich economic potential of the region would ultimately prove extremely lucrative for the British. But he was also aware of the formidable task before him. Soon after the resumption of Upper Assam, he painted a bleak picture of crumbling families, struggling peasantry and a nearly non-existent communication network when he wrote:

> The great roads and embankments have been neglected for years and are in a dilapidated condition. Heavy forest and reed grass intercept one part of partially cultivated territory from another ... trade has been annihilated by vexatious imposts ... the country is saddled with an immensely numerous ... aristocracy that made serf of all productive classes, and the latter, weighed down by the accumulated burdens of exaction, (have been) rendered idle, dissolute and timid ... (and) have taken to the habitual use of opium in such vast quantities that they cannot now exist without it.[1]

The difficulties that Jenkins had to face were indeed enormous. The administration was chaotic and complaints of high land assessments and of the arrogance and the corruption of the officials in power were rampant. He was required to administer a vast stretch of territory whose economy had been ruined by long periods of political instability.

The region's negligible transport and communication network made the task of administration all the more difficult. Moreover, although as the commissioner of a non-regulated[2] province Jenkins was theoretically armed with dictatorial powers, in practice he found his hands tied because he had to constantly seek the sanction of the authorities in Calcutta, especially in cases involving financial matters. This invariably resulted in inordinate delays. Jenkins was also expected to keep the authorities informed of all his activities on a regular basis. However, even basic infrastructural facilities were virtually non-existent to enable him to carry out all these tasks. He had neither a secretariat nor a team of capable assistants apart from James Matthie, the Deputy Commissioner. Whatever help was available was not qualified or efficient simply because the salaries offered were not attractive enough to get experienced persons to work in a frontier province. In the circumstances, district offices were filled largely by army officers who were liable to be recalled to their regiments at any time. The temporary nature of their tenure moreover, deprived them of the opportunity to acquire knowledge of local institutions, customs and traditions, a comprehension of which was essential for executing civil duties. Problems were compounded because the officers were burdened with multifarious duties. It was with these severe constraints that Jenkins started his work.

His first task was to instil confidence in the minds of the people. He had to assure them that the rulers were capable of maintaining law and order, that their rule would be just and liberal, that their demands would be moderate and that under them the people could hope for happiness and prosperity. With that objective in mind, he introduced certain changes in the administration.

JENKINS ADMINISTRATIVE REFORMS

The province was divided into a number of districts. Each of them was under a principal assistant who had to shoulder enormous responsibility. In addition to his normal duties as a collector, the principal assistant was also required to perform the functions of a civil judge, superintendent of police, executive engineer, education officer and post master. He was further expected to deal with the numerous problems of the tribes bordering his district and to visit the neighbouring hills from time to time to cultivate friendly relations with the tribes. This involved his being out of station, often for long periods. The principal assistant was assisted in his duties by a sub-assistant and three junior assistants. A major problem, however, lay in the paucity of capable officers. As mentioned earlier, their pay was so meagre compared to the nature and volume of their work that even army officers were reluctant to join civil duties. Local persons with knowledge of the British system of administration were few and far between.[3]

Judicial Reforms

In 1834, the principal assistant had been placed under the *Sadar* Court for both criminal and civil cases and under the Board of Revenue for revenue cases. But in 1837 a set of rules, known as Assam Rules, was enforced which laid down guidelines for the establishment of courts, their jurisdiction, mode of appointment of officers, provision for appeals, procedure to be followed in mortgage cases etc. In all cases not specifically provided for in the Assam Rules, the commissioner and his subordinate officers were expected to act according to the spirit of the Rules. Jenkins found that these Rules were followed more in breach than in observance. The sub-assistants and junior assistants were so overburdened with multiple duties that it was impossible for them to examine each case individually. This authority was normally delegated to the omlahs who were hardly qualified for the purpose. Moreover, the courts of law were not readily accessible as a result of which any litigation involved a considerable outlay of time, energy and expenditure. Justice was, therefore, a luxury beyond the reach of the poor and consequently, most people preferred to suffer patiently rather than get into legal hassles.

Jenkins realised that the first step towards consolidation was to set up an effective judiciary. It could be done only if an adequate number of moffusil courts were set up under qualified judges. This would not only expedite matters but also help in making justice easily accessible to all. He introduced several measures that have been listed below.

- In order to reduce the undue influence of the omlahs and to hasten the process of judgment in petty cases, he substituted oral examination by the magistrate in lieu of written depositions by *mohururs* (clerks).
- Panchayats were placed under munsifs.

- The post of munsif was open to all but preference was henceforth given to local persons with some social standing. Applicants from outside the province were required to have at least ten years of public service in Assam to be considered fit for selection. Assamese apprentices who had rendered assistance to European officers in the past were also considered for employment.

Jenkins hoped that these measures would break the monopoly of the Bengalis who had occupied almost all the high posts that had been available. Matthie later remarked that 'the success of the system was beyond expectation'.

Reforms in Police Administration

Jenkins' other priority was the reorganisation of the police administration. He was convinced that unless the life and property of the people were secure, he could never hope to win their confidence. The existing system was so weak and inefficient that the position of the people was extremely vulnerable. The thana was the unit of the police organisation. It was under the charge of a *thanadar* or a daroga who was empowered to arrest criminals and hold preliminary trials before sending them to the headquarters. He was aided by a jamadar or one of the mohururs and a few constables. There were no *chowkidars* or village watchmen and the revenue officials, like the choudhurys, *patgiris* and mouzadars were expected to aid the daroga in detection of crime and the apprehension of criminals. Had the jurisdiction of the daroga been restricted to a small area, this system would have been effective, but in most cases this was not so. The district of Nowgong for instance, which covered an area of approximately 9,000 square kilometres, had only three thanas. It was humanly impossible to provide security over such a large area. Moreover, the salaries of the staff were totally inadequate considering the nature of the work,[4] thereby tempting them to resort to corruption. Far away from the control of the higher authorities and vested with powers of both prosecutor and judge, the police official had become a symbol of extortion and oppression. As Anandaram Dhekial Phukan rightly pointed out, in a province full of jungles and marshes and where mobility was severely restricted, the extensive jurisdiction coupled with inadequate staff, made the police system totally ineffective.[5] Aware of the ground realities, Jenkins repeatedly brought to the notice of the government that unless more thanas were set up and the salaries increased substantially, the situation was not likely to improve. Much to his disappointment, the government, was reluctant to incur further expenditure and merely upgraded the salary of the daroga from 25 rupees to 100 rupees.

Revenue Reforms

Jenkins had to face problems in the revenue sector as well. Soon after the British took over the administration of Assam, they had introduced certain radical revenue reforms. The paik system, which had involved payment in the form of personal service to the king, had been replaced by taxes. Although attempts had been made from time to time to prevent forceful exactions, the interests of the ryots were not always protected. Assessments were made at the headquarters on the report of petty officials and investigations were ordered only in cases of serious doubts. Even then, the enquiry was not conducted by the officer in charge, but by a subordinate person. Allegations of over assessments, illegal imposts, corruption and bribery were rampant but it was practically impossible for a ryot to get redress for his grievances. In spite of such gross anomalies, the government had, from time to time, seriously considered the enhancement of revenue on rupit lands on the plea that the rates prevalent in Assam were too low in comparison to other provinces. Jenkins opposed this move persistently. He was convinced that in the existing circumstances, the enhancement of revenue would have the reverse effect of driving the ryots away from the cultivation of rice. In his opinion, it would have been possible to increase the revenue only by bringing more land under cultivation. His views were corroborated by Captain Butler, the principal assistant commissioner of Nowgong, who wrote:

> It is not our *Ryotwaree* system that retards the increase in revenue, but the want of a large population; our extensive wastes or jungles cannot be cultivated with a scanty population decreased by epidemics. The people are not industrious or enterprising, and will not cultivate more land than is sufficient for their own wants; unless Assam is colonised from Bengal, there is no prospect or hope of the province being brought fully under cultivation for centuries to come.[6]

Jenkins further insisted that if at all rates had to be enhanced, it had to be on those non-rupit lands which had shown an increase in production in the years immediately past. He, moreover, pointed out that in view of the differences in the development and paying capacities of the ryots in the different districts, a uniform rate was in any case not feasible. Keeping these in mind, he put forth several measures to improve the revenue administration.

- In 1852, Jenkins raised the revenue on non-rupit lands in all the districts except Kamrup. In recommending the tax on *bari* lands, Jenkins stated his desire to convert the wastelands and 'haunts of wild beasts into fruitful fields of sugarcane, mustard, mulberry, lac, tobacco and vegetables'. He believed that taxation would motivate the people to increase the productivity of their bari lands.
- In an effort to further increase revenue receipts, he introduced a number of additional taxes. For instance, gold washing and fishing rights were farmed out to the highest bidder, taxes were levied on reeds and timber and excise and stamp duties were introduced on the plea of discouraging litigations.
- He also provided incentives for agricultural production of food crops as well as cash crops like sugarcane, tea, coffee and indigo by initiating a set of rules known as Waste Land Rules for the settlement of the vast tracts of lands lying fallow in the province.

These Rules came into effect for the first time in March 1838.[7] By encouraging cultivation of crops that were easily marketable and creating a class of speculators to exploit the resources of the province, especially tea and coal, Jenkins attempted to increase commerce and industry in the region. But he realised that his efforts would be futile unless the communication network was improved. Hence, he introduced steamers on the Brahmaputra and tried to restore or construct a number of roads to facilitate the movement of goods and people. This had the immediate effect of not only opening up the province to the outside world but also providing an impetus to trade and industry.[8] Further, in an effort to focus the attention of the outside world on this frontier province, Jenkins wrote a series of articles in the *Journal of the Asiatic Society of Bengal* on Assam and her history.

Reforms in Education

When Jenkins took over as commissioner of Assam, he was alarmed at the predominance of non-Assamese people in all government offices.

He strongly believed that 'the natives of the soil' must be relied upon and that it was necessary for the government to educate and train them to take positions of responsibility. He said that it was essential to win the confidence of the erstwhile aristocracy by providing them employment, even if in the subordinate ranks of public service. The early anti-British uprisings had made it clear to the colonial administration that it was unsafe to withdraw the privileges that the upper classes had enjoyed for generations. It was, therefore, essential to accommodate them as far as possible in the new administrative set up and this called for the introduction of a modern system of education. Jenkins realised that unless the prevailing system was remedied, the future of the British in Assam was 'bleak and fraught with problems'. Writing to the government in 1834, he remarked: 'This state of things appears to me pregnant with evil (consequences) and I know no other method by which it could be remedied than by the Government taking some active measure to provide instruction to Assamese youth.'[9]

In the same dispatch, Jenkins strongly recommended the establishment of schools to impart English education at each of the *sadar* stations of Gauhati, Darrang, Nowgong and Bishwanath. Jenkins believed that these institutions would produce local teachers within a short time during which period teachers capable of teaching English and Bengali could be procured from outside. As anticipated by Jenkins, the response was very encouraging and the demand for English education was so high that many schools, funded entirely by the public, began to spring up. Most of these laid considerable stress on the study of English, because it was commonly believed that knowledge of the language was the gateway for obtaining employment in the government offices.

James Matthie, the district collector of Gauhati, however, believed that the solution lay not in setting up English schools but in establishing anglo-vernacular schools. Accordingly, he formulated certain proposals which, in fact, formed the foundation for the genesis of primary schools in Assam.[10] But unfortunately, most of these schools did not follow a uniform system. There was neither a fixed curriculum nor adequate textbooks. William Robinson, Inspector of Schools, reported that 'even the most advanced students were just able to read only a few pages of their textbooks without any comprehension whatsoever of their meaning ... their handwriting was illegible, orthography much worse, and of arithmetic they literally knew nothing'.[11] Thus, it is apparent that in spite of the efforts of Jenkins, the educational system was far from encouraging. Mills observed that not a single student from Assam had qualified for a government junior scholarship till the time of his filing the Report.[12]

Like David Scott, Jenkins too was deeply concerned about the people of the region. Considering the severe limitations under which he worked, his achievements were indeed significant. S. K. Bhuyan has observed: 'His philanthropy and magnificence combined with his intimate knowledge of the history, habits and feelings of the governed as well as his zealous watchfulness of their interests made him, in the imagination of the people, a worthy successor of the Assamese *Swargadeos* and *Barphukans*.'[13]

MILLS' REPORT ON THE PROVINCE OF ASSAM

In 1853, the Lieutenant Governor of Bengal desired to visit Assam. But before his visit, it was considered essential that an officer should precede him 'to institute a closer and more detailed enquiry into the local state of the administration'. Accordingly, a judge of the *Sadar Diwani Adalat*, A. J. Moffatt Mills, was deputed for the purpose. Mills arrived at Sibsagar in June 1853 and toured the province extensively. After a survey of the different districts, Mills recorded his findings in an exhaustive report which he submitted to the government towards the close of 1853. This report, commonly known as *Mills' Report on Assam*, is an important source for the study of the administrative history of the period. Most of the information was obtained by Mills himself, but he also incorporated the observations of various officials and non-officials while compiling the report.

Mills' Report deals with the districts of Goalpara, Kamrup, Darrang, Nowgong, Sibsagar and Lakhimpur. He gathered information on a variety of subjects such as land settlements, the revenue system, modes of assessment, the judicial system, population patterns, means of communication, education facilities, manufactures etc. He made insightful criticisms on different aspects of the government and offered suggestions for improvement of the administration. The importance of this document is that it is the first authentic and unbiased report on the province and as such it is an invaluable historical document. Mills was overwhelmed with petitions and memoranda wherever he went.

Most of them were from the disgruntled nobility but a few deserve mention. One was a memorandum submitted by Anandaram Dhekial Phukan[14] while two others were from Maniram Barua.[15]

Anandaram's Petition

Anandaram was pained to see that British rule in Assam had not brought the anticipated peace and prosperity to the people. He, therefore, decided to take advantage of Mills'visit to apprise the Government of the actual conditions prevailing in the province. Anandaram's *Observations on the Administration of the Province of Assam*[16] was based on personal knowledge and experience and provides an in-depth insight into the various aspects of British administration in Assam. While submitting his observations, he made it very clear that his intention was not to merely highlight the 'imperfections' of British rule in the province but 'to give a succinct view of the present state of the country'. He suggested certain 'reforming measures' that have been listed below.

- The reduction of taxes.
- Increase in the number of moffusil courts and appointment of more judges from among the native population.
- Improvements in agriculture.
- Establishment of technical schools and English schools.
- Supervision of religious and charitable institutions by the government.
- The restoration of Assamese as the language of the province, etc.

His observations were unbiased, based on facts and extremely forceful.

Maniram's Petitions

Maniram submitted two petitions. In one of them he prayed for some personal favours after having enumerated his loyal services to the Crown.[17] The second was more significant. In it he gave a detailed account of the rule of the East India Company in the preceding three decades. While highlighting the positive effects of British rule, he did not fail to emphasise upon the negative effects, especially in relation to the nobility and the higher classes. He observed:

> we are just now, as it were, in the belly of a tiger; and if our misfortunes yielded any advantage to the Government, we should be content; but the fact is, there is neither gain to the people nor the government; and so long as the present state of things continue, we can see no prospect of improvement in the future ... The abolition of old customs and establishment in their stead of courts and unjust taxation, the introduction of opium in the district ... and discontinuing the *pujas* at Kamakhya [has subjected the country] to various calamities, the people to every species of suffering and distress, and the annual crops to a constantly recurring failure ... The upper and middle classes have seen their offices abolished, their slaves set free, their rights removed and their fame and honour destroyed .... It might be supposed that by having given pensions to some of the respectable Assamese, great benefit has been conferred on them, but the fact is that those who have ought to get pensions did not get any while those whose services have been of short duration and their claims insignificant, proved most successful.[18]

Maniram also pointed out the evils resulting from the introduction of abkari opium, the destruction of indigenous crafts, the neglect of the *satras* and the appointment of Bengali and Marwari mouzadars. He was convinced that so long as the existing state of affairs continued, the people of Assam could not hope for a better future. He, therefore, made a strong plea for the restoration of the Ahom monarchy by supporting the cause of both Ghanakanta Singha, son of former Raja Chandrakanta Singha, and Kandarpeswar Singha, grandson of Purandar Singha. He suggested that the selected prince be aided by a European officer who would be in charge of a regiment deployed for the defence of the province. It appears that Maniram had no particular affinity towards either of the two princes and that his main intention was to see the restoration of the monarchy.

Mills paid no heed to Maniram's petition. On the contrary, he believed that Maniram was 'a clever but untrustworthy and intriguing person', that he was largely responsible for fomenting discontent and disturbing the tranquillity of the province and that as such, he could not be relied upon. In any case, Mills' intention was to suggest ways to strengthen the administration and to consolidate the British possessions in the region. He, therefore, suggested to the government to inform the royalty not to entertain hopes of restoration in the future. The report shattered the hopes of the nobility and made

Maniram the arch enemy of the British. Disappointed and frustrated in his efforts to impress Mills, he decided to plead the case of Prince Kandarpeswar personally before the authorities at Calcutta, but was unable to meet the lieutenant governor in spite of repeated attempts. Maniram realised the futility of relying on appeals and petitions. His disillusionment coincided with the Sepoy Revolt that had broken out in northern India and Maniram decided to use it to his advantage. What he could not achieve through prayers, petitions and memoranda, he decided to achieve through rebellion.

REPERCUSSIONS OF THE REVOLT OF 1857 ON ASSAM

The defence of the Company's dominions on the northeast frontier had been entrusted to the Assam Light Infantry Battalion and contingents supplied by the Muttocks and the Khamtis since the withdrawal of the Company's regular troops in 1828.[19] In addition, there was a body of irregulars in Lower Assam which was organised in 1835 as a regiment known as the Lower Assam *Sebundies*. By 1836, both the Muttocks and the Khamtis had commuted the services of their military paiks for a fixed payment. In order to guard the extreme frontier, Major Hannay raised another levy of irregulars in 1847 named the *Doaneah* Militia, comprising mainly of Singphos. Eventually this regiment was incorporated in the Upper Assam *Sebundy* which was set up with a view to providing employment to the local tribes and thereby winning their confidence. In course of time, however, it was found that these local tribes who had been used to a life of freedom, found military discipline too irksome and had withdrawn from the services. As a consequence, the Upper Assam Sebundy had to be disbanded in 1844. At the same time, the Lower Assam Sebundy was upgraded as the Second Assam Light Infantry Battalion under the command of Major Richardson with its headquarters at Gauhati.

Thus, in 1857, there were two main regiments stationed in Assam: The First Assam Light Infantry Battalion under Major Hannay with headquarters at Dibrugarh and the Second Assam Light Infantry Battalion with headquarters at Gauhati. Besides these, detachments were posted at some sadar stations and strategically located outposts on the frontier. Until June 1857, the sepoys in the Brahmaputra Valley had on the whole remained loyal to the government although news of the Revolt had percolated into the Valley. The difficult terrain of the frontier and hostile climate had compelled the government to rely primarily on the local corps for the defence of the frontier. As such, there were very few north Indian sepoys in Assam. Moreover, the heterogeneous nature of the regiments, comprising of Gurkhas, Manipuris, Singphos etc., was also not seen as likely to create disaffection. Hence, by and large the situation in Assam was peaceful till the middle of 1857.

Maniram's Revolt

The situation, however, changed quickly in the subsequent weeks. Rumours that British rule had come to an end in northern India with the restoration of Bahadur Shah Zafar spread among the sepoys of the Brahmaputra Valley. Considering this an opportune moment, Maniram Barua, who harboured various grievances against the British, goaded Kandarpeswar Singha to raise the standard of revolt. He persuaded Kandarpeswar to send two confidential agents, Nirmal Hazari and Peali Barua, to the military lines at Golaghat, Sibsagar, Dibrugarh and Saikhowa with tempting offers of high remuneration to anyone who would join his army. Meanwhile Maniram, with the aid of Madhu Mallick, Peali Barua, Nowbaisha Phukan and several others, prepared the ground for the insurrection. Maniram believed that the timing was appropriate. There was not a single European soldier along the entire northeastern frontier and even if the authorities in Calcutta had been able to spare some troops, it would have been extremely difficult to send in reinforcements and supplies. Hence, he was convinced that if the sepoys of Assam collaborated with the rebels, the British could be easily dislodged. He prepared for an uprising during the *Durga puja* in October 1857. It was assumed that once the call was given, the sepoys would rise simultaneously in their respective outposts, seize the magazines and treasuries, kill the Europeans and burn their houses. After that, Kandarpeswar would be installed as the monarch and Maniram would be the prime minister.

Matters, however, were not so simple. As news of the preparations leaked, panic stricken European planters left their gardens and missionaries abandoned their churches to take refuge in Gauhati where security was relatively stronger.[20] Major Hannay, with the help of Captain Lowther of Sadiya, placed pickets at strategic locations.

Map 4.1: Assam under the Jurisdiction of the Chief Commissioner, 1875

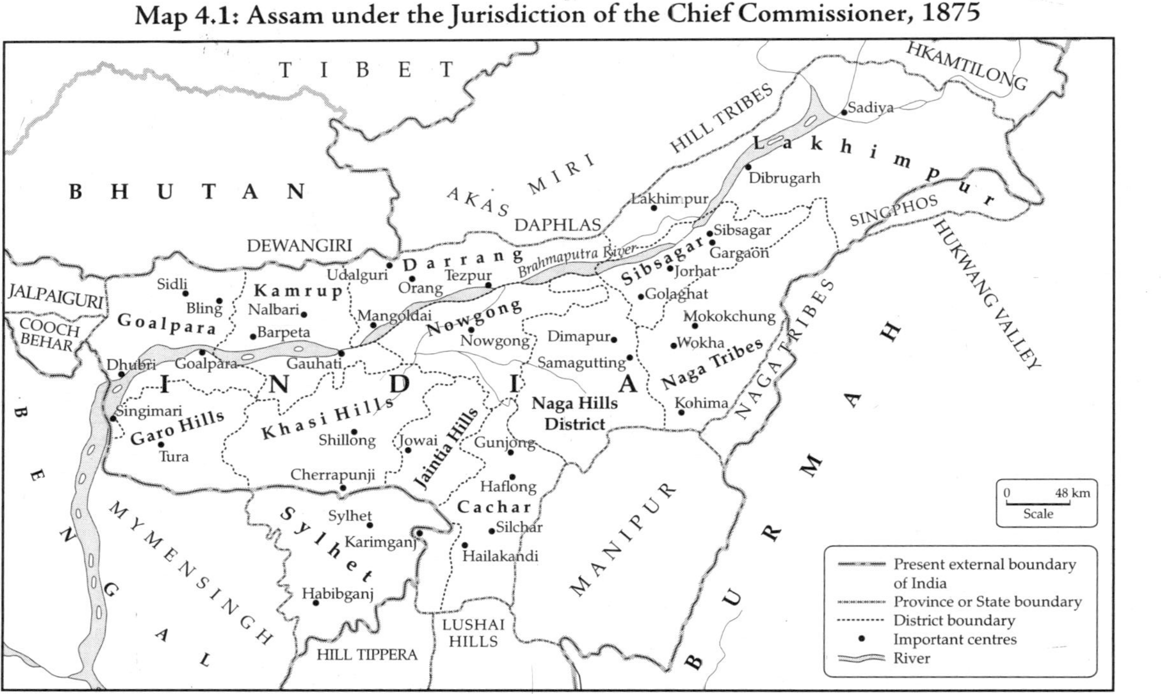

Source: Adapted from map drawn by Mohammed Taher, Professor Emeritus, Department of Geography, Gauhati University for H. K. Barpujari (ed.), The Political History of Assam Vol. I.

Morton, Principal Assistant Nowgong district, destroyed the bridges over the rivers Misa and Diju and cut off communications with Jorhat in order to foil any attempted attacks from that direction. Jenkins drew the attention of the government to the seriousness of the situation and urged upon them to dispatch a European force immediately. Although the government realised the urgency of the situation, they were unable to send a large force because of the simultaneous revolt of sepoys in different parts of northern India. Nevertheless, a small European force of 104 hurriedly gathered recruits were immediately dispatched to Dibrugarh.

After the Revolt

Maniram's strategy did not work as planned. In early September 1857, a bundle of letters he had written was intercepted and they proved beyond doubt his conspiracy with Kandarpeswar to overthrow British rule. Jenkins directed Captain Holyroyd to apprehend the conspirators immediately. Kandarpeswar and Madhu Mallick were arrested near Jorhat and sent to the Central Jail at Alipur. Maniram and several of his co-conspirators were arrested in Calcutta. With the leaders behind the bars, there remained little cause for further apprehension. Towards the close of 1857, Maniram and Peali Barua were tried, found guilty of treason and sentenced to death. Madhu Mallick, Dutiram Barua, Formud Ali, Bahadur Gaonburah and several others were tried on charges of conspiracy and sentenced to transportation for life to the Andamans. In Calcutta, Kandarpeswar Singha appealed to the government for his release. Realising that he was merely a tool in the hands of the conspirators, Kandarpeswar was released from prison but was kept under surveillance in Burdwan. When Queen Victoria of England granted general amnesty in her Proclamation of 1858, all those who were exiled were allowed to return to Assam. Kandarpeswar's petition requesting the government to allow him to return to his ancestral home at Jorhat was, however, turned down but he was allowed to settle in Gauhati where he died in 1880.

Assam was governed as a part of Bengal by the British till 1874. In that year they separated it from Bengal, added Sylhet to the province and brought the whole area under a chief commissioner who had his headquarters at Shillong.

NOTES AND REFERENCES

1. *Indian Political Consultations*, 6 March 1839, Jenkins to Secretary, Government of India, 21 February, cited in H. K. Barpujari, *Assam in the Days of the Company*, Guwahati, 1963, p. 164.
2. The Bengal Regulations promulgated by Lord Cornwallis in 1793 provided a code of Regulations for the administration of the areas under the Presidency of Fort William. These Regulations were soon found to be 'wholly inapplicable' to backward areas like those of the northeastern frontier. Hence, under Regulation X of 1822, such areas were brought under an executive who was to conduct the administration 'by the principles and spirit of the Regulations' subject to certain modifications. R. Clarke, *The Regulations of the Government of Fort William in Bengal 1793–1853*, London, 1854, p. 659–3.
3. It was only in 1850 that Anandaram Dhekial Phukan was appointed as sub-assistant of Nowgong district on a monthly salary of 250 rupees.
4. The monthly salary of the staff were as follows: daroga 20 rupees; jamadar ten rupees; mohurur three rupees.
5. For details, refer to observations of Anandaram Dhekial Phukan in A. J. M Mills, *Report on the Province of Assam, 1854*, Guwahati, (Reprint)1984, Appendix J.
6. Ibid., p. 455.
7. *Assam Land Revenue Manual*, (Eighth edition), Shillong, 1968, p. vi.
8. For details refer chapter on Economic Transformation.
9. *Political Consultations Bengal*, 10 July 1834, No. 211.
10. For details, refer to H. K. Barpujari (ed.) *The Comprehensive History of Assam*, Vol. IV, Guwahati, 1992, pp. 348–62.
11. *Report on Public Instruction*, Bengal,1845, Appendix 4, Robinson to Jenkins.
12. Mills, *Report on the Province of Assam*, Appendix J.
13. S. K. Bhuyan, *Early British Relations with Assam*, Shillong, 1928, p. 31.
14. Anandaram Dhekial Phukan, son of Haliram Dhekial Phukan was born in 1829. He joined government service as a munsif in 1849. In 1852 he became sub-assistant, Nowgong, and subsequently, officiating junior assistant.
15. Maniram Barua joined the services of the East India Company as sheristadar-tehsildar of Upper Assam in 1828. During the reign of Purandar Singha, he was entrusted with the additional duty of supervising several fiscal units. However, with the annexation of Upper Assam in 1838, he was deprived of most of his fiscal charges. Subsequently, he joined the Assam Company as *dewan*. After serving there for a few years he tried to set up a few tea gardens of his own at Jorhat but was unsuccessful because the authorities refused to grant him waste lands at the concessional rate that was being offered to Europeans.
16. This lengthy memorial was subsequently published as Appendix J in Mills' Report. For a critical evaluation of the Memorandum, refer to S. D. Goswami, 'Anandaram Dhekial Phukan's "Observations on the Administration of the Province of Assam:" A Classic Document for Rewriting the Social History of Modern Assam' in Ranju Bezbaruah, Priyam Goswami and Dipankar Banerjee (eds), *North East India: Interpreting the Sources of its History*, New Delhi, 2008, pp. 189–96.

17. Mills, *Report on the Province of Assam*, pp. 603–4.
18. Ibid., pp. 605–9.
19. It was believed that local corps, raised in the area in which they were located, would be advantageous for the government in many respects. (i) Locally recruited sepoys would be able to endure the climate better than their counterparts from other regions of India; (ii) considering the shortage of manpower in the Company's troops, this was a great relief; (iii) since the number of British officers required was less, it was economically advantageous.
20. The adult European population of Gauhati at this time was only around 25 persons, and all of them undertook mock drills regularly in preparation for any untoward eventuality.

SUGGESTED READINGS

Barpujari, H. K., *The Comprehensive History of Assam* Vol. IV, Guwahati, 1992.

Bhuyan, S. K., *Early British Relations with Assam*, Shillong, 1928.

Mills, A. J. M., *Report on the Province of Assam*, Calcutta, 1854, (Reprint), Guwahati, 1984.

5

Expansion to the South: Cachar and the Central Hills

Chapter Highlights

- Treaty of Badarpur between the British and Raja of Cachar
- Rule of Govinda Chandra of Cachar
- Question of succession and annexation of Cachar
- Cachar post-annexation
- British relations with Raja Ram Singh of Jayantia
- Annexation of Jayantia
- Reaction to British rule and Jayantia rebellions
- Revolt of U Kiang Nongbah in Jayantia
- British expansion in Khasi Hills
- Revolt of U Tirot Singh, chief of Nongkhlaw
- British interest in Garo Hills
- Subjugation of the Garo Hills

CACHAR AND JAYANTIA BEFORE 1824

To the south of the Brahmaputra Valley were the kingdoms of Cachar and Jayantia and the hilly tracts inhabited by the Khasis and Garos. The British policy of non- intervention followed since the time of John Shore, the Governor-General of India (1793–7), had encouraged the Burmese to overrun not only Assam but also to encroach upon the neighbouring kingdoms of Cachar and Jayantia. The Burmese claimed Cachar saying that the territory had been recognised as part of Burma since the rule of their king, Hshin-byu-shin.[1] They claimed Jayantia on the ground that it was a feudatory of the Ahom kingdom and, therefore, it automatically came under their rule when they occupied Assam. Both claims rested on flimsy grounds, yet the attitude of the Burmese king, Ba-gyi-daw, was so aggressive that by 1823, the situation in the entire area had become extremely volatile.

Lord Amherst, the Governor-General of India (1823–8), seriously considered extending British protection to Cachar because he felt that British troops in the region would deter the Burmese from further intrusion into the Brahmaputra Valley. He had even written to the Court of Directors about it. But before any decision could be taken, Burmese forces invaded Cachar in January 1824. At a battle fought at Badarpur, on the banks of the Surma river, the Burmese were defeated and compelled to retreat. Realising that this was probably just a temporary respite, Amherst immediately resumed his earlier correspondences and impressed upon the authorities in England the necessity of maintaining British influence in this strategic region.[2] The Court of Directors took up the matter more seriously this time and instructed the governor-general to settle the terms of future relations with Govinda Chandra, the Raja of Cachar.

Treaty of Badarpur

David Scott concluded the Treaty of Badarpur with Govinda Chandra on 6 March 1824 on behalf of the East India Company.[3] By the terms of this treaty:

- The Raja acknowledged his allegiance to the East India Company and agreed to abide by the advice of the Governor-General-in-Council.
- He also agreed to pay the Company an annual tribute of 10,000 rupees.
- In return, the British undertook to protect Cachar from all external aggressions and to arbitrate any differences that may arise between Govinda Chandra and the neighbouring principalities.
- In case the Raja defaulted on his payments, the Company was 'at liberty to occupy and attach, in perpetuity, to their other possessions, a sufficient tract of Cachar country, to provide for the future realisation of the tribute'.[4]

Thus, Govinda Chandra virtually became a puppet in the hands of the Company's government. The internal condition of the kingdom was so chaotic that it rendered the Raja's sovereignty meaningless.

In order to further strengthen its position in the region, the Company's government concluded a similar treaty with Ram Singh, the Raja of Jayantia, on 10 March 1824.[5] The Raja acknowledged the suzerainty of the British in return for protection against all external enemies. No tribute was demanded of him but he was expected to assist the British, 'with all his forces and to afford every other facility in his power' in the case of military operations to the east of the Brahmaputra.

Thus, both Cachar (Figure 5.1) and Jayantia (Figure 5.2) became part of the general system of defence for the protection of the eastern frontier of British India. During the First Anglo-Burmese War (1824–6) that followed, both these kingdoms were the arenas of a series of Anglo-Burmese encounters. The eventual defeat of the Burmese and the subsequent Treaty of Yandabo dramatically altered the course of history in the region.

CACHAR

By the terms of Article II of the Treaty of Yandabo, the king of Burma renounced his claims upon Cachar and promised to abstain from all future interference in the kingdom. Hence, in accordance with the terms of the Treaty of Badarpur (1824), Govinda Chandra continued as king of Cachar in return for an annual tribute of 10,000 rupees to the British. The authorities in Calcutta were doubtful of his ability to administer the kingdom effectively, especially in view of the aggressive attitude of two of his neighbours, Gambhir Singh of

Figure 5.1: Annexation of Cachar

Year	Event	Consequence
1824	Treaty of Badarpur	Govinda Chandra, Raja of Cachar becomes a vassal of the British government
1830	Assassination of Govinda Chandra	Administration of Cachar placed under Lieutenant Fisher who is given charge as magistrate and collector
1832	Annexation of Cachar	Lieutenant Fisher made superintendent and civil judge with his headquarters at Dudpatil
1836	Cachar placed under Commissioner of Dacca	It continues to be a non-regulated province
1854	Annexation of North Cachar	Made part of North Cachar sub-division with headquarters at Asalu

Manipur and Tularam Senapati, a chief in the hills of North Cachar. It was obvious that Govinda Chandra's position was very insecure and that he would always be dependent on British support for his existence. But the Company's government felt that it would be both politically and economically unwise to revoke the status quo at that stage. But Govinda Chandra's position was shaky from the beginning. Apart from the fact that he was fairly old, he was indecisive and lacked administrative ability. He found it extremely difficult to deal effectively with the innumerable problems that he faced and although his actions were well-meaning, he was unable to tackle the challenges that confronted him.

Govinda Chandra and the British

The Raja's major problem was that of finance. Like Assam, Cachar had been ravaged and depleted by long years of internecine strife. The economy was in ruins, law and order practically non-existent and large stretches of land virtually depopulated. In spite of this, Govinda Chandra agreed to pay the stipulated tribute of 10,000 rupees from the annual revenue estimated by Lieutenant Fisher at three lakh rupees. Scott had pointed out at that time that the estimated amount of revenue was 'greatly over rated' and that it would be absolutely impossible for the Raja to pay the tribute without oppressing his subjects. He was convinced that the maximum earnings of the Raja would not be more than one lakh rupees even at the best of times. The government, heavily in debt after the Burmese War, needed to mobilise all resources and therefore conveniently accepted Fisher's estimate. Surprisingly, Govinda Chandra acceded to the demand without any protest.

Govinda Chandra's Revenue Reforms

The Raja soon realised the immensity of the task and immediately took up measures to improve his finances. In order to achieve this, he had to resort to drastic measures to curtail existing expenditure and also had to levy additional taxes. His measures to improve revenue have been given below.

- He reduced the number of ministers and judges and also dispensed with the services of revenue officers attached to the members of the royalty.

- All rent-free grants allotted to dignitaries were withdrawn and strict instructions were laid for the collection of revenue.
- The land tax was retained at the earlier rate of five rupees per *kulbah* (one *kulbah* = 4.2 acres); but additional taxes were levied for the cultivation of poppy, fruits and vegetables, for manufacturing salt, and for certain social privileges like holding titles, riding a *dola,* wearing gold ornaments and having music during festivities.
- Customs duties were levied at the river ghats on articles of export which were invariably farmed out to the highest bidder. The king also had monopoly of trade in certain commodities like grain which he acquired from the merchants at fixed rates.

Despite these stringent measures, Govinda Chandra was unable to raise adequate money to pay the stipulated tribute regularly. In 1827, he pleaded to the government for exemption of tributes for the two preceding years. He was granted remission on the recommendations of David Scott. But the Raja was required to construct a good road between Sylhet and Manipur across his country.

Political Rivalries

Tularam Senapati

Financial difficulties, however, were only a part of Govinda Chandra's problems. His insecurity, caused by inadequate funds, was further aggravated by two persistent enemies, Gambhir Singh and Tularam who repeatedly made incursions into his territory. Tularam traced his roots to the Kachari king, Tamradhwaj, a contemporary of the Ahom monarch, Rudra Singha. His father, Kahi Das, was originally a *khidmatgar* (servant) of Govinda Chandra but had rebelled against the Raja and established himself as an independent ruler in the hills of North Cachar. He was assassinated by Govinda Chandra but his son, Tularam, resumed hostilities. Backed by the entire Dimasa population in the hills and the Forty *Sempungs*, or Council of the Forty Dimasa tribes, Tularam challenged the authority of the Raja. He frequently swooped down on the plains districts and created havoc by looting, plundering and committing numerous outrages. The large-scale depredations committed by Tularam's lieutenants in the areas bordering the hills were a source of constant harassment to

Govinda Chandra. Claiming that the British were under obligation to help him in the event of external aggression according to the terms of the treaty, he pleaded to the government for help. But he was disappointed with the response. Instead of the military help that he had anticipated, they merely instructed David Scott to bring about a compromise between the two chiefs. Accordingly, on 28 July 1829, Scott pressurised Govinda Chandra into recognising Tularam as *senapati* of the territory in the hills. Govinda Chandra had no option but to agree, thereby legitimising Tularam's position. Tularam was confirmed in his possession on condition that he would refrain from further encroachment on the territory of the Raja. He was threatened with expulsion from the territory under his control if he violated the terms laid down.

Gambhir Singh

A more formidable enemy was Gambhir Singh of Manipur whose territory lay to the east of Cachar. Gambhir Singh's claim to Manipur had been explicitly recognised by the Treaty of Yandabo, but the treaty was silent on the crucial question of his status vis-à-vis the Burmese monarchy. For years prior to the Treaty of Yandabo, Manipur had been a dependency of Burma but in the post-war scenario, the British did not think it wise to recognise Burmese suzerainty in Manipur. This was because it would have exposed the Sylhet frontier to renewed incursions. During the Anglo-Burmese War, Gambhir Singh had been of considerable help to the British and it was generally assumed that in the event of another Burmese invasion, Manipur would form a strong bulwark against Burmese aggression. The Company's government, therefore, considered it essential to strengthen the position of Gambhir Singh who was, in effect, the political and military warden of a strategically important principality separating the Burmese from the British territories. Under the circumstances, it preferred to recognise Gambhir Singh as an independent ruler rather than a protected one. Lieutenant Fisher, however, had doubts about Manipur's supposed military strength and believed that the Manipuris would be more useful as agriculturists and that the state could serve as a granary for British troops. Gambhir Singh was, therefore, considered an important ally in their scheme of strategic defence. It was because of this that the British showed extreme indulgence towards him even at the cost of harming the interests of the feeble Govinda Chandra from whom they did not expect much help. Gambhir Singh was aware of this and was not slow in taking advantage of it.

An ambitious and unscrupulous person, Gambhir Singh had always harboured intentions of including Cachar in his dominions. Post Yandabo, he found himself in a very comfortable position. Secure on his throne and backed by British support, he had the added advantage of being allowed to maintain an army of 3,000 soldiers who were to be trained and equipped by the Company. It was in these circumstances that Gambhir Singh cast his eyes on Cachar. Govinda Chandra proved to be an easy prey. Indecisive, aged, weak and practically bankrupt, he was no match for the shrewd Manipuri Raja. Moreover, the extreme indulgence shown by the government to Gambhir Singh at different stages encouraged him to encroach upon territory belonging to Cachar.

Since 1827, Gambhir Singh had steadily penetrated into the area west of the Barak river which was generally recognised as the boundary between Cachar and Manipur. This area, rich in natural resources, had been inhabited for generations by several Naga tribes who owed nominal allegiance to the ruler of Cachar. Gambhir Singh, by virtue of the superior arms at his command, compelled the Nagas to acknowledge his authority. Govinda Chandra lodged a complaint with the British following which the commissioner of Sylhet was instructed to make an enquiry. Gambhir Singh explained that the Barak had never been the boundary between the two kingdoms and that since the territory actually belonged to him, he was merely asserting his influence over the recalcitrant Nagas. The government accepted this flimsy explanation and did not pursue the matter further. Emboldened by British indulgence, Gambhir Singh proceeded to forcibly acquire Chandrapur. He claimed that the area was a piece of his ancestral property and insisted that it was a gift from the earlier Kachari king, Krishna Chandra. As he failed to produce any documentary evidence to this effect, Scott dismissed his claim, but in order to pacify him, Govinda Chandra was pressurised into parting with 50 *kulbahs* of land in the same tract for constructing a government magazine. Govinda Chandra protested vehemently but had to eventually agree. The Raja granted the land for the construction of a government magazine in his territory for fifteen years by an agreement. Significantly, this tract was soon given away to Gambhir Singh.

The British policy of appeasement towards Manipur strengthened Gambhir Singh's position. Encouraged by their attitude, he gradually became more and more aggressive.

- He sent his sepoys to the frontier villages of Cachar and exacted forced labour from the Nagas inhabiting the area.
- He levied unauthorised tolls at Chandrapur.
- He encouraged the Manipuris in Cachar to evade transit duties at the river ghats.
- He compelled the hill men to sell their produce to him at rates arbitrarily fixed by his agents.
- He made it mandatory for all trade with Manipur to pass through him.

All this was done openly. A helpless Govinda Chandra repeatedly appealed to the British to intervene, but they were slow to respond. Eventually, David Scott issued a strict warning to Gambhir Singh that if he did not desist from further acts of aggression, all Manpiuri setters in Cachar would be evicted. Even this failed to have much impact on the Raja.

Govinda Chandra's Assassination

Faced with external aggression, financial bankruptcy and administrative confusion, Govinda Chandra's position was indeed precarious. The people were unhappy with the large number of taxes and the influx of outsiders whom Govinda Chandra had recruited into the administration. The Forty Sempungs, charged Govinda Chandra with direct contravention of the norms of the Heramba kingdom (The Kacharis claimed their descent from Ghatotkacha, the son of Bhima, (Mahabharata) and Hidimbi. The kingdom his descendents ruled was called the Heramba kingdom) by being a nominee of the British and for having married his brother's widow, Indraprabha, a Manipuri princess, instead of a Kachari princess from the Hassoncha tribe. Added to all this was the fact that Govinda Chandra was childless. This complicated matters further. In such circumstances, the government toyed with the idea of bringing the area under its control and instructed Tucker, the Commissioner of Sylhet, to enquire whether the Raja would be willing to sign a deed handing over Cachar to the British after his death in lieu of which the government would relinquish his annual tribute for the remaining years of his life. The offer was tempting but Govinda Chandra declined. He stated that the payment of the tribute was 'the sheet anchor for the retention of his power' and that he was likely to lose all power and respect among his subjects and his neighbours as soon as he stopped paying tribute to the British government. He proposed that in accordance with the accepted Hindu tradition, he may be allowed to adopt a son from amongst the royal families to succeed him. After reviewing the situation, Tucker informed the governor-general that until the question of succession was settled, Cachar would continue to be a prey for disturbing elements and 'turbulent characters'. The governor-general also felt it expedient to arrive at an immediate solution and asked for Scott's comments on the matter. Scott reported that the government could not prevent the Raja from adopting an heir as he had the sanction of the Hindu law, but he believed that the Raja might be persuaded to cede Cachar in consideration of an adequate payment of money and the assignment of a jagir where he might reside with security.[6]

Gambhir Singh soon realised the implication of these moves. He was desperate for he knew that the adoption of an heir by Govinda Chandra would mean an end to his plans for annexing Cachar. Therefore, before Govinda Chandra and the British could arrived at any settlement, he engineered a plot whereby a gang of Manipuris, in collaboration with a few of Govinda Chandra's own officials, entered the palace on the night of 24 April 1830, hacked Govinda Chandra to pieces and set fire to the palace complex. This brutal attack created a situation of panic and terror. The commissioner of Sylhet immediately posted a military detachment in Cachar and reported the matter to the Government of Bengal. Scott's opinion that the incident gave the government a justifiable ground for intervention in the affairs of Cachar prompted them to step in to fill the political void. The administration of Cachar was immediately placed under Lieutenant Fisher who was invested with the powers of magistrate and collector with a monthly salary of 1,000 rupees. The moral responsibility for Govinda Chandra's death must lie with the British because by consistently appeasing Gambhir Singh they had encouraged him to believe that on the formers demise he might be allowed to take possession of Cachar.

An enquiry into the incident proved the complicity of Gambhir Singh beyond doubt, but no action was taken against him. In fact Scott was even prevented from remonstrating him verbally. And

Accordingly, by a Proclamation dated 14 August 1832, the plains of Cachar were annexed to the Company's dominion. Govinda Chandra's widows and close relatives were provided with cash allowances and rent-free grants. Tularam was allowed to retain the portion of the hill tracts under his possession though no formal agreement was entered into immediately.

Fisher, who had earlier been invested with the powers of magistrate and collector, was now made superintendent and given the additional responsibility of civil judge. He was also empowered to exercise political authority over the hill tribes of the frontier. Fisher's headquarters was at Dudpatil and he was placed under the supervision of the agent to the governor-general. The question of the eastern boundary of Cachar was also taken up and they arrived at a decision on the Jiri-Barak tract in November 1832. The authorities accepted Pemberton's view on the subject and formally ceded this tract of territory measuring 60 miles in length and eight miles in breadth to Gambhir Singh subject to certain conditions.

- He was asked to withdraw his thana from Chandrapur.
- He agreed not to obstruct the trade between Manipur and Cachar by imposing exorbitant duties.
- He would not prevent the Nagas residing in that tract from free access to the plains for the purpose of trade.
- He would be ready at all times to afford the assistance of a portion of the Manipur levy and also to furnish porters and labourers whenever their services might be required by the government.

The decision on the Jiri-Barak tract marked the climax of the policy of appeasement consistently followed by the British towards Gambhir Singh. The Court of Directors was not convinced with the arguments put forward by the government and observed that '... the same reasons which existed against granting the whole of Cachar were proportionately strong against the cession of a part'. Such a disapproval that was delayed in coming was, of course, meaningless.

Cachar Post-annexation

Cachar was placed under the agent to the governor-general, north-east frontier, whose jurisdiction extended over Assam, Cachar,

Manipur, Jayantia, Cooch Behar and the other independent principalities in the region. Like Assam, Cachar was also declared a non-regulated province under Regulation X of 1822.[9] In view of the manifold problems of the province, it was essential to entrust the superintendent with wide powers. So in addition to his duties as collector, magistrate and civil judge, Fisher was also entrusted with the functions of a police officer, an executive engineer, education officer and a post master. He had to enquire into the local systems, customs and usages and set up a government suitable for the people. His work was all the more difficult because most of the official documents had been burnt or destroyed at the time of the assassination of the late Raja. As the first superintendent of the non-regulated province of Cachar, Fisher's task was indeed stupendous. The rival claimants to the throne continued to foster internal disaffection while the persistent raids of the frontier tribes added to the chaos. He was kept extremely busy initiating police enquiries or undertaking expeditions against the refractory tribes.

In 1836 Cachar was placed under the Commissioner of Dacca. This eased the situation to a certain extent because many of the departmental heads like the superintendent of police, sessions judge and excise superintendent were common to both Sylhet and Cachar. Moreover, the services of the Sylhet Light Infantry could be requisitioned whenever necessary. Cachar, however, continued to remain a Non-regulated province or provinces that had been recently brought under the British.[10] These provinces had a different set of rules for their governance. Act V of 1835 placed Cachar under the Board of Revenue for Lower Bengal in fiscal matters.

Annexation of North Cachar

But in the meanwhile, the situation in North Cachar had drifted from bad to worse. Tularam's arrogance and the atrocities he wreaked on his people cost him not only the goodwill of the government but also a significant portion of his territory. Tired of his haughty ways, the inhabitants of the western hill tracts of his territory expressed their desire to be brought under British administration. This provided the Company's government the opportunity to bring the area under their control. A meeting ground of Assam, Khasi and Jayantia Hills, and Manipur, the area was useful for purposes of both commerce and defence. In 1834 Tularam was pressurised into concluding a treaty.[11] The terms of the treaty dictated that he:

- He surrendered a substantial portion of the western tract of his territory in return for a monthly pension of 50 rupees.
- He also agreed to pay a yearly tribute of four elephant tusks which was later commuted to a monetary payment of 490 rupees annually.
- He would not be given the title 'Raja' or permitted to deal with criminal matters other than those of a trivial nature.

He was reduced to a position no better than that of a *sirdar*, or a mere caretaker of the estates under him. His passive acceptance of a truncated territory along with the financial and military clauses imposed on him, deprived him of any real political or administrative powers. He became a puppet in the hands of the British. With a revenue collection that did not exceed 1,000 rupees, he found it increasingly difficult to manage his estate. Old, feeble and miserable, Tularam died in 1851. His two sons, Nakul Ram Barman and Brajanath Barman who succeeded him, proved totally incapable of administering the country. Repeated incursions of the Angami Nagas and internal squabbles worsened the situation. It became increasingly important to bring the frontier outposts under direct British control in order to maintain law and order in North Cachar and to reduce the Angami Nagas to submission. Moreover, operations in the area had revealed that the region abounded in coal, limestone, iron ore, salt, ivory, lac and wax.[12] Meanwhile, Jenkins, Agent to the Governor-General and A. J. Moffatt Mills, judge of the *Sadar Dewani Adalat*, had submitted their detailed reports to the government. Taking into consideration all factors, Dalhousie, the Governor-General of India (1848–56), observed that the occupation of the territory was 'a less objectionable alternative than letting it alone', and granted his approval for the annexation of Tularam's territory to the Company's dominion in early 1854. With this, the paramountcy of the Company's government over Cachar was complete.

Cachar 1854–1947

The tract was added to the North Cachar sub-division, the headquarters of which was then at Asalu. When the Naga Hills District was formed in 1866, the sub-division ceased to exist and the territory included in it was distributed among the neighbouring districts. It was re-established in 1880 and placed in charge of a junior police officer who was at first stationed at Gunjong and later Haflong. The sub-division represented the last home of the erstwhile Kachari rulers of the Bodo race.

The administration of Cachar, as in the rest of India, was highly bureaucratic. Here too, the high offices were invariably occupied by Europeans, but owing to the peculiar nature of the traditional socio-political structure[13] with which the British were unfamiliar, they had no alternative but to appoint local persons in certain responsible posts.[14] In 1861 the office of the superintendent was re-designated as deputy commissioner and that of the assistant superintendent as assistant commissioner. From time to time minor changes were made in the administrative set up to accommodate the changing patterns in administration but by and large, the same arrangements continued till the creation of the chief commissionership in 1874.

Rebellions in Cachar (1854–1947)

Although Cachar was by and large peaceful, one section continued to harbour grievances against British rule. In January 1882, a curious happening occurred in the North Cachar Hills. A Dimacha named Sambudhan, claiming divine inspiration and miraculous powers, took the title of *Deo* and attracted a large number of followers among the hill people. Many saw in Sambudhan and his movement an opportunity to revive the local institutions. He set up an ashram at Maibong, the old Kachari capital. Allegations of extortion of money by Sambudhan were made to Major Boyd, the Deputy Commissioner of Cachar, who proceeded to Maibong with a party of armed policemen. In the skirmish that followed, around nine Kacharis lost their lives. Both the Deputy Commissioner and Sambudhan succumbed to their injuries.[15]

The Lushais and Kukis, who occupied the hills to the southeast of Cachar often carried out plundering raids on the plains. Occasional raids were also reported from Manipur, Naga Hills and Tripura. The frontier problem was thus a constant menace to the authorities in Cachar. In 1927, Jadonang, a Kabui Naga, professed a new faith and claimed to have magical powers. With the active support of Nagas belonging to various tribes, including the Kacha Nagas of Cachar, he proclaimed a Kabui Naga Raj on the Cachar–Manipur Road.[16] In order to consolidate his position, he demanded the revenue from the people dwelling in the area. Jadonang's activities were a cause of serious concern to the authorities who were not prepared to accept any form of defiance. In June 1931 Jadonang was arrested and sentenced to death on charges of murder.[17] The movement was carried on by Rani Gaidinlieu, who eluded arrest for some time but was eventually apprehended and transported for life in 1932.[18] In order to prevent the recurrence of such incidents in future and to guard the frontier, a battalion of the Assam Rifles was stationed at Cachar with cantonments at Maniarkhal, Alinagar and Chargola.

Although the uprisings of Sambudhan and Jadonong were short-lived, they were of considerable cultural significance. As Fredrick Downs commented:

> Messianic leaders like Sambudhan of North Cachar Hills and Jadonong of Manipur sent a large number of their followers to death against British arms by assuring them that magic spells would dissolve the bullets. The old magic was impotent against the new reality. Hence, the preservation of a distinctive identity was not so much a matter of preserving the old ways as it was a matter of maintaining mastery in their own house, and control of their own destiny.[19]

JAYANTIA

Paramountcy over Cachar was only a step in the process of British colonial expansion in northeast India, a process which had started with

Figure 5.2: Annexation of Jayantia

Year	Event	Consequence
1824	The British sign a treaty with Ram Singh, Raja of Jayantia	The Raja now owes allegiance to the British
1830	Ram Singh establishes a *chokey* at Chaparmukh; Two British subjects kidnapped by Jayantias	Deterioration of relations with the British
1832	Ram Singh dies	Ram Singh's nephew Rajendra Singh succeeds him
1835	The British annex the plains district of Jayantia	Rajendra Singh voluntarily surrenders the rest of his territory to the British

the annexation of Lower Assam in 1828. In less than three decades, all the principalities in and around Cachar, barring Manipur, were brought under British administration one after the other.

Treaty with Raja Ram Singh

The kingdom of Jayantia was one such principality. During the Burmese incursions, Raja Ram Singh of Jayantia, like Raja Govinda Chandra of Cachar, had signed a treaty with the East India Company's government in March 1824[20] whereby he was assured of protection against external enemies in return for which he had agreed to abide by the advice of the Governor-General-in-Council in all cases of differences with other states and to assist the Company's government with all possible help, military and otherwise, in the event of military operations against the Burmese. The Company did not demand a tribute from him. Scott was under the impression that the Jayantias were a race of warriors and that as such they would be invaluable in his scheme of frontier defence. In 1826, subsequent to the Treaty of Yandabo, Ram Singh was recognised as the ruler of Jayantia. He had not been of much help during the Anglo-Burmese war, but the location of his territory was of strategic importance and Scott realised this. Soon after the war was over, the British constructed a road connecting Sylhet to Assam via Jayantia.

The principality of Jayantia was not large and comprised both plains and hilly tracts. But it did not have a strong economy. Monetary economy was unknown and the little trade that took place was in the form of barter. The ryots, therefore, paid no taxes in cash. The principality was made up of a number of small tribal republics each under a chief known as doloi. These dolois constituted the *durbar*, an institution similar to that of the cabinet of ministers in modern times. The king was merely the constitutional head and he had to refer all important matters to the durbar whose consent was essential for any important decision. The government initially refrained from interfering in the internal affairs of the principality. The relationship with Jayantia was fairly cordial and Raja Ram Singh had even sent a contingent of troops to aid the British troops in quelling the Khasi disturbances.

Deterioration in Relations

But this soon changed and from 1830, however, the relationship became rather strained. The first cause was a dispute between the

Raja and the British in connection with the establishment of a chokey at Chaparmukh at the confluence of the Kapili and Doyang rivers. The British claimed that the Raja had encroached upon a considerable tract of territory on the southern border of the Nowgong district and that he had no right to levy taxes in that area. There were also complaints of extortion by the Raja's collectors. Ram Singh was asked to remove his chokey from Chaparmukh. The Raja insisted that the chokey was within his jurisdiction and saw no reason why he should comply with the request. The British were not prepared to accept Ram Singh's arguments and a lengthy correspondence ensued resulting in bitter animosity between the two parties.

The second cause was more serious. Two British subjects were kidnapped by a group of Jayantias from Sylhet apparently to be sacrificed at the shrine of goddess *Kali*. The two victims escaped, but Cracroft, Agent to the Governor-General, warned Ram Singh to take adequate steps to prevent the recurrence of such incidents in future. Human sacrifices associated with the *shakti* cult was an age old custom in Jayantia. Thus, even though Ram Singh promised to abolish this custom, it was doubtful whether he could have succeeded even if he made a sincere effort. A few months after this incident, four more British subjects were kidnapped and this time three of them were actually sacrificed. Ram Singh was accused of carrying out the crime in conspiracy with his dependent chief, the Raja of Gobha. Ram Singh once again pleaded his innocence and promised to institute an enquiry into the matter. However, before any action could be taken, he died in 1832.

Raja Rajendra Singh and the British

Ram Singh had no sons and according to the traditions of the land was succeeded by his seventeen year old grand-nephew, Rajendra Singh. Taking advantage of his minority, the British government decided to impose a new treaty on him that was more favourable to them. This decision was largely influenced by the reports of Robertson and Fisher who pointed out that the Raja possessed, besides the hills, two fertile tracts which were capable of yielding revenue sufficient to maintain about four or five companies of troops. They also observed that the Raja's revenue in cash alone amounted to 30,000 rupees annually, in addition to what was paid in kind, and that he had treasure amounting to nearly 20 lakh rupees in the royal vault. Taking these facts into account, the authorities were of the opinion that 'a very unsatisfactory bargain in accepting military service for tribute' had been made. They felt that that a better bargain could now be struck with the accession of a minor ruler. Accordingly, Robertson recommended to the government that the treaty be revised to provide for an annual tribute of 10,000 rupees. The official ground put forward was that the treaty with Ram Singh was a personal one and therefore, liable to revision at his demise.

Rajendra Singh, the new Raja, was shocked by the unreasonable and unjustified demand. He pointed out that it was for the first time that the question of tribute from the Jayantia kingdom had arisen. He felt that compliance with such a demand would lower his position not only among his subjects but among the neighbouring chiefs as well. Moreover, he pointed out that technically he had no right to take such an important decision himself. Since the matter had to be referred to the dolois, he asked for some time. Robertson[21] was in no mood to consider such tribal customs and declared that until he signed the proposed treaty, he would be recognised merely as 'a relative of the late Raja in temporary charge of the country'. He renewed the earlier demand for the surrender of the culprits involved in the human sacrifice within 20 days. Rajendra Singh did not consider it necessary to abide by this directive since the incident had not occurred during his reign. Robertson, however, believed that failure to comply meant an indirect admission of guilt and recommended deposing the Raja. The government, however, was not prepared to take such a hasty decision and instructed Robertson to give the Raja another chance.

In January 1834, Rajendra Singh submitted a representation to the governor-general enumerating the following:

- That the Agent had lowered his position by referring him as a manager of the Jayantia country.
- That the demand for tribute was in direct contravention to the earlier treaty.
- That his principality was in no position to pay an annual tribute of 10,000 rupees.

The government called upon Francis Jenkins, who had succeeded Robertson,[22] to look into the matter and make suitable recommendations. Jenkins was of the opinion that since Rajendra Singh's succession had been approved by the *durbar*, the British government had no right to depose him. Moreover, Rajendra Singh had not violated any of the terms of the earlier treaty which, at any rate, could not be considered a 'personal treaty'. The terms of the treaty might have been unfavourable to the British but that did not warrant the imposition of a new treaty with unreasonable and unrealistic demands. He offered three suggestions:

1. Place the Raja of Gobha on trial and punish him directly.
2. Persuade Rajendra Singh to surrender the criminals.
3. Convince him to make voluntary payments in cash in lieu of military service.

Annexation of Jayantia

The government did not agree with Jenkins' suggestions. They revived the old dispute about the Jayantia Raja's chokey at Chaparmukh. In August 1834, Rajendra Singh surrendered the four criminal who were supposed to have been involved in the sacrifice of British subjects. Thus, one of the major grounds of dispute between the Raja and the British was removed, though belatedly. The natural course now would have been to settle the question of tribute. But the British made no fresh demands. Instead they annexed the plains district of the Jayantia territory on 15 March 1835 without any intimation to the Raja. The dependency of Gobha was taken over a few weeks later.[23] As the resources of the hill districts were inadequate to maintain the Raja's family and the administrative establishment,[24] Rajendra Singh voluntarily surrendered the remaining territory to the British government.

The confiscation of the Jayantia territory was criticised by the Court of Directors of the Company. They observed that it was a very 'summary measure and one of doubtful propriety'. The irregularity of the transaction incurred their displeasure to such an extent that they were constrained to issue a directive that no further annexation could take place without prior consultation with them. The annexation of Jayantia caused strong resentment among the *syntengs*, as the Jayantias were called. It was not so much the annexation as the conduct of the local authorities that strained the relations between the syntengs and the British. The political agent not only assumed charge of the territory but also seized the personal effects of the chief. Fearing an intrusion into their traditional way of life, the Jayantias rebelled. They were first suppressed and later temporarily won over with liberal concessions.

The traditional institution of the dolois[25] was initially retained. They were entrusted with the administration of civil and criminal justice within their respective areas subject to the authority of the political agent.[26] The dolois in return paid one male goat for each village under their control, this being their only contribution to the government. The dolois were remunerated from the amount collected from fines imposed for offences and duties on haats.[27] In 1849, Colonel Lister suggested the imposition of a house tax on the inhabitants in view of the temperament of some people to assert their independence. He believed that it was essential to exact some payment, however trifling it might be, as a token of submission.[28] The government, however, considered this unwise at the time.

Disaffection with the British

Meanwhile allegations of 'lawless proceedings' and 'corrupt practices' of the dolois poured in. Lister's suggestion of the imposition of a tax as a means of asserting authority increasingly gained ground in official circles and in 1860, they introduced a house tax. The Jayantias strongly opposed this new tax, expelled the tax collector and even resorted to armed resistance. But the government came down heavily on the protestors. They were disbanded and the civil authorities were empowered to dismiss the dolois and other local officials in cases of insubordination. The hostile attitude, however, continued. There were several reasons for this and they were:

- The British introduced additional taxes such as income tax, judicial stamps duty and agricultural income tax. The new taxes caused widespread resentment among the people who had never been subjected to any taxation earlier.
- The forests were auctioned to the highest bidder.
- The introduction of the British judicial system involved a lengthy process of litigation which was totally unfamiliar to the people. In the circumstances, they often had to take recourse to bribes to settle disputes.
- The dolois were unhappy because they were no longer recognised as chiefs but merely as managers of their estates for a period of three years. They could not reconcile to the rule of the

English who had deprived them of all their earlier power and privileges. They also resented the fact that in the new setup their importance had been undermined by the presence of the daroga with whom the aggrieved invariably lodged their complaints.
- The advent of the Welsh Presbyterian missionaries who began to interfere with the traditions and customs of the people aggravated the tense situation.

The situation was indeed volatile and when the deputy commissioner gave orders for the confiscation of all the swords and shields, which were used not only for self-defence but also in their religious ceremonies, rebellion broke out in 1860.

The Jayantia Rebellion

The rebels were dealt with sternly and warned against any further seditious activities. The high-handed manner in which the uprising was dealt with provoked a leader called U Kiang Nongbah to organise the Jayantias to challenge British authority. Brisk preparations were made for the war of liberation by assembling men, erecting stockades, storing grains and sending emissaries even to Burma.[29] The objective of this revolt was to oust the British and to restore Rajendra Singh as their Raja. U Kiang Nongbah was able to garner mass support and the uprising of the Jayantias continued in spite of reinforcements brought in by the British. Brigadier G. D. Showers of the Eastern Command was entrusted with exclusive civil and military charge to quell the rebellion. A general amnesty was announced for those who surrendered voluntarily and the authorities declared a reward of 1,000 rupees for the capture of U Kiang Nongbah.

The government unleashed a virtual reign of terror. U Kiang Nongbah was eventually captured, tried by a military court and publicly hanged at Jowai on 30 December 1862. The resistance, however, continued for some time even after his execution. Eventually, as their stockades collapsed one by one, the Jayantias were forced to surrender.

After the suppression of the rebellion, the government posted an assistant commissioner, vested with the powers of a magistrate at Jowai. The district remained under the overall control of the deputy commissioner, Khasi-Jayantia Hills, who exercised concurrent authority with the assistant commissioner on all matters. The dolois continued to be responsible for the maintenance of law and order and the collection of revenue. European officers were instructed to make frequent tours to the places under their jurisdiction and mix freely with the people so as to encourage interaction and instil confidence in them. The income tax, which had been a major source of discontent, was withdrawn but the poll tax was retained. In this way, the village authorities and chiefs were gradually brought under the effective control of the assistant commissioner.

KHASI HILLS

The Khasis lived in the area known as Naduars,[30] south of Kamrup in Assam. During Ahom rule, the Khasi chiefs received their titles from the Ahom monarchy in return for a fixed amount as tribute. Until the beginning of the nineteenth century, British relations with the Khasi states, except with those bordering Sylhet, were practically non-existent. The Anglo-Burmese War of 1824–6, however, resulted in a changed situation. David Scott, who had resided in the hills for a time during parleys with the Jayantia raja, was delighted by the climate of the hills. He brought it to the notice of the government that

Figure 5.3: Annexation of Khasi Hills

Year	Event	Consequence
1824	David Scott signs treaties with chiefs of Mariaw, Nongkhlaw and Rambrai	The chiefs now owe allegiance to the British
1825	David Scott proposes a road through the Khasi Hills	Barmanik, chief of Khyrim opposes the plan
1826	Chattar Singh, chief of Nongkhlaw dies	U Tirot Singh elected next chief of Nongkhlaw. The British ask him to persuade other chiefs to agree to the road through the hills
1828	The British refuse to help U Tirot Singh in his dispute with the Raja of Rani	U Tirot Singh declares invalid the treaty with the British
1829	Khasi resistance to British	Led by U Tirot Singh, they burn the sanatorium, free the convicts working on the road etc.
1833	U Tirot Sigh surrenders	Complete surrender of all Khasi chiefs to the British

locations in the Khasi Hills could be developed for 'sanitary stations' for Europeans. He also suggested that a road be constructed through the Khasi Hills to connect Sylhet and Assam since the one started through Jayantia Hills had been discontinued.

In 1824, the Khasis were in possession of only three *duars*, viz., Maurapur, under Sadu Singh of Mariaw; Barduar under Chattar Singh of Nongkhlaw; and Pantan under Lal Singh of Rambrai. David Scott had entered into treaties with these chiefs during 1824–5 promising them British protection against external aggression in lieu of a fixed payment in cash (see Figure 5.3). Demorua, situated to the east of Naduar, was traditionally under the chief of Khyrim, but it was occupied by the Burmese in 1825, and subsequent to the Treaty of Yandabo, it passed into British hands.

The Khasi territory was administered by a number of chiefs known as *syiems*, who ruled with the help of durbars comprising of representatives of various clans. The durbars were democratic institutions and decisions were arrived at after much debate. Commenting on this aspect, Adam White wrote:

> I was struck with astonishment at the order and decorum which characterised these debates. No shouts of exultation or indecent attempts to put down the orator of the opposite party; on the contrary, every speaker was fairly heard out. I have often witnessed debates in St Stephen's Chapel, but those of the Cassya Parliament appeared to me to be conducted with more dignity of manner.[31]

White also observed that he had been under the impression that the government was 'lodged in a widely extended Aristocracy', but that in reality 'it was of a much more Republican cast'.[32] The syiem managed the administration through his durbar though in some villages much of the responsibility was shouldered by the village headman, known as the sirdar. There was also an official, called *lyngskor*, who supervised the work of the different sirdars and acted as the syiem's deputy.[33] Some of the petty principalities were presided over by *lyngdohs*, sirdars and *wahadadars*. Khasi society being matrilineal in nature, the heir to the syiem-ship was invariably from the female line of descent.

Administration under the Syiems

- Land was generally the property of the different villages and clans although certain estates were also owned by individuals. No land revenue was imposed on the cultivators.

- The syiem's income was derived from the produce on the state lands and from the tolls levied at the markets in his territory.
- The Khasis did not have a monetary economy and barter was the mode of trade. Transaction with the plains people were carried out through the duars.

British interest in the Khasi Hills primarily lay in the logic of its geographical location, although the limestone reserves available in the region had also attracted their attention. David Scott deemed it of utmost importance to have a direct line of communication connecting the Brahmaputra Valley with the Surma Valley. But his proposal to construct a road through the Khasi Hills as early as 1825 had fallen through because it had met with stiff resistance by Barmanik, the chief of Khyrim. So when Chattar Singh, the chief of Nongkhlaw, died in 1826, Scott agreed to recognise his successor only on condition that he would grant the British access through his territory to construct the above mentioned road. Meanwhile, U Tirot Singh was elected chief of Nongkhlaw. In order to make his position secure, he had no other option but to agree to Scott's proposal. He was also directed to use his influence with the other chiefs to agree to the proposal. After considerable persuasion, the Khasi chiefs agreed to the British proposal and approval was granted for the construction of a road from Sylhet to Gauhati via Cherrapunji, Mawphlang and Mairang. Delighted at this achievement, Scott immediately started negotiations to acquire a piece of land at Nongkhlaw to establish a sanatorium. Permission for this was also granted though not without initial hesitation. The British, thus, created a strong foothold for themselves in the Khasi Hills.

Barmanik had always been suspicious of the intentions of the British. Their attempts to tighten control over the Khasi Hills after the construction of the road further confirmed his suspicions. In neighbouring Nogkhlaw, U Tirot Singh also began to experience certain constraints. His disillusionment was complete when the British refused to assist him in 1828 in his dispute with the ruler of Rani. Instead of assisting him according to the terms of the existing treaty, the British supported his enemy. U Tirot Singh considered this a grave breach of trust on the part of the British. Declaring that he was no longer bound by the treaty with the British, he threw in his lot with Barmanik and other chiefs.

Khasi Resistance

In 1829, the Khasis, led by U Tirot Singh, burnt the sanatorium at Nongkhlaw, set free the convicts employed in the construction of the road and massacred several British subjects including two European officers. The Nongkhlaw outrage marked the beginning of a prolonged Khasi resistance to British expansionism. Captain Fredrick Lister of the Sylhet Light Infantry was immediately dispatched to restore order in the Khasi Hills. By the end of the year many of the hostile chiefs were reduced to submission. Barmanik was also apprehended and a treaty was imposed on him whereby he was compelled to acknowledge British authority, pay a fine of 5,000[34] rupees and renounce all claims over Demorua. In spite of the fact that most of his allies had surrendered, U Tirot Singh continued to resist the British. David Scott's successor, Robertson, realising that military operations alone were inadequate, decided to use economic pressure. He closed all the markets on the duars bordering the Khasi Hills, thereby completely disrupting the fragile economy of the Hills. Prolonged resistance had weakened the Khasis. Unable to bear the pressure, Tirot Singh surrendered in June 1833.

Khasi States after the Rebellion

The subsequent peace process initiated by the British resulted in the complete subordination of all the Khasi chiefs.[35] Those states that had actively participated in the struggle lost a portion of their territory or paid a fine, or a combination of both. No state was annexed to the British dominion of India other than three small villages—Mawsmai, Mawmluh and Sohbar—the first two by conquest and the third by treaty. Scott personally believed that it was more expedient to impose fines than collect tribute because the cost of collection would outweigh the receipts apart from the risks involved in its collection.[36] The authorities at Calcutta, while agreeing with this in principle, cautioned the officers to use their discretion while imposing the fines. The British recognised 25 Khasi states as either semi-independent or dependent ones. Cherra, Khyrim, Nogstoin, Langrin and Nongspun were referred to as independent states as they had never been actually coerced by a British force. The remaining 20 states, recognised as dependent states, were those that had been restored to their chiefs or in the case of five sirdar-ships, been created by the British.[37] In 1835, a separate political agency under Captain Lister was created for the Khasi Hills with headquarters at Cherrapunji. Although the traditional administrative structure was retained, the syiems were reduced to mere figure heads by divesting them and their durbars of most of the powers that they had hitherto exercised.

It is apparent from the above that the British administered the whole of the Khasi Hills, except the Cherrapunji station, indirectly through the traditional administrative structure. They arrived at a balance of distribution of power and authority without assuming responsibility for all aspects of administration. As the number of British officials was limited, it necessitated collaboration with Khasi chiefs. The relationship with these Khasi chiefs, however, was not clearly defined and Dalhousie considered it of utmost importance to assert and proclaim the paramountcy of the British in legal terms. In 1859, they made it mandatory for the Khasi chiefs to enter into a formal agreement with the deputy commissioner who was entrusted with the functions of the government's political officer in relation to these states.[38] Periodic changes in terms of agreements with the chiefs were made in the subsequent years. In 1867, the syiems were placed under the deputy commissioner whose orders they were bound to obey. Moreover, the syiems had to cede to the British all waste lands, forests and areas having limestone, coal and other minerals in return for half the profits gained from any monetary transaction. They were also prohibited from alienating property without the consent of the government. In 1875, the system of agreements with the chiefs was replaced by a sanad conferred by the chief commissioner in the case of syiems and deputy commissioner in the case of lyngdohs, sirdars, and wahadadars.[39] Thus within a fairly short time, the Khasis were effectively brought under British control.

British control implied intervention in the internal affairs of the states, for instance, in cases of maladministration, questions of law and order, public grievances and, most of all, on questions relating to succession. Very often, they took advantage of internal dissensions and inter-village disputes to allow villages to secede from the Khasi states and become British villages.[40] This naturally caused resentment among certain sections of the people and in course of time, as in the rest of India, the policy of interference and disregard for local customs led to the gradual emergence of political awareness in the Khasi Hills.

GARO HILLS

The estates of Karaibari, Kalumalupara, Habraghat, Mechpara, Sherpur, Susung and Bijni lay between the plains of East Bengal and the Khasi Hills. The hilly tract in this region was inhabited by various clans of the Garo tribe. The zamindars of the above estates, known as choudhury and raja, were responsible for the collection of revenue[41] from the Garos and for the maintenance of law and order in the area. They made no attempt to secure any footing in the hills at first and were satisfied with the profits that they earned from the trade and money lending activities in the low lying areas adjoining their estates. In any case, they had little control over the hill people who regularly made incursions into the plains below. The villages at the border were often compelled to buy their security by paying a tax known as *matharakha*. Meanwhile, cotton from the hills had become an important item of trade and the emergence of British commercial interest in cotton pressurised the zamindars to expand and strengthen their jurisdiction in the region. Subsequent attempts by them to force the tribes into submission and their high handedness had provoked retaliatory raids by the hill people. This obviously led to much turmoil in the frontier and the Company's government began to seriously doubt the expediency of leaving the Garos under the control of the zamindars.

In 1816, the East India Company assumed administrative responsibility over the tract of land inhabited by the Garos as part of the district of Rangpur. The Garos were then divided into three categories, viz.,

1. The Zamindari Garos who lived within the estates of the former zamindars.
2. The *Nazarana* or tributary Garos who had acknowledged the authority of the government by paying an annual tribute; and
3. The *Bemulwa* or independent Garos.

The Bengal Regulations were made operative here for administrative purposes. However, David Scott, who was in charge of the region, soon realised that the Bengal Regulations were totally unsuitable for this area and recommended the creation of a separate administrative unit for the frontier tract comprising Goalpara, Dhubri and Karaibari, to be named North East Parts of Rangpur, and placed under the jurisdiction of a civil commissioner. The idea was to bring all the Garos under the direct control of the British without zamindars as intermediaries and to make the commissioner the supreme judicator. Scott also proposed that wherever possible, Garos should be employed in the police and judicial services. The Bengal Regulations were replaced by Regulation X of 1822,[42] embodying Scott's proposals, in the new administrative unit. Scott was given a free hand to implement the scheme.[43] But before he could take any action he was appointed as agent to the governor-general, northeastern frontier, in addition to his existing offices. The Burmese invasion meanwhile called for his undivided attention and the Garo problem was sidetracked for the time being. This provided the Garos with the opportunity to carry on their plunder.

British supremacy in the Khasi Hills had exposed another frontier to the plundering raids of the Garos, but the authorities in Fort William were very cautious in their dealings with them. Although coercive measures were sanctioned from time to time on grounds of expediency, the policy in general was conciliatory. Repeated raids and murders of British subjects in the Garo Hills eventually convinced the authorities that the Garo problem needed urgent attention. Lord Dalhousie, the Governor-General, took a strong view of the situation and recommended the immediate dispatch of an expedition to quell the tribes. He observed that the ruling principle of the frontier policy must be to compel the Garos into submission, to enforce tranquillity and to protect the lives and property of the British subjects.

Dalhousie's policy was indeed a departure from the earlier policy followed by the government. Curiously, neither he nor his predecessors attempted to identify the real causes of the depredations. On earlier occasions, the government had attributed the outrages to the high handedness and extortions of the zamindars, but since the time of David Scott, the feudal elements had been replaced by the Company's government. Yet the outrages committed in 1852 were unprecedented, leading Jenkins to comment: 'There had never been a time in which they have committed more numerous and more atrocious murders during so short a period.'[44] Lieutenant Agnew, Commander of the Assam Light Infantry, believed that the root of all the trouble lay in the poverty and backwardness of the people. He observed that unless the economic and social problems were addressed, the situation was not likely to change. Therefore, he suggested that a special officer be appointed to deal exclusively with Garo affairs. It was also recommended that a road be constructed through the hills to facilitate closer contact and steps be taken to spread education.[45]

Dalhousie did not agree with these recommendations. He considered the disturbed conditions as essentially a question of law and order and firmly believed that peace could be obtained only by quelling the rebellious tribes through military operations. Accordingly, an expedition was sent, but much to Dalhousie's dismay, it was not successful in achieving its aims. As a result, relations between the Garos and the English drifted from bad to worse. Realising the futility of coercive actions against the Garos, Dalhousie decided that the only other way to curb the increasing lawlessness on the frontier was to set up an economic blockade. The frontier markets were closed and the Garos confined to the hills, but even this measure proved to be only partly effective. Both Jenkins and Mofatt Mills reported that in the circumstances, the only hope of securing permanent tranquillity on the frontier lay in the military occupation of the Garo Hills. The governor-general, however, did not share this view. Taking advantage of the government's indecision, the Garos intensified their raids into the frontier villages.

Repeated outrages eventually compelled the authorities at Fort William to arrive at a firm decision. Henry Hopkinson, who succeeded Jenkins as agent to the governor-general and commissioner of Assam in1861, subscribed to the views of his predecessor who had recommended military occupation of the hills. Hopkinson was not in favour of sending occasional expeditions. He pointed out that past experience had shown that such expeditions had no lasting effect whatsoever and that the hill people resumed hostilities as soon as the troops were withdrawn. He further believed that the absence of a fixed policy towards the hill tribes was responsible to a large extent for the predatory raids. He disapproved of the government's policy of separating hill people from those of the plains as inconsistent because no distinct frontier existed between the tracts. He felt that the annexation of Assam could not be considered complete without territorial acquisitions in the neighbouring hills since the government had assumed the responsibility of protecting the life and property of its subjects. He, therefore, advocated a radical policy towards the hill tribes. He reiterated the earlier suggestion for the appointment of a special officer exclusively for the Garo Hills and also stressed the necessity of constructing two roads; one from Karaibari to the boundary of Sylhet along the Garo frontier and another right across the Garo Hills from Goalpara to Mymensing.

The government also realised the necessity of asserting it's authority in the hills, but did not approve of the policy of armed intervention or the appointment of a European officer in the hills. The idea of opening up the hills through roads was, however, appreciated because it was felt that it would facilitate the promotion of trade. The secretary of state for India, while observing that there was 'nothing which would lend more to the general improvement and civilization of the country than the increase of commerce', advised that the Garos be encouraged to grow more cotton by extending all possible aid for its cultivation. Hopkinson outlined the government's new policy[46] towards the hill tribes in these words:

> Sometimes we must employ coercion, pure and simple, sometimes blockades; very often a judicious system of subsidising will keep the tribes quiet for a while, but still the surest foundation on which to build our control over them will be their fear of us. It is not coercion that has often failed us but failure to coerce.

He also observed:

> We must cease to regard them as aliens or even as enemies, but acknowledge them as subjects, seek to establish ourselves amongst them, to extend our influence over them and bring them under our control and within the pale of civilization ... we must be responsible for their condition; ... and we are as answerable for their continuance in their present state as it used to be held that the states of north America were answerable for the continuance of slavery in the South.

In 1865, B. W. D. Morton, Deputy Commissioner of Goalpara, proposed the setting up of a police organisation under which the *laskars* would be responsible for the collection of taxes and the maintenance of law and order within their respective jurisdictions. The proposal was approved by the government. Morton was directed to re-designate the laskars as *zimmadars* and to arm them with civil and military powers necessary for maintaining law and order. Accordingly, Lieutenant W. J. Williamson, Assistant Commissioner, Goalpara, entered into written engagements with thirty four chiefs who were appointed as zimmadars on a fixed salary.

This arrangement worked well in the northern part of the Garo Hills but in the southern part troubles continued. Reports of continuing outrages convinced the government that the only solution to the Garo problem lay in the assertion of British sovereignty over the hills. In July 1866 the Garo Hills were made a separate administrative unit. Williamson was appointed assistant commissioner, Garo Hills with headquarters initially at Singimari and later at Tura. In 1869, under Act XXII, the Garo Hills became a full-fledged district with Williamson as its deputy commissioner. This marked the formal assertion of British authority over the Garo hills.

But there were several hostile villages within the boundary demarcated by the government. The inhabitants of those villages were determined to remain independent. In December 1872, an expedition was sent to coerce them into submission. After an initial resistance, the villages eventually surrendered in January 1873. With this the subjugation of the Garo Hills was complete. It was brought under the chief commissioner of Assam in 1874.

British interest in the Garo Hills lay in the logic of its imperialist policy. The subjugation of the Garo Hills was imperative as it was surrounded by British territory. The primary object of the government was not so much the realisation of revenue from the region as ensuring peace on the frontier and the exploitation of the economic resources. Sir George Campbell, the Lieutenant-Governor of Bengal, put this very succinctly when he observed:

> ... instead of our having to burn large quantities of cotton in punishment of outrages, as was unhappily necessary for a few instances, we may find a new source of supply to Manchester ... the timber of the hills is also expected to prove valuable, and while preserving all reasonable jungle rights of the Garos, the Government may expect a fair return of judicious forest operations. Wild elephants are said to be very numerous, and probably *kheddah* operations would be profitable at an early date.[47]

In order to exploit the economic resources and to prevent encroachments from across the borders, the government enacted the Inner Line Regulations in 1873 which prohibited British subjects and other classified persons from moving beyond a certain line. This was replaced by Regulation I of 1876 and subsequently by Regulation I of 1882 which authorised the chief commissioner to prohibit all persons who were not natives of the Garo Hills, from exploiting the forest resources within the district without a valid licence. Even the Garos were required to obtain permission for frequenting the hills. On the strength of this Regulation, the government reserved 14 forests where even the Garos had no rights. This naturally resulted in strong resentment. Led by Sonaram Sangma, they submitted a memorandum to the Viceroy claiming compensation against the unilateral extinction of their rights in the reserved forests. As in the Khasi Hills, simmering discontent in the Garo Hills had also resulted in the emergence of political awareness. Under the leadership of Sonaram, around 700 Garos invaded Habraghat pargana in Bijni, overpowered opposition and proclaimed a 'Garo Raj' in 1902. Sonaram even posted notices ordering the tenants not to pay rent to the zamindars.[48] Fearing severe adverse consequences if the agitation was not nipped at the bud, the government convicted Sonaram and his accomplices. Further, in order to placate the Garos, the government relented to most of their demands.[49]

The incorporation of the Cachar, Jayantia, the Khasi Hills and the Garo Hills into the British Dominion marks an important phase in Britain's colonial penetration in India's northeastern region. As each of these principalities came under British paramountcy one after the other, it became clear that the government was largely influenced by economic factors when taking major policy decisions. Areas which started off as spheres of influence gradually became areas of political and economic control.

NOTES AND REFERENCES

1. It was claimed that as early as the reign of the Burmese king, Hshin-byu-shin, the Raja of Cachar had handed over to the victorious Burmese general a tree with roots as recognition of surrendering himself and his land to the Burmese. A. C. Banerjee, *The Eastern Frontier of British India,* (Third edition), Calcutta, 1964, pp. 112–14.
2. For details, refer to J. B. Bhattacharjee, *Cachar under British Rule in North East India,* Delhi, 1977, pp. 32–6.
3. For full text of Treaty refer C. U. Aitchison, *Treaties, Engagements and Sanads,* Vol. XII, Delhi (Revised reprinted edition), 1983, p. 117.
4. Ibid.
5. For full text, refer to ibid., p. 118.
6. J. B. Bhattacharjee, *Cachar under British Rule in North East India,* p. 52. Scott fixed the value of Cachar at 20 times the amount of the existing revenue.

7. Refer Chapter 6 for details.
8. A. C. Banerjee in H. K. Barpujari (ed.), *Comprehensive History of Assam,* Vol. IV, p. 65.
9. Regulation X exempted the operations of normal rules and provided for administration by an executive who was expected to harmonise the spirit of the Regulations with native institutions.
10. The Non-Regulated System in Cachar was abolished in 1921.
11. For details, refer to Aitchinson, *Treaties, Engagements and Sanads,* Vol. XII.
12. J. B. Bhattacharjee, *Cachar under British Rule in North East India* , p. 68.
13. The population of Cachar was not large, but it comprised of several distinct racial, cultural and religious elements. Apart from the indigenous people, there were a number of migrants, both Hindu and Muslim, from the neighbouring districts of Bengal. The Kachari Rajas were very tolerant and these immigrants lived as free settlers so long as they paid their dues to the government. Many of the local people, including the royalty who embraced Hinduism, adopted the customs and traditions of the Hindu migrants to some extent, but in general, all the communities lived together peacefully.

    There was a gradation of officers who looked after the interests of the different sections of the people. The *barbhandari* or prime minister, the *patras* or ministers, the senapati or the commander-in-chief, the *raj pandit* or the royal priest, besides several others, looked after the welfare of the Dimachas, Kukis and Nagas or the *parbatiyas* (hill men) as they were referred to. The affairs of the immigrants were controlled by units known as khels which were formed for common objectives and were heterogeneous groups comprising of members from different social and religious communities. The channel of communication between the raja and the ryots was the mukhtar who collected the government revenue and supervised the affairs of the khels. As the number of khels increased, adjacent khels were grouped together to form larger units called *raj* or pargana. The mukhtars of the constituent khels elected the *raj mukhtar* who were given various titles like choudhury, *majumdar,* laskar, *barabhuyan, chotabhuyan* etc., in accordance with the social status and importance of the unit of which he was the elected representative.
14. In addition to the judges of the panchayat courts and tahsildar munsiffs, Goluk Chandra Bol, for example, was appointed as Deputy Collector in 1841 and Dr S. M. Sarkar as Assistant Surgeon of Cachar Civil Hospital in 1856.
15. *Assam Secretariat Proceedings,* Appointments and Political Department, September 1931, Appendix , N. C. Hills, p. 10; also L. W. Shakespeare, *History of the Assam Rifles,* 1929, Guwahati (reprint), 1980, pp. 80–1. .Also, S. K. Barpujari (ed.), *History of the Dimasas,* Guwahati, 1997, pp. 116–8.
16. Piketo Sema, *British Policy and Administration in Nagaland, 1881–1947,* Delhi, 1992, pp. 144–7. Also, L. W.Shakespeare, *History of the Assam Rifles,* pp. 80–1.
17. B. C. Chakravorty, *British Relations with the Hill Tribes of Assam since 1858,* Calcutta (reprint) 1981, p. 191.
18. For details, refer to Robert Reid, *History of the Frontier Areas Bordering on Assam from 1883–1941,* Guwahati (Reprint) 1997, pp. 167–72.
19. F. S. Downs, *Christianity in North East India,* Guwahati, 1983, p. 192.

20. C. U. Aitchinson, *Treaties, Engagements and Sanads,* Vol. XII.
21. In April 1832, T. C. Robertson succeeded W. Cracroft as Agent to the Governor-General, North East Frontier and Commissioner of Rangpur.
22. In January 1834, the Company's government abolished the office of the Political Agent to the North East Frontier of Bengal and Commissioner of Rangpur and created the distinct office of the Commissioner and Agent to the Governor General for Assam and North East of Rangpur. In April 1834, Jenkins succeeded Robertson.
23. No formal declaration by the government was made to this effect. It appears that 'on 15 March 1835, Captain Lister took formal possession of Jaintiapur and issued a proclamation announcing the annexation of the Jaintia parganas to the British Dominion. The dependency of Gobha met with the same fate a few weeks later'. R. M. Lahiri, *The Annexation of Assam,* Calcutta, 1954, p. 157.
24. The only income derived by the Raja from the hills was one male goat from each village annually and a small quantity of parched rice and firewood for his annual religious ceremonies. The villagers were also bound to cultivate the crown lands. E. A. Gait, *A History of Assam,* (Reprint), Guwahati, 2008, p. 302.
25. At the time of British annexation, there were 15 dolois. For details see H. K. Barpujari, *Problem of the Hill Tribes North East Frontier,* Vol. II, Guwahati, 1976, p. 76.
26. The Jayantia parganas were transferred to Sylhet district and the Gobha area to Nowgong. But in effect, Jayantia remained under the *de facto* control of Lister. Eventually, the Khasi and Jayantia Hills became his common charge.
27. Periodical markets.
28. A. J. M Mills, *Report of the Khasi and Jaintia Hills 1853,* (edited version) NEHU, p. 13.
29. H. K. Barpujari, *Political History of Assam,* Vol. I, Guwahati, 1999, p. 85.
30. Duar is a mountain pass. Naduar literally means nine passes.
31. Adam White, *A Memoir of Late David Scott,* DHAS, 1988 p. 12.
32. Ibid.
33. For details, refer to P. R. Gurdon, *The Khasis,* 1907, Reprint, New Delhi,1987, pp. 66–75.
34. Subsequently this fine was commuted to constructing a road from Mooleem to Cherra. See Mills, *Report of the Khasi and Jaintia Hills, 1853,* p. 42.
35. At that time there were 16 syiemships, 1 wahadadarship, 1 lyngdohship and 2 sirdarships in the Khasi Hills. For details, refer to Hamlet Bareh, *The History and Culture of the Khasi People,* Shillong, 1967, pp. 106–31. There were 564 villages with a total population of around 82, 400. Mills, *Report of the Khasi and Jaintia Hills 1853.,* p. 44.
36. Foreign Political Consultations, 27 May 1834, No. 78.
37. Aitchison, *Treaties, Engagements and Sanads,* Vol. XII , p. 122–3.
38. David Syemlieh, 'British Policy Towards the Khasis' in J. B. Bhattacharjee (ed.) *Studies in the History of North East India,* Shillong, 1986, pp. 188–9.
39. This system continued till 1912. Ibid.
40. Ibid.

41. The interest of the zamindars was mainly economic. The trade in cotton, elephants, timber, *agar* and other indigenous products was so lucrative that the zamindars set up a string of haats at the hill passes in their respective estates. Besides, periodical markets were also held to attract both Bengali and Garo traders. While the Garos paid duty in kind, others were expected to pay both in cash and kind. *Haat mohururs* were appointed for the collection of the taxes. For details, refer to J. B. Bhattacharjee, *The Garos and the English,* New Delhi, 1978, pp. 20–2.
42. 'A Regulation for exempting the Garrow mountaineers and other rude tribes on the North Eastern Frontier of Rangpur from the operation of the existing Regulations.' The objectives of the Regulations were stated in the Preamble as follows: 'To promote the desirable object of reclaiming these tribes to habits of civilized lives, it seems necessary that a special plan for the administration of justice of a kind peculiar to their customs and prejudices, be arranged and concerted with the headmen; and that measures should at the same time be taken for freeing them from any dependence on the *zamindars* of the British provinces.' R. Clarke, *The Regulations of the Government of Fort William in Bengal 1793–1853,* London, 1854, p. 659.
43. The new regulation provided for the recognition of the existing *sirdars* and *laskars* and for the nomination of fit persons to such posts by the inhabitants of a village or the *sirdars.* Ibid., pp. 67–8.
44. *Judicial Department Proceedings,* January. 1853, No. 5, National Archives of India.
45. Ibid., No. 120–32.
46. For details, refer to J. B. Bhattacharjee, *Studies in the History of North East India,* pp. 160–8.
47. Bengal Report 1872–3.
48. Santo Barman, *Zamindari System in Assam during British Rule (A Case Study of Goalpara District),* Guwahati, 1994, p. 84.
49. P. C. Kar, *British Annexation of Garo Hills,* Calcutta 1970, pp. 75–6.

SUGGESTED READINGS

Barpujari, H. K., *Problem of the Hill Tribes North East Frontier,* Vol II, Guwahati, 1976.

———, *Political History of Assam,* Vol I, Guwahati, 1999.

Bhattacharjee, J. B. (ed.), *Studies in the History of North East India,* Shillong, 1986.

6

Expansion to the South and Manipur and the Frontier Tribes

Chapter Highlights

- Relations with Manipur
- Relations with the Lushais and occupation of Lushai Hills
- Relations with the Nagas and occupation of Naga Hills
- Relations with Bhutan—Treaty of Sinchula
- Penetration into the sub-Himalayan tracts east of Bhutan

The annexation of Assam had brought the British into close contact with Manipur and the different tribes inhabiting the northeastern frontier. Manipur was recognised as a 'Subordinate Native State' since the end of the First Anglo-Burmese War and every succession to the throne required British endorsement. The British also had to frequently interfere in the affairs of Manipur with regard to other matters also. Their policy towards the frontier tribes, on the other hand, was different. The British were initially reluctant to have any close contacts with the frontier tribes and preferred to exercise only as much control as was necessary to maintain peace and security on the border. The tribal people had always been independent. Their age-old customs and traditions determined their social, political and economic lives and they were completely averse to any interference. Moreover, the areas were inhospitable, communication facilities virtually non-existent and the known economic resources very limited. Further, the terrain was such that campaigning in the hills was bound to be an extremely difficult task. Therefore, the British were not keen to extend their direct administration over the hill people. In fact even an expansionist like Dalhousie wanted to leave the hill tribes alone. Whenever the frontier was in turmoil, the British tried to sort out the problem by sending peace missions. Outlining the general British policy, Woodthorpe observed, 'The Government does not wish to exterminate these frontier tribes, but by converting them into our allies, [intends] to raise a barrier between our frontier districts and other more distant races'.[1]

However, by 1860 the situation in the border areas had deteriorated dramatically. The expansion of British dominion in the plains resulted in constant friction with the adjoining hill tribes. In the absence of a well-demarcated boundary, the extension of tea plantations by European entrepreneurs was seen by the tribes as an encroachment on their territory. Repeated raids into British territory and the consequent insecurity of the entire frontier necessitated a permanent solution to the problem. In the circumstances, the Government was compelled to abandon its policy of non-intervention and adopt one of active interference. The problem of law and order was the primary reason for the change in British policy towards the frontier tribes. But there were other reasons as well. By the second half of the nineteenth century, the British had received several reports of the economic potential of the region. It was believed that the region's valuable resources, like cotton, limestone, salt, coal and rubber, could be commercially exploited to serve British interests. Moreover, the opening up of a trade route to Tibet had also become a distinct possibility. In this context, control over this region was of vital importance.

Theoretically, the British claimed the entire region west of Burma as belonging to them. However, only those territories that were identified as being economically or strategically important was brought under their direct rule. In course of time, those areas which were not considered as vital or significant were left alone. Inner Lines, as distinguished from the outer-most limits of British territories, were drawn between the regularly administered tracts and the neighbouring hills in order to safeguard colonial administrative and economic interests. In 1903 the Government of India declared that beyond the 'administrative' frontier, the 'tribes may do as they please'. Two years later, however, it was made clear that non-interference would be followed only till such time that the tribes occupying the tracts refrained 'from raids within the administered areas'. Elaborating this policy, the government stated:

> The Government of India ... recognise that occasions may arise when the action of a barbarous neighbour may compel them temporarily to abandon their policy of non-intervention, whether in pursuance of their duty as a civilized power, to deter the tribes from the repetition of their barbarities, or to allay serious unrest caused among their own

> subjects by the immunity enjoyed by the offenders. Each case must be decided however, according to its special circumstances....[2]

The possibilities of British subjects being involved in trans-frontier quarrels resulting in the violation of the border by the people from the 'unadministered'[3] tracts constantly kept the district authorities on their heels throughout the entire period of colonial rule.

MANIPUR

We have observed earlier[4] that the British policy of appeasement towards Gambhir Singh had strengthened his hands and that he had taken advantage of this to pursue his aggressive designs on Cachar. Gambhir Singh died in 1834 and was succeeded by his two year old son, Chandrakirti. The real authority, however, rested with Nar Singh, the regent, who subsequently usurped the throne and ruled till his death in 1850 despite attempts by Chandrakirti and his mother to remove him. When Nur Singh died, the British at first recognised his brother Debendra Singh as the new ruler, much to Chandrakirti's chagrin. He then launched a major offensive to recover his lost throne. In the wake of the onslaught, Debendra Singh fled from Manipur leaving the throne to Chandrakirti. Chandrakirti's reign (1850–86) was one of political restlessness marked by plots and attempted assassinations, but with the help of the British he managed to retain his position. He reciprocated the favours by helping the British with military aid on several occasions. When Chandrakirti died, his eldest son, Surachandra, succeeded him. The rival claimant who tried to seize the throne was defeated by a police force from Cachar and deported to Hazaribagh.

Surachandra was a weak ruler who was more concerned with religious affairs than with the governance of the country. In September 1890, his brother Tikendrajit led a revolt against him. Surachandra took refuge with the political agent, declared his intention of abdicating and left Manipur for Vrindavan (see Figure 6.1). But when he reached British territory, he appealed to the Viceroy to be reinstated saying that he had been misunderstood about his plans for abdication. Meanwhile, his brother Kulachandra proclaimed himself maharaja before intimating the government at Fort William. Considering this a breach of the code of conduct, the Government of India 'declined

Figure 6.1: Manipur

Year	Event	Consequence
1834	Gambhir Singh, ruler of Manipur, dies	Chandrakirti, his two year old son crowned king. But real power with Nar Singh, the regent who rules till 1850
1850	Chandrakirti crowned ruler	Rule marked by internal strife. Holds onto the throne with British help
1886	Surachandra, Chandrakirti's son, succeeds him	Surachandra a weak ruler
1890	Surachandra's brother Tikendrajit rebels against him	Surachandra seeks asylum with the British
1890	Kulachandra, another of Chandrakirti's sons ascends the throne	The British decide to acknowledge him as the ruler
1891	Tikendrajit foments more trouble	The British decide to install Churachand Singh, a six-year-old relative of Nar Singh, on the throne; administration placed under the British superintendent
1907	Churachand Singh formally crowned ruler	The superintendent's administration ends but the president of the Raja's durbar to be an Indian Civil Service officer

to pass orders regarding the succession or to acknowledge the letters received from Kulachandra whom the Chief Commissioner of Assam had recognised as Regent pending the orders of the Government'.[5]

For a while, the new administration functioned fairly well but the hesitation by the authorities at Fort William in recognising Kulachandra as the maharaja encouraged the growth of divisive forces within the state. Tikendrajit was believed to be at the root of all the problems. The government, therefore, decided to strengthen the position of Kulachandra by recognising him as the rightful heir to the throne and ordered Tikendrajit to be deported. The Chief Commissioner, J. W. Quinton, proceeded to Manipur with an escort to execute this order. Tikendrajit refused to surrender and an attempt to capture him also failed. The rebels attacked the Residency and rounded up Quinton, Colonel Skene, Lieutenant Simpsons and Cossins, all British officers. Grimwood, the Political Agent, was killed on the spot. The four other officers were tried by the Manipuri Court according to the local law, sentenced to death and executed. The attack on the Residency was resumed and the defenders, unable to hold out, retreated to Cachar. The British Government then declared war on Manipur and sent three columns from Cachar, Kohima and Burma to occupy Manipur. The rebel leaders were tried under the Indian Penal Code, the code of laws enacted by the British in 1860. Tikendrajit and his close confidants, found guilty of waging war against the Empress of India and abetment of murder of four British officers were sentenced to death.[6] The others were deported for life and Gambhir Singh's family was debarred from ascending the throne.

The removal of the royal family brought the question of the future settlement of Manipur. A proclamation issued in August 1891 stated that although Manipur was liable to be penalised with annexation, they had decided to re-establish native rule. Accordingly, Churachand Singh, a six year old descendent of Nar Singh, was declared as the new ruler. The sanad granted to the new king imposed not only an annual tribute but also the condition that the Raja and his successors would carry out 'all orders given by the British Government with regard to the administration ... and any other matters in which the British Government may be pleased to intervene'. As the new Raja was a minor, Major Maxwell, the political agent, also assumed dual charge of superintendent with full administrative powers. A collective fine was imposed on the people of Manipur for their misconduct.[7] The British initiated numerous reforms.

- They set up better judicial tribunals.
- Revised the land revenue administration and abolished the old system of forced labour for the state (*lallup*).[8]
- They also defined the boundaries of the state and took steps to disarm the hill tribes.
- They also opened a cart road from Imphal to Kohima.

In 1907 Churachand Singh[9] was formally crowned the king of Manipur andthe administration of the superintendent came to an end. The president of the Raja's durbar, was a member of the Indian Civil Service. He was responsible not only for the administration of the hill tribes living within the state but also for all financial and revenue matters. He made certain changes in the judicial administration. The number of *chirap* courts, which tried both civil and criminal cases earlier, was reduced and lower courts, known as panchayat courts, were instituted. Sentences exceeding five years of rigorous imprisonment required the Raja's assent while death sentences had to be confirmed by the governor of Assam. These administrative arrangements, with partial modifications from time to time, continued till the end of British rule in India.[10]

The abolition of lallup and *pothang*[11] and their substitution with monetary payment served long-term colonial interests. Monetisation and the consequent circulation of money led to the development of trade and commerce and the opening up of Manipur as a lucrative market for British goods. The economic and social changes also resulted in the gradual emergence of a middle class. The imposition of the house tax without reciprocal welfare measures, however, caused acute resentment among the people. The accumulated resentment triggered an anti-British agitation during 1917–19 when there was an attempt to recruit *coolies* to Europe during World War I. The Kuki Uprising [12] soon assumed the form of an armed struggle for national liberation. Although the agitation was crushed, the government realised once again that it could not ride roughshod over the sentiments of the people. The chief commissioner recorded, 'The tribesmen had contributed some 70,000 rupees a year in the form of house tax, but had received in return practically no benefits: neither roads, nor education, nor medical education.'[13] It was, therefore, decided to initiate steps to extend to them some 'benefits of civilization'.

THE LUSHAI HILLS

The Lushais inhabited the hill tracts adjoining Cachar. The British only had vague knowledge of these tribes since their occupation of Bengal after the Battle of Plassey in 1757, but it was only after the annexation of Cachar that the British came into direct contact with them. Yet, for many years, their information on the Lushais continued to remain rudimentary. The economic resources of the hill tracts inhabited by the Lushais were very limited and disputes over control of resources often led to inter-clan feuds. The Lushais also raided neighbouring British territory in the plains often for their sustenance.[14] Until the early years of the 1840s, these depredations were sporadic. Subsequently however, as the raids became more frequent, violent and deeper into British territory, the Government of Bengal decided to send a punitive expedition into Lushai territory. Accordingly, in January 1850, Captain Lister was dispatched with a force of the Sylhet Light Infantry. Despite a strong contingent at his command, Lister found the task extremely challenging. He realised that the Lushais were much more powerful than estimated by local officers, and thought it more prudent to retire to Silchar.[15] This futile expedition convinced the government that extensive operations in difficult terrain were not only an economic strain but impractical as well. It was, therefore, decided to erect a number of armed outposts of friendly Kukis for the defence of the Cachar frontier. They set up three stockades garrisoned by four companies of the Sylhet Light Infantry at the most vulnerable points along the southern frontier. They also set up a 200 member Kuki Levy for the defence of the frontier.

These actions yielded results immediately. In December 1850, the deputies of several Lushai Chiefs came to Silchar with an offer of tribute in return for British aid against their enemies. But while accepting the offer of friendship, the government refused to get entangled in inter-tribal feuds. It ordered the demarcation of the boundary line and assured the delegates that no action would be taken against them so long as they remained peaceful. But peace on the frontier which followed this agreement was short-lived. In 1862 groups of Lushais swooped into Kachari villages, plundered them, killed several inhabitants and took many more as captives. The immediate reaction of the collector of Sylhet was to send another expedition against the offending clans. The authorities at Fort William decided otherwise. The superintendent of Cachar, Captain Stewart, was instructed to induce Sukpilal, one of the main chiefs, to release the captives and maintain peace on the frontier in lieu of a fixed annual payment.[16] Thus, in 1864, they entered into an agreement with Sukpilal whereby he agreed to maintain peace and offer certain tributes to the British in return for an annual payment of 600 rupees.

But contrary to expectations, Sukpilal did not fulfil his obligations. The extension of tea plantations to the foot of the hills was seen as an infringement of Lushai territory and Sukpilal no longer considered himself bound by any obligation. The fugitive Manipuri princes in Cachar also instigated the Lushai chiefs whom they used in their attempts to dislodge Chandrakirti from the throne in Manipur. The situation became so alarming that the government was compelled to sanction another expedition into the Lushai Hills in 1869. The

Figure 6.2: Lushai Hills

Year	Event	Consequence
1850	British send Captain Lister in a punitive raid to the Lushai Hills to stop Lushai raids	Lister unable to quell the Lushais; The British instead set up three stockades garrisoned by the Sylhet Light Infantry
1850	Lushais offer to pay tributes to the British	British accept the hand of friendship but refuse to get involved in inter-tribal feuds
1862	Lushais conduct more raids	The British decide to induce Sukpilal, one of the main Lushai chiefs to maintain peace in return for an annual payment
1864	Captain Stewart signs an agreement with Sukpilal	Sukpilal reneges on agreement; more trouble on the frontier
1869	Another British expedition sent to the Hills	Though initially successful, the British forces withdraw due to bad weather; government appoints a special officer to deal with the area; He concludes treaties with several chiefs in the Hills including Sukpilal
1881	Sukpilal dies	Renewal of inter-tribe feuds
1890	Another British expedition sent to the Hills	All the main tribal chiefs surrender; North Lushai Hills brought under a British political officer
1891	South Lushai Hills and the Chittagong Hill Tracts formed into a separate district	The district has its new headquarters at Lungleh
1898	Chin Lushai Hills added to the above district	The whole region placed under the chief commissioner of Assam; Internal strife to be dealt with by the chiefs

expedition, which proceeded in three columns, met with initial success but incessant rain and the difficult terrain eventually compelled the British army to withdraw (see Figure 6.2). As partial solution to the problem, the government appointed an officer exclusively to deal with the tribes on this frontier. He was directed to meet the chiefs and induce them to sign agreements of good conduct. In addition, he was instructed to strengthen outposts at the frontier and take necessary measures to prevent the smuggling of arms into the hills.

In accordance with this directive, they arrived at agreements with several chiefs, including Sukpilal.[17] But these arrangements did not last long despite their high hopes. The defensive measures taken from time to time by the government failed to contain Lushai aggression. Repeated raids convinced them that unless some strong measures were immediately taken, the Lushais would be emboldened to renew their attacks on a larger scale. Hence, in 1871, they sent a military expedition into the hills in an attempt to deal with the Lushais more effectively. This expedition was a success and most of the chiefs surrendered to the British. Military occupation of the territory was ruled out but they once again made attempts to bring the Lushais under effective control through friendly relations. Sukpilal had his own vested interests in maintaining good relations with the British.[18] Hence, he assisted the local authorities in detecting and punishing those Lushais who committed acts of aggression against the British.

Sukpilal's death in 1881, saw the renewal of inter-clan feuds. The recurrence of outrages on British territory and British subjects convinced the government of the necessity of reconsidering its policy towards the Lushais. In the circumstances, another military expedition against them was inevitable and accordingly a strong force was sent into the Lushai Hills. The object was threefold:

1. To subjugate the recalcitrant clans.
2. To explore and open out the territory as far as possible.
3. To establish semi-permanent posts in the region so as to ensure their complete subjugation by the British.

The operations against the Lushais ended by 1890 with the surrender of the main chiefs. Captain H. R. Browne was appointed political officer, North Lushai Hills, with headquarters at Aizwal. He was directed to exercise his influence over the tribes with the object of establishing political control over them. At the same time, he was instructed 'not to accept any revenue or tribute or obligation of a nature which might render future fulfilment a matter of difficulty'.[19] Browne stipulated that henceforth all inter-clan feuds would have to be submitted to the political officer for arbitration. The chiefs were further instructed to guarantee, within their territory, security of life and property and allow free access to traders and travellers from British territory. Browne levied a house tax and also demanded supply of free labour disregarding instructions about the imposition of taxes. These were seen as an infringement of the liberties of the people and Browne was killed in an ambush soon after.

The following year, the South Lushai Hills, along with the Chittagong Hill Tracts, was formed into a separate district, with headquarters at Lungleh, under C. S. Murray as Superintendent. In 1898, the Chin Lushai Hills, which had hitherto been administered partly by Assam and partly by Bengal, was incorporated with the above territory. The whole of the Lushai Hills were then placed under the chief commissioner of Assam. The internal management of the villages was left to the chiefs subject to the control of the superintendent and his assistants, in whom the administration of civil and criminal justice was vested. But sporadic rebellions among the Lushais resulted in the government's decision to confiscate all unlicensed guns. The subsequent improvement of law and order, the introduction of administrative changes and the activities of the Christian missionaries, together helped to integrate the Lushai Hills into the British dominion in course of time. As peace returned to the region, the government began to look beyond the frontier. With the completion of the Calcutta–Chittagong Railway, the government considered opening up communications between Calcutta and Mandalay through the Lushai Hills. The Chief Commissioner of Assam, C. J. Lyall, observed:

> A feasible line for a cart road or a railway can be discovered from Chittagong to Mandalay, the land route to Upper Burma will enable the surplus population of Bengal, who refuse to cross the sea, to spread into Upper Burma, benefiting both provinces. The trade of Upper Burma will also gain much by the possibility of easy communication between Calcutta and Mandalay.[20]

Thus, British policy in the Lushai Hills from the second decade of the twentieth century onwards was influenced more by economic considerations rather than the strategic considerations which had predominated earlier. In the backdrop of perennial inter-tribal feuds and migration to and from the neighbouring Burma districts of Chin Hills and Northern Arakan, one major concern of the authorities of the Lushai Hills District was to identify a suitable southern boundary, which was finally settled in 1931.[21] Further, under pressure from a section of Christian missionaries, the district administration had initiated important steps to regulate a 'system approximating slavery' in the Lushai society, which was known as the *bawi* or *boi* system.[22] The system, in effect, was more humanised.

NAGA HILLS

The extension of the frontier in Upper Assam brought the British into direct contact with the Nagas who dwelt in the hills adjacent to Sibsagar district. The Nagas were divided into a number of clans such as Angami, Sema, Ao and Lotha, each under a chief. Residents of a particular village comprised various clans. Inter-clan feuds were a common feature. Very often these feuds did not remain confined to a particular village but spilt over to other villages because of kinship ties. Like the other hill tribes in the region, the Nagas also made plundering raids into the villages in the plains. The frontier thus remained in a constant state of upheaval.

The British policy towards the Nagas was initially one of non-intervention. The enormity of the task of campaigning in the hills was apparent. Apart from the inhospitable terrain, the Nagas were known to be formidable warriors. Moreover, inter-clan feuds were so frequent and distrust among the clans very deep rooted, that it was impossible to keep them under control. Therefore, the British decided that the best way to deal with them was to establish personal contact with the chiefs and bind the Nagas under them through conciliatory gestures to stop them from attacking neighbouring British territory.[23] In 1851, the government laid down the following policy that was to be followed with regard to the Nagas.

> To confine ourselves to the frontier, to protect it as it could and ought to be protected, never to meddle in fights and feuds of those savages, to encourage trade with them so long as they are peaceful towards us and rigidly to exclude all communications on their becoming turbulent or troublesome.[24]

However, the policy did not produce the desired results. Depredations into British territory in general, and raids on the tea growing areas of Cachar, in particular, recurred with alarming frequency. It was clear that defensive measures alone would not ensure the security of the frontier. In the circumstances, the government was forced to abandon its policy of non-intervention. Explaining the position, Henry Hopkinson, who had succeeded Jenkins in 1861, observed:

> It is not creditable to our Government that such atrocities should recur annually with unvarying certainty, and that we should be powerless alike to protect our subjects or to punish the aggressors. It is quite certain that our relations with the Nagas could not possibly be on a worse footing than they are now. The non-intervention policy is excellent in theory, but Government will probably be inclined to think that it must be abandoned.[25]

Hopkinson further pointed out that the government had no alternative except to occupy the territory or leave them alone altogether. Taking these into consideration, he believed that until the government laid down a clear-cut policy, it would be impossible to propose measures for the security of the border . Both J. P. Grant, the Lieutenant-Governor of Bengal, and his successor, Cecil Beadon (1862–71), agreed with the views of Hopkinson. In fact Beadon wanted to extend British influence over the Nagas by degrees with the ultimate objective of bringing them under the effective control of the British.[26] The arguments of the local authorities convinced them to reconsider the policy towards the hill tribes. The new policy can best be summarised in the words of Hopkinson who wrote:

> We must cease to regard them as aliens or even as enemies, but acknowledge them as subjects, seek to establish ourselves amongst them, to extend our influence over them and bring the under our control with the pace of civilization.[27]

The deputy commissioner, Sibsagar district, A. E. Campbell, pointed out that the Nagas could be satisfactorily dealt with only if they were brought under British political control without direct administrative interference. This would only be possible if the boundary was clearly demarcated. Accordingly, they drew the Inner Line in 1873 beyond which tribes were left to mind their own affairs.[28] The British gave protection to those Naga villages which agreed to pay a house tax. By 1878, 17 Naga villages had come under British protection. A few powerful villages, however, refused to succumb to the pressure and maintained their independence (see Figure 6.3)

When G. H. Damant took over as political officer of Naga Hills in 1878, he found the attitude of the powerful Angamis very aggressive. Despite this, he shifted his headquarters from Sumaguting to Kohima

Figure 6.3: Naga Hills

Year	Event	Consequence
1851	British policy towards the Nagas laid down	They decide to follow a strict policy of non-interference
1873	Inner Line Regulation enacted	Demarcated the boundary between British administered areas and those under the tribes; British protection extended to those Naga villages who paid a house tax
1878	17 Naga villages under British protection	Some villages continue to remain independent
1878	G. H. Damant takes over as political officer of Naga Hills	He demands revenue from all villages, including the independent ones; His demand causes widespread discontent
1879	Damant murdered by the Nagas	The Nagas lay siege to Kohima
1880	Brigadier-General Nation sent to cow the Nagas into submission	The British restore their influence around the areas of Kohima, Khonoma, Wokha and Golaghat; The outlying villages continue to cause trouble

to be in their midst. He divided the Naga Hills into three tracts for administrative purposes, viz:

1. The westernmost tract comprising the villages which paid the house tax and acknowledged British authority.
2. The central tract which paid the tax but acknowledged British authority only partially.
3. The easternmost tract which was completely outside the pale of British administration.

Damant decided against imposing direct British administration; but he attached great importance to the collection of revenue, more as a symbol of discipline and authority rather than for any fiscal benefits. As such, he was determined to realise the total revenue from the central tract as well, even by force if necessary.

Damant's revenue demands and the transfer of his headquarters to Kohima caused widespread resentment among the tribes. The independent villages regarded these measures as a deliberate attempt to subjugate them. They prepared to revolt, fearing that their independence was at stake. In October 1879, Damant, along with his escorts, was murdered at Khonoma where he had gone to enquire into a dispute. The death of the political officer emboldened the Nagas to group together and around 6,000 of them laid siege on Kohima. Frantic messages were sent by the besieged inhabitants to the authorities for reinforcement of troops. After ten days of total uncertainty and immense hardship, help arrived in the form of a strong contingent under James Johnstone, the political officer of Manipur. As soon as they came to know of Johnstone's arrival, the Nagas lifted their siege and dispersed. The incident left the British embarrassed and humiliated.

It became imperative for the authorities to reassert their position. The government sent Brigadier-General Nation on an expedition to cow the Nagas into submission. In March 1880, after several hostile villages were levelled to the ground, most of them were compelled to surrender. The British restored their influence in the neighbourhood of Kohima, Wokha, Khonoma and Golaghat. But the outlying villages remained beyond control and outrages continued in these areas. In 1881, the designation of the political officer was changed to that of deputy commissioner. The requirements of the tea industry and competition among the Europeans for the exploitation of coal and other resources in the Naga Hills gradually led to the extension of the administrative boundary of the district. By the beginning of the twentieth century, the major portion of the Naga Hills came under British administrative control.

The British did not introduce any significant changes in the administration of the Nagas. They considered it politically and economically expedient not to interfere directly in the administration at this stage. Hence, they allowed the Nagas to continue to administer their villages according to their respective customs and traditions with only 'loose control' by the government.[29] Thus, they tried to integrate the existing leadership into the colonial administrative framework by recognising the traditional administrative set up.[30]

BHUTAN

The Bhutiyas inhabited the hills situated on the northern frontier of Kamrup and Darrang east of the Manas river. It covered an area of around 1,000 square miles intersected by a number of passes or duars connecting the hills to the plains. The frontier contained seven duars, in Assam (five in Kamrup and two in Darrang) and eleven in Bengal. During the rule of the Ahoms, Bhutan enjoyed exclusive control of the duars in Kamrup and partial control over those in Darrang in return for a fixed amount of tribute.[31] Bhutan's economy was very fragile. As such, the people were almost completely dependent on these duars for their livelihood. This made Bhutan's position extremely vulnerable to coercion if there was an economic blockade by an adversary. The existing arrangements with Bhutan regarding the duars continued even when the British occupied Assam. However, it soon became apparent that conditions on the frontier were far from satisfactory. Theoretically, the governor of eastern Bhutan, the *Tongso Penlop*, was in charge of the duars. But for all practical purposes, these were controlled by a few frontier officials. In addition to indulging in lucrative personal trade, these officers indirectly encouraged plundering raids into the neighbouring villages with an eye on the share of the loot.[32] Thus, complete lawlessness prevailed on the frontier.

By 1837, the question was not merely one of law and order. The financial aspect also played a significant role. The tribute that had been agreed upon (It included cowries, ponies, cowtails, musks, gold dust, blankets and daggers. The total value of these goods was fixed at 4,785 rupees and four annas annually) had not been paid regularly and the arrears had accumulated to over 20,000 rupees. The government, however, preferred a negotiated settlement. Robertson, Agent to the Governor-General, explained that apart from the huge expenditure that a military expedition would entail rupture with Bhutan would affect British commercial interests as well. He wrote:

> The Booteahs not only require the produce of the plains for their support, but seem disposed to become customers of the Assamese for various commodities, which the latter can either supply by their own industry or procure from Bengal, to be exchanged, among other articles, for gold, of which metal there seems reason to suspect that the regions to the north of Bootan yield no inconsiderable quantity.... Years of disturbance and foreign invasion have interrupted the intercourse between the mountains and the plains, but it has never been entirely broken off and will now, I trust, if not checked by any political misunderstanding, annually increase.[33]

The government, therefore, decided to send a mission under Robert Pemberton to negotiate a settlement with the Bhutanese Raja. Pemberton was instructed to:

- Try and persuade the Bhutanese government to hand over the management of the duars to the British in lieu of a mutually agreeable fixed annual payment
- Categorically state that the British did not wish to acquire any additional territory in Bhutan.
- Impress upon the Raja that the British only wished to cultivate friendly relations with his country.
- Insist upon commutation of the tribute for a tract of land or a fixed amount of money.

The mission failed to achieve its objectives. Although Pemberton was able to arrive at an agreement with the Raja, the Tongso Penlop strongly opposed the draft proposal as his vested interests were directly at stake. Negotiations, therefore, fell through.

The problems on the Bhutan border dragged on. In 1862, Cecil Beadon, the Lieutenant-Governor of Bengal, agreed to a suggestion of Henry Hopkinson that a mission should be dispatched to Bhutan to resolve the pending disputes over the duars. He also suggested that the Raja should be persuaded to accept a permanent British envoy in his court.[34] Acting on these recommendations, the government decided to send a mission under Ashley Eden, Secretary to the Governor of Bengal, to Bhutan for an amicable resolution to all disputes between the two. When Eden arrived at Punakha, the Bhutanese capital in 1864, he found that the Raja and his officers were mere puppets in the hands of the Tongso Penlop who had in the meantime usurped all authority. He refused to negotiate with Eden. He turned tables on Eden and forced him to sign a dictated agreement. Eden returned totally humiliated.

On his return, Eden submitted a memorandum to the Government wherein he suggested the following three alternatives:

1. Permanent annexation of Bhutan.
2. Temporary annexation to be followed by withdrawal after destruction of all military constructions.

3. Permanent occupation of the Bengal duars and the economic blockade of the duars in Assam.

While commenting on the advantages of the occupation of the duars by the British, Eden wrote:

> These *duars* contain some of the finest cotton and timber lands in Bengal.... The province is one of the finest in India and under our Government would in a few years become one of the wealthiest. It is the only place I have seen in India in which the theory of European settlement could, in my opinion, take a really practical form.[35]

These arguments influenced the Viceroy, Lord Lawrence, who was convinced of the need for strong retaliatory measures against Bhutan. He ordered the mobilisation of troops on the Bhutanese frontier. Within a few weeks of the commencement of military operations in November 1864, the duars and the hill forts came under British control. The Bhutiyas refused to surrender inspite of the losses they had suffered. The government then planned a major assault on Bhutan. The superiority of the British military strength and their large-scale preparedness eventually compelled the Raja to make peace. The Treaty of Sinchula, signed on 18 November 1865, had the following terms:

1. The Bhutan government agreed to surrender all duars and hill tracts between the rivers Teesta and Jaldhaka. In return, the Government of India agreed to pay the Bhutan government an annual sum of 25,000 rupees in the first year, 35,000 rupees in the second year, 45,000 rupees in the third year and 50,000 rupees every succeeding year. But the payment was liable to be discontinued in the event of misconduct on the part of Bhutan government or the people.
2. The Butanese declared the document which had been imposed on Eden earlier null and void.
3. Bhutan agreed to release all British subjects in their captivity and enter into arrangements for the extradition of criminals in future.
4. The Bhutanese government agreed to the arbitration of the Government of India in all disputes between the Bhutanese government and the chiefs of Cooch Behar and Sikkim.

The Treaty of Sinchula was an important landmark in Anglo-Bhutanese relations. The problem was eventually solved after much turmoil on the frontier. The British gained both politically and economically. The territory surrendered to the British was rich in timber and there was the added possibility of tea cultivation. The annual revenue from the area was estimated at one and a half lakh rupees. More importantly, it provided the British with a road to Lhasa and placed them at a strategically advantageous position. The British policy towards Bhutan henceforth was one of conciliation and non-intervention. The commercial interests in Tibet and Central Asia demanded that cordial relations be maintained with Bhutan as trade routes to those areas lay through the country.

SUB-HIMALAYAN TRACTS EAST OF BHUTAN

The Abors (Adis), Daflas (Nyishis), Akas (Hrusso) and Miris (Misings) were a few of the major tribes that inhabited the hilly tracts of the northeastern frontier east of Bhutan. These areas were also poverty stricken and therefore, like the other neighbouring tribes, they too resorted to plundering raids on the villages in the plains. The Ahoms, in order to prevent the occurrence of such raids, had introduced the system of *posa* whereby the tribal chiefs were entitled to visit the plains annually and levy a tax on every household in specified villages. For instance, the Daflas of Charduar levied a posa consisting of one *seer* of salt, five seers of rice and a tax of one anna on every household in certain villages. In addition, a village tax of seven rupees and 10 annas was levied on every 20 houses.[36] This system appeared to be the most practical way of conciliating the tribes. Therefore, the British decided to follow a similar policy when they occupied Assam. Realising the difficulties of campaigning in the hills, they believed that their interests would be best served if their relations with these tribes were defensive and conciliatory. With the passage of time it became apparent that even after levying posa, the plundering raids into British territory continued. Repercussions of inter-tribal feuds in the hills moreover, were also felt in the villages in the plains. The British were, therefore, compelled to apply retributive measures to subdue the tribes. In normal circumstances economic pressure was applied to coerce them into submission. If a blockade or withdrawal of posa failed to bring them to terms, only then was military pressure used.

The posa system had its inherent drawbacks. David Scott soon realised this after he took over the administration of Assam. Therefore, he initiated a system whereby the collection of posa in kind was substituted by monetary payment. In 1842, for instance, they arrived at an agreement with the Akas whereby they agreed to maintain peace on the border in lieu of payment of 180 rupees annually. Similar agreements were made with other tribes as well.[37] Despite these agreements, trouble erupted from time to time primarily over demands for enhancement of posa and the re-drawing of boundaries. On other occasions, there were disturbances arising out of inter-tribal feuds or over collection of forest produce by British subjects. When the application of economic pressure in the form of closure of the duars, was unsuccessful in compelling the chiefs to submit, military expeditions had to be sent into the hills before agreements of good behaviour could be obtained. Many tribes succumbed to the pressure, but others like the Abors and Daflas held out. Thus, the history of British relations with these frontier tribes is one of raids into British territory by the more war-like tribes, of innumerable isolated murders of British subjects and of retaliatory measures taken by the British. The murder of Williamson, the assistant political officer posted at Sadiya, and Dr Gregorson in March 1911[38] marked the culmination of these attacks.

The British viewed the attack on Williamson and his party as a challenge to British authority which had to be avenged at all costs. It was perceived in official circles that inaction would be seen as a sign of weakness. They decided to use military pressure to cow the tribes into submission. The expedition into the Abor Hills (1911–12) that followed was primarily intended as a demonstration of strength. In view of Chinese activities in neighbouring Tibet,[39] British assertion of power in these frontier tracts was of vital importance. However, force had to be supplemented by immediate administrative reorganisation of the region if control was to be effective.

Accordingly, in October 1912, the government introduced certain administrative changes. The tract east of the Subansiri river was placed in charge of Dundas with headquarters at Sadiya, while the tract west of the Subansiri was placed under Neville who was directly under the chief commissioner. In order to ensure effective political control in a 'regular manner', the government set up, in 1914, three new charges, viz., (1.) Central and Eastern Section(comprising the erstwhile Dibrugarh Frontier Tract, created in 1882, along with some other areas in the south), (2.) Lakhimpur Frontier Tract and (3.) Western Section, each under a political officer. In 1919, the Central and Eastern Section was renamed Sadiya Frontier Tract, while the Western Section was renamed Balipara Frontier Tract.[40] Under the provisions of the Government of India Act, 1935, the Sadiya and Balipara Frontier Tracts, along with Lakhimpur Frontier Tract, came to be collectively referred to as the 'Excluded Areas of the Province of Assam'. In 1943, the government created the Tirap Frontier Tract, comprising certain portions of the Eastern Section and the Lakhimpur Frontier Tract. With these changes, British paramountcy in the region was assured.

CONCLUSION

The northeastern boundary of Assam under colonial rule did not have a fixed frontier. While several tribes lived on both sides of the Indo–Burmese border, many others inhabited the hills on both sides of the northern boundary of Assam. Moreover, *jhum* cultivation often entailed a shift in the population from one region to another. In the circumstances, it was impossible to draw uniform ethnic lines while laying down the boundaries. Problems were further aggravated because the frontier along the tract of 'unadministered' territory between Tibet and India was vague and undefined. Inter-tribal feuds often spilt into British territory while plundering raids into villages in the plains were frequent occurrences.

For decades, the local authorities in Assam had advocated a policy of intervention towards the hill tribes, but the Government at Fort William believed that intervention would not only be financially detrimental but politically inexpedient as well. Considering the difficulties of campaigning in the hills, the government sought to solve the problems through negotiations and peace missions. However, this policy was only partially effective and resulted merely in temporary relief. As turmoil on the frontier continued unabated, the government eventually decided to abandon its policy of non-intervention and gradually adopt one of active interference.

In course of time, British policy towards the frontier tribes resulted in a slow but steady penetration into the hills of the northeastern frontier of India. The government strengthened its hold on the region by demarcating the boundaries of the territories under their control and by laying down the Inner Line. This was crucial, especially in the context of international rivalries across the Indian border in neighbouring Tibet. Economic and strategic considerations once again predominated.

NOTES AND REFERENCES

1. R. G. Woodthorpe, *The Lushai Expedition 1871–72*, London 1873, (Indian reprint) Calcutta 1978, p. 6.
2. Cited in Ranju Bezbaruah, *The Pursuit of Colonial Interests in India's North East*, Guwahati, 2010, p. 98.
3. The term 'unadministered' was used to denote 'outside the administration of the British' and not lack of administration in any form.
4. See Chapter 5 for details.
5. Cited in R. C.Majumdar (ed.), *British Paramountcy and Indian Renaissance*, Part I, Bombay, 1963, p. 716.
6. The manner in which the trial of Tikendrajit and his accomplices was conducted was subjected to much criticism. Captain Hearsey, described the trial as 'one of the most outrageous farces and parodies of justice that have ever yet been exhibited'. For details refer Ibid., pp. 732–9.
7. Ibid., p. 731.
8. A uniform system of land revenue in cash five rupees per *pari* (2.5 acres) was introduced. *Lallup* was replaced by a house tax of two rupees per annum in the Manipur Valley and three rupees per annum in the Hills.
9. The young Raja was educated at Mayo College at Ajmer between 1895–1901 and then joined the I. C. Corps.
10. Ranju Bezbaruah, *The Pursuit of Colonial Interests in India's North East*, pp. 219–20.
11. Compulsory village duties; free carriage of the baggage of state officials.
12. The Kukis were a hill tribe of Manipur. Apart from Manipur, Kuki settlements existed in the neighbouring Naga Hills and Lushai Hills. For an account of the Kuki Uprising see Ranju Bezbaruah, *The Pursuit of Colonial Interests in India's North East*, pp. 165–75.
13. *Assam Secretariat Political Proceedings A*, Extract from the Proceedings of the Chief Commissioner Assam, No. 8856P, dated 27 September 1920.
14. Sylhet often faced such border raids and it is recorded that in the 1830s, the authorities at Cachar distributed muskets to the villages exposed to such raids.
15. For the background of the expedition, refer to Suhas Chatterjee, *Mizoram Under British Rule*, Delhi, 1985, pp. 25 *ff*. For the expedition, refer to R. G. Woodthorpe, *The Lushai Expedition 1871–72*, pp. 13–14.
16. Annual payments were made to the chiefs of tribes not in order to enable them to organise among themselves a force for the preservation of law and order, but

with the intention that the well-disposed among them may influence their more turbulent colleagues to maintain peace. R. G. Woodthorpe, *The Lushai Expedition 1871–72*, p. 4.

17. Charters were granted to the chiefs specifying the conditions on which they would be left in undisturbed possession of their territory, the levy of tolls by them on people who went to the hills for the purpose of trade, the settlement of the villages along the frontier, the appointment of a Political Agent in Tripura and the opening of two roads, one from Maniarkhal to Bongkong and the other from Dwarband to the Rengti Range. H. K. Barpujari (ed.), *The Comprehensive History of Assam Vol. IV*, Guwahati, 1992, p. 180.
18. There were endless disputes over control of jhum lands between the western chiefs, Sukpilal, Khalkom and Lankhunga and the eastern chiefs, Langkham, Lalbura and Chengliena. The continued enmity with the eastern chiefs compelled Sukpilal to be on good terms with the British.
19. H. K. Barpujari (ed.), *The Comprehensive History of Assam* Vol. IV, Guwahati, p. 241.
20. Cited in B. C. Chakravorty, *British Relations with the Hill Tribes of Assam since 1858*, (Reprint), 1881, p. 79.
21. Ranju Bezbaruah, *The Pursuit of Colonial Interests in India's North East*, Chapters 6, 7 and 8.
22. For details, refer to Ranju Bezbaruah, 'Dr. Fraser's Crusade and Bawi Correspondences 1909–1923', in Ranju Bezbaruah *et al* (ed.), *North East India: Interpreting the Sources of its History*, New Delhi, 2008, pp. 225–47.
23. The government also tried recruiting Angamis to the Frontier Police but met with little success. They could not be induced to remain long under military discipline, and among the 37 recruits, the average tenure of service was only eight months. B. C. Chakravorty, *British Relations with the Hill Tribes of Assam since 1858*, p 84.
24. Cited in A. Mackenzie, *History of the Relations of the Government with the Hill Tribes of the North-East Frontier of Bengal*, Calcutta 1881, (Reprint), 1981, p. 114.
25. *Assam State Archives*, Political Proceedings, April 1861, Nos 4-5
26. H. K. Barpujari, *Problem of the Hill Tribes North East Frontier*, Vol. II, Guwahati, 1976, pp. 65–6.
27. H. K. Barpujari (ed.) *The Comprehensive History of Assam* Vol. IV, Guwahati, p. 159.
28. Ranju Bezbaruah, *The Pursuit of Colonial Interests in India's North East*, Chapter 5.
29. Loose control implied the maintenance of law and order, collection of annual house tax, and supervising the general administration of the district but leaving the day to day administration to the local *Gaonburas*.
30. For details of the pattern of native administration see P. Sema, *British Policy and Administration in Nagaland 1881–1947*, Delhi, 1992, Appendix III.
31. The Bhutiyas had exclusive control over the duars in Kamrup , but the two duars of Guma and Killing were occupied by the Bhutiyas from December to July and by the Ahoms for the rest of the year. Tributes were paid in kind. Very often disputes arose as to the value of the articles paid by way of tribute. R. C. Majumdar (ed.), *British Paramountcy and Indian Renaissance*, p. 1022.
32. R. B. Pemberton, *Report on Bootan*, Calcutta 1839, (Reprint), 1966, p. 8.

33. Robertson to Government of India, cited in ibid., p. 27.
34. H. K. Barpujari (ed.), *The Comprehensive History of Assam* Vol. IV, p. 164.
35. Cited in R. C. Majumdar (ed.), *British Paramountcy and Indian Renaissance*, pp. 1022–3.
36. J. F. Michell, *The North-East Frontier of India*, Calcutta 1883, (Reprint), 1973, p. 264.
37. C. U. Aitchinson, *A Collection of Treaties, Engagements and Sanads*, Vol XII, Calcutta, 1929, (Reprint), 1983, p. 77, M. L. Bose, *History of Arunachal Pradesh*, Delhi, 1997, p. 61.
38. L. W. Shakespear, *History of the Assam Rifles*, Guwahati, Reprint 1980, p. 125.
39. In 1908, the Imperial Commissioner of Tibet, overran eastern Tibet and entered Lhasa forcing the Dalai Lama to take refuge in India. Two years later they penetrated through Yunan into Upper Burma and threatened even Upper Assam. It was even reported that the Chinese were planning to construct a road from Tibet to Assam. For further details, refer to Dorothy Woodman, *Himalayan Frontiers: A Political Review of British, Chinese, Indian and Russian Rivalries*, London ,1969, pp. 127 *ff*; Also, Robert Reid, *History of the Frontier Areas Bordering on Assam from 1883–1941*, Guwahati (Reprint), 1997, pp. 217–18, 221, 226–7.
40. Ranju Bezbaruah, *The Pursuit of Colonial Interests in India's North East*, pp. 59–61: Reid, *History of the Frontier Areas Bordering on Assam from 1883–1941*, Guwahati, Reprint 1997, pp. 240 *ff*, 280 *ff*: K. K. Bhattacharjee, *North East India: Political and Administrative History*, New Delhi, 1983, p. 100.

SUGGESTED READINGS

Barpujari, H. K., *Problem of the Hill Tribes North East Frontier*, Vol I, NEHU, reprint 1998.

Barpujari, H. K., *Problem of the Hill Tribes North East Frontier*, Vol II, Guwahati, 1976.

Bezbaruah, Ranju, *The Pursuit of Colonial Interests in India's North East*, Guwahati, 2010.

7
Economic Transformation of Assam

Chapter Highlights

- Pre-colonial economy
- Changes in agriculture
- De-industrialisation
- Establishment of new industries: tea, coal, oil, timber, plywood, Indian rubber, rhea, and jute
- Regeneration of indigenous industries
- Development of the communication network: Waterways, roadways and railways

Colonialism has had tremendous and far reaching influence in the making of the contemporary world. Colonies underwent a fundamental transformation and witnessed remarkable changes, but this transformation was in limited areas and bore little resemblance to the colonising countries that were responsible for initiating the process. Development occurred only in pockets and was specifically geared to cater to imperial demands. All the colonies were exploited for their resources and were underdeveloped. Thus, in the history of former colonial societies, colonialism is a distinctive phase. It has an added significance because in any study of a post colonial society, all major economic, political, social, cultural and intellectual developments can be understood only by keeping in mind colonialism as the backdrop. It is only then that the terms 'developed', 'underdeveloped', 'developing' or 'backward' can be fully comprehended. The study of colonial Assam is, therefore, of great significance in this context.

Colonial penetration into Assam and the neighbouring hill areas was accompanied by sweeping political, economic and social changes resulting in a radical transformation of the region within a very short time. Many of the changes were positive, when seen in isolation, but when viewed in the overall colonial framework, it is apparent that they were part of the general process of underdevelopment that accompanied imperialist forces. The former autonomy of the villages was eroded; indigenous crafts declined; the introduction of monetary economy and systematic revenue maximisation led to escalating poverty while industrialisation resulted in dramatic demographic changes. Along with all these changes, came improvements in the transportation and communication network which broke down the isolation of the provinces, both physically and metaphorically, and opened them up for new forces, ideas and thoughts to percolate. The cumulative impact of all this was immense and far-reaching.

PRE-COLONIAL ECONOMY

However, in order to fully gauge the impact of the changes, it is important to have an overview of the pre-colonial economic structure. We have already observed earlier[1] that agriculture was the mainstay of the people and that the basic pattern of the land system and distribution rested on the concept of communal ownership of land. We have also seen that land revenue consisted of the personal labour services of the peasant cultivator. Another significant feature of Assamese rural society was the fact that although primarily agriculturists, the people combined agriculture with other trades. There are many references to weavers, spinners, blacksmiths, potters, goldsmiths and workers in ivory, wood, dyes, hide and cane. Almost all the people were self-employed and manufactured their products at home, generally for their own use. There was little specialisation and indigenous crafts formed an integral part of every household. Spinning and weaving, for instance, were a part of every woman's work irrespective of caste or class. Similarly, the extraction of mustard oil or jaggery (*gur*) from sugar cane was generally carried out in individual households. The little specialisation that did exist was in the production of goods like bell metal utensils, pottery and gold jewellery. In contrast, the manufacture of guns and cannon balls, an industry controlled by the state, had acquired a high degree of perfection.[2] Generally speaking, each village was a self-sustaining unit and its autonomy was a significant feature of medieval Assamese society. Further, unlike in many other parts of India, no worker in Assam was hereditarily attached to any particular trade in such a way as to tie him down to any community.[3] Hence, there was considerable flexibility in the social structure so far as the practice of trade was concerned.

Within this overall framework of a subsistence economy, where surplus was limited, the scope for trade and commerce was naturally restricted. Certain other important factors like the geographical isolation of the region, the isolationist tendencies of her rulers and the consequent insular attitude of the people, also contributed to the unique nature of the Ahom economy. Six centuries of Ahom rule had produced shrewd statesmen whose actions were determined not by sentiment but by political considerations and practical expediency. They were equally adept in their commercial policy. Though they favoured a policy of isolation, they did encourage limited trade[4] so that traders from neighbouring territories could do limited transactions and thereby, contribute towards the maintenance of a steady income from market duties and customs revenue. This trade, which was accomplished through an organised market system in the adjoining foothills and plains, passed through the duars or mountain passes in the northeastern and northwestern borders of the Brahmaputra Valley. Besides the periodical markets, annual fairs were held at important duars like Udalguri and Doimara. Udalguri was especially important because the whole of the Tibeto-Assamese trade was conducted there. Silk, rice, iron, lac and pearls were traded for rock salt, gold dust, Chinese silks, woollens and horses. In fact, trade with the Tibetan merchants fetched gold and silver worth nearly 170,000[5] rupees. For the Ahom Government, however, the frontier trade, which formed the basis of the plains-hills contact, meant much more than a source of revenue. It was a symbol of the assertion of their power beyond the physical limits of their kingdom.

Apart from commercial relations with the hill tribes, the Ahoms also engaged in trade with Bengal, though again in a limited manner. This was necessary because of the limited availability of salt in the region.[6] Hence, trade with Bengal was primarily in salt which was bartered for a range of assorted products from Assam. What is of significance is the fact that apart from certain agricultural products like mustard seeds and black pepper, important items of export from Assam were silk cloths, lac, dyes, ivory, iron hoes, bell metal utensils and cotton broadcloth—all manufactured items. It is therefore, apparent that within limited parameters, manufactured items from Assam were in considerable demand in the neighbouring regions and

Table 7.1: Trade with Bengal 1808–9

Imports From Bengal		*Exports To Bengal*	
Item	*Value (Rs)*	*Item*	*Value (Rs)*
Salt	192,500	Stick Lac	35,000
Ghee	1,000	Muga Silk	11,350
Pulse	800	Muga Cloth	17,350
Sugar	1,000	Munjeet	500
Beads	2,000	Black Pepper	500
Coral	1,000	Long Pepper	300
Jewels	5,000	Cotton	35,000
European Glass & Cutlery	500	Ivory	6,500
Taffetas	2,000	Bell Metal Vessels	1,500
Spices	1,000	Mustard Seeds	20,000
Shells	100	Iron Hoes	600
Paints	500	Slaves	2,000
Copper	4,800	Fruit	150
Red Lead	1,000		
English Woollens	2,000		
Benaras Khinkobs	500		
Satin	1,000		
Gold & Silver cloth	1,000		
Muslin	10,000		
TOTAL	**228,300**	**TOTAL**	**130,900**

formed an important component of the trade. Table 7.1[7] illustrates the point.

Trade was mostly through barter. Whatever little currency was in circulation consisted of gold and silver coins although they were not used much.[8] These were probably in addition to those coins brought in from neighbouring Bengal and Bihar for trade and also payments like taxes.[9] *Cowries* were also used as an equivalent of money but copper coins were unknown in the region.[10] It is thus apparent that prior to the Burmese invasions, Assam was on the whole, prosperous.

However, when the British occupied Assam after the Treaty of Yandabo, they found that years of disruption and turmoil had wrought havoc in the medieval kingdom. The administrative structure was practically non-existent, the economy was in shambles, the country was in a precariously depopulated state, important administrative and trading centres had been reduced to mere clusters of dilapidated houses, while most of the roads were overgrown with deep and sometimes, impenetrable jungles. Yet, despite these conditions, the British decided to stay on. As the threat of renewed Burmese incursions receded, initial concerns about the security of the frontier gradually faded making way for the more predominant economic concerns. The region held out promises of huge economic potential waiting to be exploited.

AGRICULTURE

I have mentioned in the preceding chapters that one of the first measures of David Scott took was the abolition of the paik system and the introduction of a monetary economy. In fact, one of the major arguments put forward for the annexation of Lower Assam in 1828 was the calculation that the region would yield annual revenue of at least three lakh rupees. Similar considerations had eventually led to British penetration in the entire Brahmaputra Valley and beyond. They initially imposed a poll tax of three rupees per paik in lieu of personal service. This was soon abandoned for a regular assessment of land revenue based on the measurement of the land. The mode of collection was fully monetised by 1840 and the tax was paid by individual landholders. But the assessments were made without an accurate survey as a result of which, the tax levied had little relation to the actual area under cultivation. Further, the introduction of a monetary economy placed the ryots under severe strain. The peasants had no accumulated capital and it was extremely difficult for them to procure cash. That apart, the monetary value of the produce that was usually the peasant's medium of tax payment, fluctuated widely depending on the prices of other commodities including those imported from outside.[11] Very often the major part of the peasants' meagre produce had to be sold off simply to meet the land revenue demand.[12]

There were three distinct classes of tenures in the Brahmaputra Valley, viz., ryotwari, *nisf-khiraj* or half-assessed tenures, and lakhiraj or revenue-free tenures. The general tenure was ryotwari whereby the tenant had the right of occupation in the land covered by his lease so long as he paid the government revenue regularly. The Assam Settlement Rules declared holdings settled for a set term of years to be heritable provided the transfer was registered. The nisf-khiraj and lakhiraj lands were those generally given for religious and charitable purposes. A district was divided into *mauza*s or revenue circles, each under a *mauzadar* who collected the revenue. The mauzadar was obliged to pay the entire land revenue due from his mauza by April of each year. For his services, he received a commission of ten per cent on the first 10,000 rupees and five per cent on the balance amount. He was normally succeeded by one of his family members. The mauzadar occupied a very influential position in the village. Thus, apart from the financial benefit of the system, it also fostered the growth of a stable and loyal gentry owing allegiance to the administration.[13]

The average rates of revenue for the districts in the Brahmaputra Valley were initially fixed at six annas per bigha for basti (homestead land), five annas per bigha for rupit (wet paddy land) and four annas per bigha[14] for *pharingati* (dry highland). In 1861, Colonel Hopkinson put forward for a proposal for raising the revenue of Assam on the ground that it was unreasonably low.[15] Acting on these proposals, the Government doubled the rates in 1867. As a result of these enhanced rates, implemented during 1868–71, the total revenue jumped from 1,001,733 in 1864–5 to 2,165,157 rupees in 1872–3.[16] The Assamese generally had small holdings that grew two types of crops, viz., food crops like rice which were first in order of the cultivated area and importance, and cash crops, like opium, jute and oil seeds which the cultivator sold to pay the revenue demand. As food crops occupied the major portion of the cultivable land, the peasant was often hard pressed to pay the revenue demand. He had to resort to borrowing from the moneylender at exorbitant rates of interest, especially during times of scarcity. There were also instances of confiscation of private property on failure to pay the revenue.[17] During 1891–2, the land revenue demand was 4,214,067 as against 4,127,328 rupees in 1890–1.[18] The following year the amount increased by 60,769 rupees.[19] The government now decided to revise the rates of revenue. The Chief Commissioner, William Ward, recommended the enhancement of the revenue within the framework of the existing classification of the land, viz., basti, rupit and pharingati. The existing rates were doubled in the case of the first category; for the second category the revenue was increased by 50 per cent and for the third, by 25 per cent. New assessments were made in 1893 which resulted in an almost 33 per cent increase in the land revenue collection of the Brahmaputra Valley.[20] This burden fell heavily on the peasants, especially at a time when cash was a scarce commodity. With the limited paying capacity of the peasant cultivators, the land revenue was transformed into a virtual rack-rent that impoverished them.

It did not help that the systematic revenue maximisation was not matched by government efforts to help peasants increase productivity of their land. Hunter's observations in 1874 that there were no irrigation facilities, manure was not used and that the system of rotation of crops was practically unknown, also held good at the turn of the century. There were also no attempts to deal with the recurring floods and the few embankments that were built were only makeshift arrangements. Strangely, the revenue was periodically increased despite the fact that there was neither any change in the general crop pattern nor any noticeable extension of cultivation. The high rates of land revenue siphoned away a large portion of what could have been the cultivator's possible savings, and in the process, drained capital away from the countryside.

The levy of certain additional taxes further aggravated the economic condition of the ryots. One such tax was the grazing tax which was levied annually as a cattle fee. First introduced in 1888 at the rate of eight annas per head of cattle that grazed in the forests, the tax was increased in 1907 to one rupee per head of buffalo and eight annas per head of other horned cattle. The tax was unpopular from its inception. In spite of strong protests, the tax continued to be increased periodically to such an extent that by 1912 it stood at eight rupees per buffalo and one rupee per head of other horned cattle. Such arbitrary increments naturally caused tremendous discontent. Continued protests and mobilisation of public opinion eventually led to a temporary reduction in 1914 to two rupees per buffalo and six annas per other cattle, pending further enquiry. The following year, however, the tax on buffalos was increased to three rupees.[21]

The government's excise duty on opium was another heavy burden on the peasant. During the early years of British rule, opium production and consumption had continued unhindered. In fact, both David Scott and Francis Jenkins had advised the government against sudden restrictions on poppy cultivation and had instead recommended a tax on it, to be gradually increased over the years, until the province was considered ready to be subjected to the general laws of the government with regard to opium.[22] They believed that if cultivation of opium, the most important cash crop grown locally, was suppressed, the problem of shortage of money would become more acute. Many cultivators would lose their only source of cash income, while those addicted to opium would require additional money to buy abkari opium. In course of time, however, the authorities realised that they were losing a considerable amount of excise revenue by allowing the local cultivation of opium to continue. Moreover, the chapari and basti[23] lands on which the poppy was generally cultivated, was assessed at lower rates than the rice fields. Therefore, the government made arrangements to sell Bengal opium through government treasuries at cheaper rates than the local opium. It was hoped that the availability of the cheaper imported opium would deter the peasants from cultivating the crop locally and thus make them totally dependent on imported opium. This policy, however, failed to have the desired effect. The growing monetisation of the economy induced the farmers to grow more poppy for cash, sometimes even at the cost of food crops. The importance of poppy as a cash crop became so pronounced over the years that traders regularly distributed advances to the cultivators to ensure timely deliveries. Realising that it was losing out on a valuable source of revenue, the British banned the cultivation of opium in 1860. On the other hand, trade in opium was intensified with the government acquiring a monopoly over it. In 1864–5, the total quantity of abkari opium sold in the Brahmaputra Valley amounted to 1,939 *maunds*. The excise collected from opium during the same period was almost 170,500 rupees more than the land revenue collection. In an effort to further increase the excise revenue, the price of opium was raised from 14 rupees a seer in 1862 to 23 rupees a seer in 1873 and 37 rupees a seer in 1890.[24] It is interesting to note in this context that the government repeatedly justified the increments in land assessments by pointing out that high tax decreased the buying capacity of the peasants and as such served as an effective deterrent to opium consumption. But the consumption of opium continued unabated despite price hikes.[25] It is thus obvious that addiction to the drug had reached immense proportions and was consumed irrespective of the price demanded. There was much hue and cry for the abolition of the opium trade and anti-opium agitations gathered momentum during the first decade of the twentieth century. Persistent demands, including that of a formal Anti-Opium Conference held at Dibrugarh in 1907, compelled the government to appoint an Enquiry Commission with A. W. Botham as chairman.[26] Despite the Botham Committee's recommendations, the government refrained from taking any action to rationalise opium consumption by restricting its supply. Thus opium, together with the spiralling land revenue demands, reduced the masses to a state of abject poverty. The feeling of being continually exploited by an alien government was so strong that it found expression in a series of sporadic agrarian uprisings that occurred in the Brahmaputra Valley during the last four decades of the of the nineteenth century. (Details in Chapter 9)

INDUSTRY

The Industrial Revolution had seen England emerge as a major industrial power and all her commercial activities in the colonies had been geared to the growing external trade. One particularly significant outcome of this policy was the destruction of indigenous crafts and industries. The general British attitude was reflected in a statement of Doyle and Parkins, two officers of the department of customs in India, who wrote:

> As in all semi-barbarous countries the manufacturing industries of India will decline in proportion as its intercourse with a civilised manufacturing country increases, and the attention of the people will rather be turned to the improvement of raw produce exchangeable for the manufactured goods of England.[27]

Impact on Assam

Assam too fell prey to this general British policy. Faced with the onslaught of cheap, machine-made imported items, the technologically backward local industries found themselves in a precarious condition. It became increasingly difficult for the people to hold on to their crafts and within a very short period they completely lost their mastery over most of them. The healthy balance of the pre-colonial economy, maintained by the co-ordination of agriculture and industry, was totally disrupted. The countryside was witness to de-industrialisation whereby the traditional industries suffered so greatly that most of them fell sick beyond recovery or were on the path of destruction. One of the most severely affected ones was the handloom industry. British manufactured textiles did not find a ready market in Assam in the beginning.[28] However, in course of time, the unequal nature of the competition between mill-made fabrics and locally woven cloth began to have adverse effects on the local industry. In 1885, the import of cotton piece goods almost doubled in comparison to the preceding year. At the same time, huge quantities of raw cotton were taken out of the province. Hence Assam, which was at one time self- sufficient in cotton products, now had to resort to importing yarn to meet even her own requirements. Similarly, the silk industry also suffered a severe setback. There were two forms in which the silk trade was conducted. One was the export of thread and the other, the export of cocoons. Of the two, the latter was preferred because indigenous reeling was seen by English manufacturers as crude and unfit for use. Hence, a profitable trade existed in the export of cocoons as manufacture of silk fabrics out of waste cocoons was a flourishing industry in England. China was the principal source of supply of silk to England, which meant that the English manufacturers were largely dependent on Chinese suppliers. But when they discovered that the Brahmaputra Valley was abundant in the article, British traders pounced at the opportunity. The Trade Report of the province for 1906–7 shows an export of 643 maunds of raw silk from the Brahmaputra Valley.[29] Significantly, the Report does not mention any export in silk piece goods.

Silk and cotton were the two major industries that were affected by the British policy of de-industrialisation, but other industries like bell metal, brass, pottery, earthenware and the production of sugar and mustard oil also suffered a similar fate. As large sections of the people were displaced from their traditional economic activities, the erstwhile flourishing centres of trade like Sarthebari, Hajo, and Titabor dwindled into insignificance. Reeling under the weight of heavy land revenue demands, the peasant cultivators now lost even the subsidiary income they used to earn when they were able to combine industry with their agricultural pursuits. Moreover, once the indigenous base of their production was eroded, the people were left with no other alternative but to use imported products. De-industrialisation thus aggravated the process of economic exploitation.

In the meantime, the Charter Act of 1833 had resulted in the ascendance of industrial interests over mercantile interests. This had tremendous impact on the settlement of newly acquired Assam. For the first time, Europeans were allowed to hold land outside the presidency towns on long-term leases or with freehold rights. Motivated by the intention of attracting a class of European planters, along with their capital, to take up the cultivation of commercial crops like tea, coffee, indigo and sugarcane, the regulation paved the way for the establishment of a new industrial economy in the region.[30]

TEA

The discovery of the indigenous tea plant in Assam was an event of profound political and commercial significance to Britain. The East India Company had lost its monopoly of the lucrative tea trade in China on the renewal of its Charter in 1833. It had been looking furiously for probable tea growing areas within its own dominions. The importance of the discovery of the tea plant in Assam was further increased when it was proved that the local plant was identical to that of the Chinese variety and that the indigenous seeds were of a superior quality and more suitable for growing in local conditions. British private capital immediately responded to the immense prospects of opening up the vast wastelands in Assam for the cultivation of tea. Introduced in 1839, tea was firmly established as the most important cash crop by the 1870s. The first government plantation was set up at Jaypur in 1837 under the supervision of Chinese overseers but was sold off to the Assam Company[31] in 1840. It appears that the intention of the East India Company was to experiment only to prove that the tea plant would grow in Assam and that tea could be produced as a marketable commodity, and then to leave it to private enterprise to produce it on a commercial scale. The East India Company had repeatedly affirmed the principle that the 'government are eventually to withdraw from the pursuance of the scheme as soon as it may appear expedient to entrust its future success to private speculators'.[32] The Assam Company was not just the pioneering tea company in India but was also the founder of the tea industry outside China.

Plantations in general are associated with opening up wastelands at minimal costs. Consequently, large tracts, far in excess of the required minimum for viable plantations, were acquired. This naturally resulted in over-acquisition and consequent under-utilisation of the land. The total acreage under tea increased from 2,311 acres in 1841 to around 8,000 acres in 1859 and almost 31,000 acres in 1871. A set of Waste Land Settlement Rules were formulated, and then revised repeatedly to felicitate the development of the tea industry.[33] Though local aspirants were not discriminated against in theory, the clauses were such that Indian competition was excluded in practice. The terms of the Waste Land Grants were so favourable to the Europeans that a scramble for land took place among the planters. By 1872, the total area taken up by the planters in the Brahmaputra Valley was officially reported to be 364,990 acres. In 1850 there was only one tea garden; twenty years later there were 295 gardens. The planters did not intend to plant the entire area with tea and, more often than not, acquired these wastelands, which contained valuable resources, with the intention of selling off portions of it for an unearned profit. They were also motivated by the fact that by occupying extensive areas, they would be able to ward off prospective competitors. In fact, of the 364,990 acres, only 27,000 acres (i.e., eight per cent) were under tea.[34] Under-utilisation of the land had very important consequences. Although the planters formed the largest land owning class, they contributed the least to the revenue of the province. While the ordinary ryot paid between one rupee eight annas and three rupees per acre annually as land revenue, the planter held most of his land rent-free and paid, on average, only about nine annas per acre on the remaining portion. Therefore, the burden of taxation fell more heavily on the peasant cultivators.

One very important consequence of this systematic land grabbing policy was the displacement of many rural cultivators. Officially, 'wasteland' meant land that was covered with jungle or uncultivated land that would not be used for cultivation in the near future. In practice, however, many planters encroached upon the jhum rights of the shifting cultivators. There were also instances when land that had not been farmed by cultivators, was sold off as wasteland to the tea companies. This resulted in the former occupants either having to leave the place and settle in a new tract or staying back as tenants of the new owners. Moreover, it was not the case of one section of indigenous population being replaced by another because the tea gardens were worked with immigrant labour. The development of the plantation industry in the purely subsistence economy of the Brahmaputra Valley left a deep imprint on the agrarian structure of the region. The changeover from the traditional economy to commercialisation was so sudden that in many areas like Lakhimpur for example, land under tea cultivation far outstripped the area under other crops.

The tea industry opened up new avenues for the investment of Britain's surplus capital. But management and capital are just two facets of an industry. Labour is another major aspect, especially in labour intensive industries, like the plantation industry, where one requires a constant supply of labour. A characteristic feature of all plantations is that they are initially set up in sparsely populated areas, and Assam was no exception. The tea industry in Assam faced an acute shortage of labour from the beginning. In 1835, the total population of the entire Brahmaputra Valley was estimated at only 799,519.[35] We have already observed that the people were primarily agriculturists though they combined agriculture with traditional industry. Rice, the staple crop, was cultivated at small risk and while its cultivation yielded large returns, it required no corresponding investment of capital. The people had limited wants, led fairly easy lives and grew nearly all articles of domestic consumption in their own fields. 'In this enlightened country', wrote G. M. Barker, a contemporary observer, 'each man is his own master.'[36] Although the Brahmaputra Valley offered all conditions conducive for material prosperity, there was no accumulation of wealth among the people. Opium, no doubt, was a heavy tax on most peasants. That apart, the enervating climate and the security that their crops would yield enough for their wants contributed to their lack of enterprise. In these circumstances, it is not surprising that when the tea gardens opened, few Assamese were willing to work as wage labourers, and certainly not at the cost of their own cultivation. In fact, the only local people who considered taking up some form of employment in the tea plantations were the Bodo-Kacharis and the Nagas. Labour, therefore, had to be imported at considerable cost from places such as Bihar, Orissa, Chota Nagpur, Dacca, Chittagong, and even distant places like Madras and the Central Provinces.

The gradual expansion of the industry in an area with acute shortage of labour created a class of agents or middlemen who supplied labourers to the gardens.[37] The planters themselves had no better connection with recruitment than was involved in paying for the labourers. This system led to disastrous consequences as the contractors began competing among themselves by offering workers for lower wages. Moreover, until the passing of the Inland Emigration Acts viz., Act III (Bengal Code) 1863 and Act IV 1865, the recruiters were not licensed and the emigrants not registered. Further, there were no standard rules regarding wages or working terms and conditions. In well-established gardens, few trustworthy men called *sirdars* were identified and they were deputed on paid leave to go to their native place and return with recruits for whom they were paid a fixed bonus. However, since this system was applicable only in a few cases, the main recruitment was done through contractors. The abuses of this system were so great that even official reports could not ignore them. The Assam Labour Enquiry Committee of 1906 reported:

> Contractors collected *coolies* by the hundreds on false promises of high pay and light work and despatched them to the tea districts without taking any sanitary precautions for their welfare on the journey; the result was shocking mortality on the voyage up, while many of the immigrants were of cast or constitution which precluded all hopes of their serving many months in the jungles of Assam.[38]

The problem of labour which perpetually haunted the planters, was to some extent their own creation. Had they been prepared to sacrifice a portion of their profits in the form of higher wages, they might have been able to attract even local labour. The reports of the Indian Tea Industry and most other official documents always claimed that the tea garden workers were paid much more than they could have earned in their native place. They pointed out that conditions of employment in the tea industry were essentially different from those that prevailed in other industries and that factors peculiar to the industry, viz., family income and not the individual income, subsidised rations, bonus, medical facilities, absenteeism, etc., should be taken into consideration while commenting on the income of the workers. They also pointed out that the hardworking labourer could always avail of the system of *ticca* wages.[39] Although there was a law prescribing minimum monthly wages of five rupees for a man, four rupees for a woman and three rupees for a child, this was never implemented. Thus, in 1864, when a male worker in the Public Works Department could earn a minimum of seven rupees a month, the corresponding rate in the Assam Company, the largest tea company in Assam, was only five rupees. It was not that the gardens were unable to pay more. The phenomenal expansion of acreage under tea led to increased production and reduction in production costs. It was true that a portion of the profits was reinvested in the industry but much of it was siphoned out of the country in the form of dividends. Thus, the plantation industry, financed and managed by Europeans and worked with immigrant labour, had few links with the local economy.

Recruitment of labour was one problem but getting them to Assam was an even greater problem. The supply of boats or boatmen who were familiar with the river and sufficient food for large numbers of people at halting points were not always available. Moreover, there were instances of the outbreak of cholera or malaria epidemics inflicting heavy casualties on the labourers. These factors were major obstacles to further recruitment, for it led to rumours in the recruiting districts that those who migrated to the tea areas were never heard of again. G. M. Barker has recorded that these immigrants were generally 'wedged in on a small dirty steamer or country boat so closely that all idea of a healthy atmosphere is out of question while the thought of moral effects are never considered'.[40] It is on record that very often the doctor attending the migrants put on shore men who were on their deathbeds but fortified to such an extent with rum that they were passed by the receiving officer as being in good condition. It is, therefore, evident that many of the newly recruited labourers were unfit for work.

In 1859, the government equalised the revenue of all the districts with that of Kamrup, which was then the highest, in an attempt to recruit local labour. They hoped that the ryots, being unable to pay the revenue, would be compelled to take up work in the tea gardens as wage labourers.[41] In fact, the government's repeated enhancement of revenue rates was largely motivated by the belief that 'if assessments upon the natives were generalised and not heavy', they would not be available as tenant cultivators. By 1872–3 there was 100 percent increase in the total revenue demand of the Brahmaputra Valley. Yet the industry was not successful at all in attracting local labour. Perhaps the main reason was that for the ryots, cultivating their own land, even if at subsistence level, was still more worthwhile, both from the social and economic point of view, than taking up jobs in plantations. This is apparent from the fact that although the adult labour force in the plantations of Assam in 1905–6 was around 417,260, only a few thousand of these were local men. With the passage of time, as the communication network improved, recruitment became slightly easier,[42] but desertions became more frequent. Further, as the skilled workers became aware of the importance of their services, it placed them in an advantageous bargaining position and planters frequently faced considerable difficulty in persuading them to renew their contracts. The enticement of skilled labour further added to the problems of the management. Unscrupulous employers often enticed labourers from their neighbours who had spent considerable sums importing them. Managers, therefore, were constrained to pay bonuses for renewal of agreements or offer inducements in the form of higher wages or lower tasks in order to retain their skilled workers. On the other hand, there were also instances of labourers being so much in debt, to the local money lender for instance, that they were forced to renew their contracts at old rates however much they may have disliked the work. Another major problem was that of absenteeism. Since work in the tea estate formed only a part, though the main part, of the occupation of the garden worker, he spent much of his time in subsidiary occupations like agriculture, household work, collection of firewood etc. Hence, he remained absent from garden work fairly often, especially during the harvesting season.

COAL

Tea led the way and other ventures like coal and oil followed. The first recorded notice of the existence of coal in Upper Assam was by Lieutenant Wilcox, the revenue surveyor posted at Sadiya, who accompanied a party of the 46th Regiment up the Disang river to Borhat in April 1825.[43] In a subsequent expedition up the Dihing River, Wilcox came across other coal bearing sites. David Scott was delighted at the prospect of procuring coal locally, because he was convinced that this would make the introduction of steamers on the Brahmaputra an economically viable proposition. In a region like Assam, where railways were unknown and roads hardly worth the name, waterways formed the main arteries of communication. One of the most important steps towards opening up the province, therefore, lay in improving the means of navigating the mighty Brahmaputra. One of the major impediments for economical steam navigation was the necessity of carrying Bengal coal upstream, not only for the entire upward voyage but for the return journey as well. Carrying coal for the 1,000 mile long journey over the water, in addition to railway charges from Raniganj, where coal was mined, to Calcutta, raised the cost of fuel to ten times its value at the mines.[44] Therefore, the introduction of steamers on the Brahmaputra would not have been economically viable unless coal was available locally. Initially, the authorities at Calcutta were hesitant about the exploration of coal resources in the region. Shortage of labour, difficult terrain, inhospitable climate, transportation difficulties and insecure political conditions, dissuaded private as well as state enterprise from undertaking coal operations. But the establishment of the tea industry changed the entire scenario and as the availability of coal at reasonable rates became an urgent necessity, the government undertook an active search for prospective coalfields.

One of the earliest extractions of coal was at Suffrai, a tributary of the Disang, in 1828, when around 5,000 maunds were mined under the direction of C. A. Bruce and loaded into canoes. But the difficulties of navigation were such that several canoes were lost on the way downstream. Those that survived the hazardous journey were dispatched to Calcutta where the trials confirmed that the coal was equal to English coal and 'the best ever found in India'. This was indeed a tremendous boost. Subsequently, several other coal beds were discovered in the vicinity of Borhat and Jaipur in Upper Assam by Lieutenant Bigge and Captain Hannay. In 1838, the government appointed a Coal Committee to make enquiries and present an official report. The Committee pointed out the advantageous position of both the Borhat and Jaipur coal seams with respect to access to waterways. The Committee was also of the opinion that in the existing state of communication between Upper Assam and other parts of India, this coal could not be supplied to Calcutta at a cheaper rate than the coal from Bengal. Nevertheless, they considered that Assam coal might be used advantageously towards supplying the steamers plying on the Ganges.[45]

The demand for coal increased with the introduction of steamer services on the Brahmaputra in 1847. As most of the coal fields were situated near the upper terminal point of the steam navigation at Dibrugarh, it was recognised that the working of coal beds would 'usher in a revolution in the carrying trade on that river'. Despite this, the government was unwilling to take any initiative. No systematic geological and economic investigation for coal was undertaken and the government depended solely on private companies[46] and contractors who agreed to supply coal to their steamers at Ghwahati or Dikhowmukh. Interestingly, even Maniram Dewan was one such contractor.[47]

In 1865, Medlicott, an officer of the Geological Survey of India, was deputed to visit the coal fields of Assam and make his recommendations. While recognising the advantages of the Jaipur coalfields so far as its position was concerned, Medlicott believed that the coal at the Makum field was much superior and in his opinion Makum was 'the coal field of Assam'.[48] A subsequent survey in 1874–76 by Mallet, also of the Geological Survey of India, confirmed Medlicott's opinion. In his report, Mallet named four other important coalfields, viz., Jaipur,

Nazira, Jhanzi and Desoi. But in spite of these repeated assertions, little progress was made in the excavation of the mineral.

A serious impediment in the development of the coal industry was the problem of transportation. In the absence of good roads, the only effective means of communication was by country boats. The Brahmaputra was no doubt navigable up to Sadiya, but during the rainy season it was almost impossible to ply the river in small country boats. While government steamers were irregular and therefore undependable, non-availability of local coal made the use of private steamers expensive and not viable economically. Thus, the lack of basic infrastructural facilities was a severe hindrance in the development of the industry.

The problem of transportation was, however, just one of the major hurdles. Another grave problem was the scarcity of labour. The coal reserves were located in isolated areas covered with dense forests and infested with a variety of insects and wild animals. Labour had to be attracted to these hostile places, their houses constructed, medical services and sanitation provided, food and other necessities supplied and training made available to the recruits. Since the local people were not interested in working as wage labourers, the coal industry, too, was compelled to recruit workers from distant places. In the early years, the colliery labour force included not only men from the United Provinces, Central Provinces and Bihar, but also Makranis, Peshwaris and Chinese.[49] The Ledo and Tikak fields were worked mainly with contract labourers under the Labour and Emigration Act. These were ignorant persons recruited from distant places and generally unaware of the conditions of the place where they opted to work. They were brought under long terms of contract and were compelled to serve out the full term under stringent criminal penalties. Under the terms of the contract, the employers were obliged to 'maintain the labourers in good health', but as the deputy commissioner, Lakhimpur District, observed, 'this obligation the Assam Railways and Trading Company have failed to discharge in regard to their labour force under Act Contracts'.[50]

The unhealthy conditions of the mining estates were pointed out in the inspection remarks of the medical officer.[51] He observed that impure water and long working hours underground were the principal causes of the high death rate in the mines. The Committee, which was subsequently set up to look into the matter, recommended among others, improved quarantine arrangements, measures for the prevention of cholera, supply of filtered water, reduction of hours of work, provision of proper sanitation facilities and the establishment of at least one clean hospital with qualified hospital assistants at each colliery. The Committee also categorically stated that coolies from the northwestern provinces , though cheaper, were not to be recruited as they were unsuitable and that 'recruitment should be restricted to Santhals, Borahs, Bournis, Dhangers etc., who are the only classes or nationalities suited to working in the mines'.[52]

The method of mining coal in Assam at that time was rather interesting. Unlike the popular conception of coal mining where the coal seam is approached from the surface by a deep vertical shaft, in Assam, the approach to mines was through a horizontal tunnel, or more precisely, one which sloped imperceptibly upwards from the mouth of the pit. A tunnel was bored into the hill until the seam was reached, at which point, underground roadways (known as main roads) were driven horizontally along the seam for a distance of up to two miles. The seam itself was at an inclination of 30 degrees to 60 degrees and inclined roadways, known as *chauries,* were constructed along it. At various points in the chauries, further roads were constructed horizontally. Coal was brought from the working faces along these horizontal roads and brought down the chauries by means of gravity operated tramways known as *jigs* to the main roads and then to the mouth of the pit. Owing to the uncertain nature of the strata, the roofs of the underground roadways were usually supported by steel arches and girders, timber and masonry. Wherever convenient, metre gauge railway sidings were constructed as near the pit as possible. Where this was not feasible, two-feet gauge tracks were constructed over difficult terrain to carry the coal from the mouth of the pit to the railhead.[53]

Initially, when the government had issued a notification offering grants of coal bearing land to the public, the response was limited. With the terms and conditions not being very attractive[54] and in the absence of proper communication facilities, it was futile to hope that many private entrepreneurs would risk their lives and money in such ventures. Only a few speculators had applied for the grants and having got them, had entered the hills for the exploitation of coal on a commercial basis. From the beginning, however, they were plagued with problems. The encroachment of tribal land for the exploitation of mines led to serious complications resulting from arguments over rent, tribute and boundary, compelling the government to intervene. Eventually, the government promulgated the Inner Line Regulations in 1873 under which the local authorities were empowered to prohibit British subjects generally, or those of specified classes, from going beyond the Line without a pass from the deputy commissioner. The new difficulties created by the Regulation stalled the commercial exploitation of the resources beyond the Inner Line.

It soon became apparent that if the valuable deposits were to be opened up by private enterprise, more favourable terms would have to be offered to the promoters of these undertakings. Stuart Bayley, the Chief Commissioner of Assam, was very forthright when he stated that 'unless the indispensable preliminary of providing cheap and certain communication from the mines to the river is first undertaken by the government, it is certain that no lease will be applied for'. He was convinced that if the government was not prepared for this, then adequate inducements would have to be given to the speculator, and in his opinion the only sufficient inducement was 'a virtual monopoly of one or other of the coalfields'.[55] This view was eventually accepted by the Government of India and in 1881 a fairly large grant was leased to Messrs Shaw Finlayson and Company in the Makum coalfield. Subsequently, the Ledo field was taken up by the Assam Railways and Trading Company which was formed in 1881. Construction work on the Dibru-Sadiya railway was immediately undertaken and in the following year, the first railway line was opened from Dibrugarh steamer ghat to Jaypur Road. Two years later, the coalfields of Upper Assam were connected by railway lines.

By the beginning of the twentieth century, Assam had become self-sufficient in coal. In 1903 the total output was 293,000 tons. There were around 1,200 miners under the supervision of nine Europeans. The coal industry was closely intertwined with the transport system and until the construction of the Assam Bengal Railway, sales were limited to the tea gardens and the steamers on the Brahmaputra. Subsequently, however, substantial quantities of coal were sent to Calcutta from where it was shipped to various shipping companies for consumption in ocean liners.

Like the tea industry, the coal industry too was a potent instrument for the promotion of Britain's colonial interest. The increasing demand for coal was met by enterprise worked with immigrant labour and initiated and run by foreign capitalists who sent their profits home, brought their manufactured goods from abroad and seldom identified with the local interest. Hence, it had little impact on the local economy.

OIL

The discovery of both tea and coal were the result of conscious efforts on the part of the British. Oil, on the other hand, was an accidental discovery. Thirty years before Colonel Drake drilled the world's first oil well at Pennsylvania, men in Assam were exploring for coal. These explorers who were mainly army officers, found oil in addition to coal by accident.

The earliest recorded notice of oil in Assam is by Lieutenant Wilcox of the 46th Regiment Native Infantry who reported findings at Supkong in 1825.[56] Subsequently, C. A. Bruce, Major White, Lieutenant Bigge, Dr Griffiths, Captain Hannay and Captain Jenkins all confirmed the presence of oil springs adjacent to several coal beds in Upper Assam. Acting on these reports, an Australian speculator, Wagentreiber, applied for leases and monopoly rights over the tract of land between Bappapong and Namchik in Lakhimpur District. After lengthy correspondences between the Board of Revenue and the Commissioner of Assam, Wagentreiber was granted a lease to operate the petroleum springs of Makum, but only for a period of three years. There is, however, no record of the experiments undertaken by him and presumably the venture failed. In 1865 Goodenough of McKillop Stewart and Company got a rent-free lease of the same area for 20 years. After a couple of unsuccessful borings, he finally struck oil at Margherita, a place named in honour of the Queen of Italy and as a tribute to the Italian engineer, Chevalier Roberto Paganini who had founded the settlement. The oil was found at a depth of 118 feet. This was the first mechanically drilled oil well in Asia.

Notwithstanding these encouraging results, Goodenough was not successful in establishing a petroleum industry in Assam primarily because of transportation difficulties which raised the cost of freight and the subsequent price of the oil at Calcutta to a figure at which it could not compete with the oil from Rangoon or America. Therefore, he handed over his rights to The Assam Mineral oil Company which also suffered a similar fate. In 1878, Messrs Balmer Lawrie and Company acquired the exclusive rights of working the springs at Naharpung and Makum for a term of 50 years, but success was limited. It was left to the Assam Railways and Trading Company, incorporated in 1881,[57] to play a pioneering role in the exploitation of the mineral resources and development of the communication network in the province.

The Assam Railways and Trading Company acquired petroleum rights over a fairly extensive area in Makum, but most of the borings resulted in dry wells. Meanwhile, as the company's engineers were constructing the railway line from Dibrugarh to Margherita, they noticed oil seepages near modern day Digboi. The generally accepted view is that elephants used for pulling timber, made the discovery by getting oil on their feet. In 1888 the company applied for and obtained a licence to bore in an area of about six miles in the vicinity of Digboi. The following year, the company struck oil at a depth of 178 feet. The company's Well No.1 produced around 200 gallons of oil per day for several months. This success ushered in the oil industry in India.[58]

Drilling for oil continued and as the business expanded, the Directors of the Assam Railways and Trading Company felt that the profitable developments of the oilfields could be best secured only if oil was the sole concern of a separate company. Accordingly, in 1899, the Assam Oil Company was formed with its headquarters at Digboi. In 1901 they commissioned the Digboi Refinery with a production capacity of 500 barrels (20 gallons) a day. The following year, the first lot of kerosene from this refinery appeared in the market. As the output increased, the refining capacity was also stepped up. By 1926 a wide variety of products like jute batching oil, wax and different lubricants, apart from kerosene, petrol and diesel, were available. The Assam Railways and Trading Company did not relinquish its interest in oil entirely. They had a large number of shares in the new company and their Boards were also connected. Continuity of interest and management survived for almost twenty years. In January 1921, the shares were sold and the Burmah Oil Company was appointed commercial and technical managers of the Assam Oil Company.

By the beginning of the twentieth century, a sophisticated industry had been set up in Assam. But all the capital invested in the ventures was European. This meant that any profit that accrued was drained out of the country. Besides, as the oil industry was highly technical, it was essential to import all the skilled workers, along with the machinery and tools required for the operation of the plants, from Europe.

Being more capital intensive than labour intensive, the scope of local involvement was in any case minimal. It has been observed that in spite of the existence of tea and coal industries, Assam continued to remain backward. Hence, apart from kerosene, there was practically no local demand for the products of the refineries. Even as late as 1905, there was only one car in Assam. For a long time, therefore, almost all the petrol was sent out to Calcutta while the entire quantity of wax was exported to Europe.

TIMBER

The development of the new economy opened up fresh avenues for the development of ancillary industries. The trade in timber, for instance, grew remarkably after the establishment of the tea, coal and oil industries. The large requirement of timber for tea chests, railway sleepers, bridges, planks, posts and numerous other uses made the exploitation of the valuable forest resources of Assam an urgent necessity. The diversified elevation of the land yielded a variety of trees, while the proximity of forests to streams and rivers provided easy access to the Brahmaputra on which the main trading stations were situated. The forests were so extensive that for a long time no serious effort was made to conserve them. In fact, the first step in the way of forest conservancy was the reservation of the Nambor forest in Sibsagar district during the commissionership of Jenkins. In 1868 the Department of Forest under a Conservator was set up and subsequently more attention was paid to this area.

The timber operations of the Forest Department were initially on a small scale. The trees were generally converted into logs in the forest and dragged by elephants to the nearest river from which they were floated down to the place of requirement. In the tea grants, the planters disposed off the timber as they wished. The usual way of getting rid of jungle trees was to enter into a contract with a local contractor to clear it at a fixed rate per acre. The most valuable timber was used for construction purposes, while others were generally used for making large crates and charcoal. The first saw mill was run by steam and established on the Dihing river to meet the requirements of the tea gardens in the vicinity. Many more mills were set up with the gradual increase in demand for railway sleepers as well. By 1901 there were 14 saw mills in the Brahmaputra Valley which turned out, on an average, 1,000 pieces of sleepers a day. Lakshminath Bezbaruah, Bholanath Barooah, Manik Chandra Baruah and Chandra Kumar Agarwala were leading timber merchants of Assam. In contrast to the other industries, the entire timber trade was local in character. The government set up certain experimental plantations for production of timber not indigenous to the region to encourage profitable exports in first-class timber. They started teak plantations at Makum, Jaypur and Kulsi, but the results were not promising. Therefore, it was decided to concentrate on the indigenous varieties and it was hoped, that with proper management, the forests of Assam 'would bring the net revenue by degrees up to several lakhs of rupees'.[59]

An offshoot of the tea industry was the plywood industry. It had a late start as the planters showed a preference for imported tea chests to the ones made from locally produced plywood. It was only after 1918, when the Assam Saw Mill and Trading Company was floated, that the indigenous plywood industry really gained momentum.

Apart from timber, the forests of Assam also contained large quantities of cane, the major portion of which was exported. A small trade also grew in *agar* wood for the manufacture of perfume, but there is no mention of the perfume being manufactured locally.

IRON

In any story of industrial development, iron and steel occupy an important place. In Assam, however, although iron was found at several places, the industry as such made a slow and hesitant start. The principal iron ores found locally were clay ironstone and an impure limonite from the sub-Himalayan strata, both of which were worked extensively in pre-colonial times. According to Captain Hannay, there were around three thousand iron workers during the period when Ahom rule flourished. Subsequently, the industry appeared to have declined and Robinson remarked that by 1841 the manufacture of iron ore in Upper Assam had practically become extinct. Renewed interest in the mineral emerged with the establishment of the tea, coal and oil industries. Specimens of iron ore which were sent to the revenue department at Fort William received very favourable comments and it was believed that with improved means of extraction and sophisticated furnaces and rolling mills, the produce of Assam could meet the demands of the entire eastern region.

The extensive availability of both iron and coal in Assam should have resulted in the establishment of a flourishing steel industry in the region, considering the substantial volume of demand. But this was not the case. The iron industry in Assam was confined to the workshop of the village blacksmith and, to a much lesser degree, to railway workshops and private enterprises. There were no large iron and steel factories comparable to those of Bengal. The only one worth mentioning was the railway workshop at Jorhat set up with European capital and under European management. Even that manufactured only small items like cast iron railings, light posts, gates and similar things but no heavy machinery.[60]

The development of the three major industries in Assam constituted the mobilisation of just a portion of the region's economic potential and it was generally recognised that much more remained to be tapped. But the mobilisation of resources was influenced by various interests. While the British investors were anxious to find an outlet for their surplus capital, their manufacturers were equally keen to preserve the Indian market as the monopoly of their products. In an attempt to safeguard the interests of both sections, the government encouraged the investment of British capital in only such areas which would not rival British products or hinder British trade in any respect.

By the beginning of the twentieth century, resource mobilisation took two broad forms: Firstly, the exploitation of the hitherto untapped sources; secondly, the regeneration of certain indigenous industries. A general survey revealed that investment in certain agro-based industries would not only serve the mercantile interest but promised to be extremely lucrative as well. Attention was accordingly given to the cultivation of products like jute, rubber, rhea and lac. It was observed that these products were available naturally, often in a wild state, and that with proper care and effective supervision, a flourishing trade could be established.

RUBBER

Indian rubber (caoutchouc) forests in Assam extended over large areas in the Kamrup, Darrang, Nowgong, Sibsagar and Lakhimpur districts. The trees were far more numerous in the forests beyond the British boundary than within, a factor which caused serious difficulties in management. As the demand for rubber increased rapidly, it became essential not only to preserve the existing trees but also to set up new plantations. Accordingly, government rubber plantations were established at Charduar near Tezpur and Kulsi in Kamrup. In course of time, the production of rubber proved so profitable that the government decided to establish a monopoly over its production. The rubber collected in Assam was said to be 'so much purer and cleaner' than other rubber that it fetched 40 per cent more than the normal market rates at Calcutta. This profitable trade, however, was short lived. The local method of tapping, especially root tapping, proved to be most destructive. Yet the government did not ban this method of collection as it did not want to lose the revenue. It was not till the second decade of the twentieth century that the government increased the duty on root rubber three times to that on tree rubber. But by then, the damage had already been done and most of the natural trees had been permanently destroyed.

RHEA

Other agro-based industries that drew the government's attention were the cultivation and manufacture of rhea (*Bohneria nivea*) and jute. Ever since the rapid growth of the shipping industry in England, there was increasing demand for canvas, sail cloths, lines, ropes and cables. These were manufactured with chinagrass or ramie imported at considerable cost from China, the Far East and Russia. It was found that in Assam, rhea was cultivated in small patches by the fishermen near their huts. Some also grew wild at the foot of the hills. Dr Forbes Royale, who was sent to Assam to discover the properties and value of this product, commented that rhea and chinagrass were identical and that 'it was likely to prove one of the most valuable products of India, for in strength it exceeds the best hemp and in firmness it rivals the superior kinds of flax'.[61] Encouraged by such positive comments, the government believed that a regular industry in rhea would not only meet British requirements but could be exported to other countries as well. However, in spite of its best efforts the government was unable to identify an economically viable machine or process for the preparation of the fibre. Hence, all attempts to set up an industry proved futile.

JUTE

The industry in jute proved more successful. Many areas in the plains districts of Assam and the plains of the Garo Hills were suitable for its cultivation, but jute was produced on a commercial scale for export mainly in the districts of Goalpara and Sylhet adjoining Bengal. It was a highly profitable cash crop and it was even suggested that since jute was almost twice as paying as *ahu,* a special variety of rice, the ryots could double their income, with a little extra investment if they substituted jute for ahu rice. F. J. Monahan, Director of Land Records and Agriculture, found this suggestion absurd for he believed that substitution of jute for rice would lead to an acute shortage of food grains. He believed that the government could play a positive role by adopting measures to encourage immigration and reclamation of waste lands, distribution of seeds to cultivators and furnishing technical information on jute cultivation and preparation of the fibre. In course of time jute production increased considerably especially after its production was taken up on a large-scale by muslim migrants from East Bengal. Most of the raw jute was sent to Calcutta. But a jute mill was established at Silghat, near Nowgong, only in 1970.

The regeneration of indigenous industries proved to be a more difficult task. The systematic de-industrialisation of the local industries has already been referred to. Their revival was not easy as is apparent from the following observation in an official report:

> The present decadent condition of the indigenous industries is the result of many economic and political causes, which have worked uninterruptedly for many generations and it will be no easy task to arrest the disruption which has followed. For while Assam has lost her own industries, other nations are in possession of her markets, and the great start which they have gained, coupled with their manifold resources in modern methods, machinery and almost unlimited capital will make the struggle a most difficult and unequal one.[62]

The indigenous industries had become relics of a past order, but their artistic excellence had never been disputed. An important question, however, was whether there was any possibility of these industries holding their own against the products of western manufacturers. If a fresh lease of life were to be given, the government would have to be prepared to devise ways and means by which the production could be made less expensive. It was, therefore necessary to ensure that that only those industries were encouraged whose products had an adequate local demand and for which raw material and labour was available locally. It was also concluded that if they could be revived, markets would have to be secured in other parts of Asia, instead of attempting to compete with similar products in Europe. The industrial development of the province so far had revealed an absence of indigenous industrial enterprise. Insufficiency of fluid capital, absence of skilled supervision in technical matters and years of stagnation had resulted in an eclipse of local enterprise in the industrial sphere. The idea behind government assistance was to attract Indian investors with whose collaboration the English merchants could set up a profitable trade in these products. Hence, there was renewed interest in regenerating industries like silk and sericulture, cotton, gold washing, leather and metal work. Strangely, government intervention did not proceed beyond instituting committees and making recommendations.

Industrialisation always brings in its train the instruments of material progress in some form or the other. The growth of industries in Assam brought about certain changes which transformed the province to a large extent, breaking not only her isolation but also earning for her a pace in the economic map of the world. Improved means of transportation and communication was a direct outcome of this new economy.

COMMUNICATION NETWORK

When the British occupied Assam, most of the areas of the province were covered by thick virgin jungle stretching for hundreds of miles over steep hills and deep valleys through which flowed torrential streams. The only means of communication available at that time was by boat, elephant and palki (palanquin), the former being preferred whenever possible. Railways were unheard of and even simple modes of wheeled traffic like bullock carts were non-existent. Roads, which figured so prominently during the heyday of Ahom rule, practically ceased to exist a century later. It was thus the Brahmaputra and it tributaries which had made industrialisation in Assam possible almost half a century before the advent of railways or proper roads.

Waterways

The Brahmaputra was the only artery which connected the province to the rest of the country and the journey, which had to be undertaken by country boat, was long and tedious. A large boat took between six and seven weeks to reach Gauhati from Calcutta, though the post, which was conveyed in small canoes, rowed by two men, (who were relieved every fifteen miles) reached Gauhati in ten days.[63] As there were no government steamers plying on the river, the tea companies had to rely largely on private boats which were not only scarce but also irregular. The acquisition of boats was not easy either.[64]

The first government inland steamer, *The Lord William Bentinck*, commenced services on the Ganges in 1834 between Calcutta and stations up to Allahabad. By 1836 the government fleet had been increased to four steamers, but they rarely plied on the Brahmaputra, and when they did so, it was only up to Gauhati. The inconvenience caused by inadequate transport facilities grew with the expansion of the tea industry. With the growth and development of the other industries, the problems multiplied. The supply of labour, essential provisions like agricultural implements, medicines and food, including rice, had to be imported from other provinces. Apart from the difficulties of transporting the factory products to the river ghats, there was also the additional problem of obtaining small coin for payment to the labourers. The government treasuries at Jorhat and Gauhati seldom had adequate coins to meet the requirement of the companies. The accountant general of Bengal would send bullion by steamer if one was available, and even that would not proceed beyond Gauhati without any security or insurance.[65] Very often the companies had to face labour unrest for long delays in the payment of dues.

The Assam Company, took the initiative in solving this acute communication problem. Urgent requests to the Board in London resulted in the acquisition in 1842 of the Company's steamer, *Assam*, which was the first commercially owned steamer to attempt the navigation of the Brahmaputra. Three years later, the first government steamer plied between Calcutta and Gauhati. The services that were subsequently introduced were not at all dependable because the vessels were not only small and ill equipped, but also not powerful enough to ply against the strong currents of the Brahmaputra. Jenkins' proposal that these steamers should nevertheless be permitted to ply up to Dibrugarh three to four times a year, was turned downed by the marine department on the ground that these voyages would not be economically feasible.[66] The government, however, changed its views when Mills, in his *Report on the Province of Assam*, strongly recommended the extension of the steamer services to Dibrugarh. Mills pointed out the advantages of the abundance of locally procurable coal and the fact that the Brahmaputra was navigable throughout the year. Further, he believed that steam navigation would not only add to the efficiency of the various departments but also reduce government expenditure in the transportation of troops.[67] When steamers started plying to Dibrugarh from 1854, the time taken for the journey from Gauhati to Dibrugarh was reduced to two weeks. This was in stark contrast to the interminable delay of the same voyage in a country boat. The cargo tendered soon exceeded the carrying capacity of the steamers. In 1885 Lieutenant Colonel Jenkins complained that vessels reached Gauhati fully laden with goods shipped for Upper Assam, with the result that Gauhati and the ports downstream derived practically no advantage from the downward service of the steamers.

In 1860, the Indian General Steamer Navigation Company entered into a contract to run two vessels every six weeks provided the government boats were taken off the route. Together with the River Steam Navigation Company, with which they were associated, a moderately regular service was at last introduced. Yet in spite of the quicker pace of private enterprise, travelling continued to be a slow and fairly expensive affair.[68] Hence, for a long time the trade of the province continued to be carried on country boat. The government soon realised that if effective communication was to be established between Bengal and Assam, then they had to provide subsidy to the existing steamer companies. They decided to pay half the subsidy, if it was of a reasonable amount, for a period of five years. Eventually, Messrs McNeil and Company, who offered to conduct a weekly service for an annual subsidy of 1,104,000 rupees or a fortnightly service for 78,000 rupees, was recommended.

With the increase in the number of steamers of the navigation companies, the situation gradually improved. A considerable amount of cargo was carried in these vessels, but special cargo steamers were pressed into service to transport bulky freight. In 1884, a daily mail service was introduced between Dibrugarh and Dhubri. It combined regularity with speed, a fact which was reflected in the postal system. The introduction of the despatch service in 1886 greatly facilitated goods traffic from Goalundo to Upper Assam. Thus from modest beginnings grew the various steamer services of later years.

Roadways

The development of roads in Assam was a very slow process. Apart from the mountainous terrain and heavy rainfall which made road construction an immensely difficult task, the cost of bridging the numerous rivers flowing from the mountains made the development of an elaborate road system quite beyond the province's limited resources. Although it is true that her innumerable waterways made Assam less dependent on roads than other places, it is equally true that road development was neglected by the government for a long time. In the circumstances, raised embankments that were constructed to prevent inundations, also served as roads, and these formed the main network for overland communication.

The tea companies did maintain roads inside the gardens to the best of their ability, but the government was reluctant to grant funds, the public roads were totally neglected. Therefore, even the bullock cart made a very late appearance in Assam. Though an improvement, the bullock cart was still a very slow and expensive means of transport. G. M. Barker, a contemporary, records:

> Each bullock *ghari* will take for shipment seven to eight chests (of tea) to the river where they await the first steamer going downstream. Factories situated close to a tributary of the Brahmaputra can ship their products to the main stream at much less expense than others who have not got the advantage of a waterway .[69]

An example here will probably enable us to appreciate fully the difficulties that were experienced owing to the absence of proper communications. A boiler was required for a tea garden situated beyond a river. Shipped from London to Calcutta, it was put aboard one of the steamers plying on the Brahmaputra. Sealed and thrown overboard, it was floated up a tributary river, and then a stream until three miles of virgin forests barred the way. A road was then cut and paved with felled trees. A team of fourteen elephants took ten days to bring the boiler to the site of the factory, and only then did the tea garden become a power driven one.[70]

As early as 1836 the necessity of 'a road for the purpose of facilitating military movements at all seasons of the year' was strongly felt.[71]

The existing road from Cherrapunjee through Nongkhlaw to Gauhati and Sylhet was considered inadequate from the security point of view and it was suggested that an alternative road from Cherrapunjee to Bishwanath through Jaintiya and Raha be immediately constructed. As no action was taken by the government, Jenkins once again stressed the need for improved road communications in Assam. From time to time correspondence on the subject was carried on with the government but nothing substantial evolved. Hopkinson, the Commissioner of Assam, tried to impress upon the government that investment on roads was a good one which would ultimately yield good returns. He even recommended that the land tax be doubled and that the additional revenue thus obtained be utilised to construct trunk roads in the province.

It was not until 1865 that steps were taken to construct a road through the length of the Brahmaputra.The road ran along the south bank of the Brahmaputra from Sadiya to Dhubri where it was connected by a steam ferry with the road system of Goalpara and northern Bengal. Gauhati was joined by a metal road to Shillong which was further connected via Cherrapunjee, Theriaghat and Companyganj with Sylhet and Cachar. From Cachar a bridle path led to Manipur. A cart road from Manipur passed through Kohima, Dimapur and Golaghat which finally led to the Brahmaputra. A second trunk Road ran along the northern bank of the Brahmaputra. Apart from these major roads, important feeder roads were the *Dhodar Ali* and the ones that connected Tura to Gauhati, Gauhati to Disangmukh, and Rangamatighat to Mangaldai . By 1903 there were 7,977 miles of roads in Assam but, of this, less than two per cent were metalled roads. In spite of Hopkinson's repeated assertions that an un-metalled road in Assam was total waste of money as it was 'bound to be destroyed in the course of one or two rainy seasons', the situation remained practically unchanged. Only those roads which were considered absolutely necessary for strategic reasons were opened up. With the intention of making the local boards partly responsible for road development along with other welfare projects, a District Cess Bill was passed in Bengal which became Act X in 1871. Under this Act, district committees were constituted, with the district magistrate as chairman, for the management of the district roads. Funds were provided from tolls and other miscellaneous sources. This was an extremely half-hearted measure on the part of the government. Firstly, the money available was totally inadequate for the amount of work involved and, secondly, the district committees had little independence of action in directing the expenditure entrusted to them, or in suggesting means for raising additional money.[72]

It is thus clear that road development in Assam continued to be neglected for a long time. Even as late as 1939, only 14 per cent of the roads were metalled. Of the rest, 20 per cent were gravelled roads while 66 per cent were earthen tracks. Thus, for all practical purposes, the majority of roads in Assam could be used for only a few months in a year and this naturally resulted in the diversion of the trade channels to waterways and railways.

Railways

As the road system proved inadequate in meeting the demands of the enterprises situated beyond the rivers, an alternate means of transport became an urgent necessity. The Sadiya Road, though raised in most sections above flood level, was not metalled and therefore, unable to bear the burden of the heavy load which resulted from the opening up of numerous tea gardens and coal beds beyond the waterways. The first rail route from Calcutta towards Assam was the single line to Paradaha, with the extension to Goalundo that was completed in 1864. The Annual Report of the Jorehaut Tea Company of 1878 stated:

> Railway communication from Calcutta to Assam has been slightly extended from Rungpore to the bank of the Teesta River; but from Teesta to Doobrie, on the Brahmaputra River, there are yet about 40 miles to be sanctioned by the Government of India , the construction of which would be a great boon to Assam, as the traffic frm the province would then be tapped by the railway at the station at Doobrie, and great facilities would then be afforded to travelers and labourers proceeding from Calcutta to Assam.[73]

In 1878, Stuart Bayley, the Chief Commissioner of Assam, proposed the construction of a metre gauge railway from Dibrugarh, under the guarantee of an annual subsidy for a term of years. Bayley's positive comments and constructive proposals led to an attempt by Dr Berry White to invite applications for shares in the proposed Assam Railways Company Limited. The main object of the company was to construct a railway line from Dibrugarh steamer ghat to the 51st mile on Sadiya Road, together with three branch lines.[74]

Unfortunately, in spite of a government subsidy of 100,000 rupees, the applications for shares in the proposed company were insufficient and the entire project fizzled out.

Towards the end of 1880, the project came to the notice of Benjamin Percy, an engineer from London, who agreed to support the scheme if it was widened to include the opening of the Makum coalfields in addition to timber and petroleum rights. He believed that the earlier attempt had failed primarily because the scheme had put forward railways unassociated with coal, timber and petroleum. The only way to attract shareholders was to include these items in the list, and he proved to be correct. After verification and a subsequent report that the scheme was likely to be a very remunerative investment, the Assam Railways and Trading Company was incorporated on 30 July 1881.

After an initial survey, the first consignment of rails, locomotives etc., shipped from London arrived at Dibrugarh. With sleepers cut locally, the first few miles of track were successfully laid. On 1 May 1882, the first metre gauge locomotive in Assam passed over the section of the line extending from the Dibrugarh steamer ghat to the Jaipur Road. By the end of the year the line was opened for goods traffic, first up to Dinjan river and then up to Chabua. Two years later, the coalfields of Upper Assam were connected by railway lines. The Jorhat Provincial Railway connected the tea gardens of Mariani and Titabar with the river port of Kakilamukh in 1885, while the Tezpur-Balipara Railway connected the tea gardens with the port of Tezpur. The investment in all these railways was subsidised by the government.[75]

It is interesting to observe that a section of the planters adopted an obstructionist attitude towards the advent of the railways because they were alarmed that railways would affect their labour force adversely. They not only feared that their labourers would be enticed away for the construction and maintenance of railways, but also believed that the advent of railways would introduce disease and seedy characters into the neighbourhood. In an attempt to thwart the introduction of railways, they demanded exorbitant prices as compensation for the land if a railway line passed through their estates.

For over decade, the railway system in the Brahmaputra Valley continued to be essentially an internal one. It was only after the formation of the Assam Bengal Railway in 1892 that steps were taken to connect the province with the rest of India through the Surma Valley. By 1896 railway lines connected Chittagong to Badarpur, Noakhali and Chandpur. The Lumding-Badarpur Hill section was extremely difficult to construct. For most of the distance, the line ran through very poor quality shale which was often mixed with bands of kaolinite that swelled when exposed. This caused heavy slips and exerted considerable pressure on the sides of the tunnels. To counteract this, very heavy masonry was required, cuttings had to be arched in and special measures taken to allow the drainage to escape. Though this section was only 113 miles long, it had 24 tunnels, 7 covered ways and 74 major bridges.[76]Apart from the engineering difficulties other inconveniences, like shortage of labour and food supplies, aggravated the problem[77]. Hence this section was completed only in 1903. The East Bengal Railway line from Calcutta was extended to Dhubri in 1902 and to Amingaon in 1909–10.

The construction of the Assam Bengal Railway was encouraged for two main reasons. Firstly, it was hoped that since the line passed through the garden tracts, it would be very convenient for the transportation of labour and other immigrants who could be tempted to settle in the land abundant Brahmaputra Valley. Secondly, it was assumed that this railway would cross the southern hills of Assam, probably at the northeast corner of the valley, and connect with the Burma Railway system. It was hoped that in the near future it would result in a great Asiatic continental highway, from Bombay or Karachi, across India through Assam to Burma and across China to Shanghai.

The extension of the Eastern Bengal Railway to Lumding established communication between Assam and Chittagong. When Bengal was partitioned in 1905, an important argument in its favour had been that since Chittagong would be the only port in the newly created province of Eastern Bengal and Assam, the Assam Bengal Railway would receive better attention from the government. In fact, Curzon himself had repeatedly stressed that the Lumding-Badarpur section needed to be speedily completed so as to enable an unbroken connection of the oil fields of Digboi, the coal mines of Makum and Margherita and the tea gardens of Upper Assam with the port of Chittagong. The board of revenue also concurred with the view that the foreign trade of Chittagong port would definitely flourish under the new administration.

From these beginnings, the railway system in Assam grew steadily. By 1943 there were more than 1,125 miles of railway lines in Assam.[78]

By the beginning of the twentieth century, the industrial belt in Assam had been connected to the rest of India through a network of railways and waterways. As the importance of the tea, coal and oil industries increased, traditional commercial centres like Hajo, Barpeta and Baligaon dwindled into insignificance. With the diversion of trade routes, junctions like Lumding and Tinsukia emerged as important trading centres where trade was usually in the hands of Marwari businessmen or the Muslim *beparis* of Dacca. Railway stations became the focal point of a town. A distinctive feature of industrialisation is the emergence of satellite towns in and around the industrial areas. In the case of Assam, the situation was just the reverse as industrialisation did not create a situation of interdependence. The industries procured almost all their supplies directly from Calcutta and had virtually no link with the surrounding areas thereby sapping all possibilities of the growth of urban centres in the vicinity.

Further, the old seats of government were replaced by new administrative centres. The 'Civil Lines' and 'Cantonments' were new innovations which existed as adjuncts to the 'native' town to accommodate the British civil and military personnel. With large open spaces and roads constructed according to plan, the Civil Lines stood apart from the rest of the town which often lacked basic amenities. The Europeans formed their own social island, a miniature England in a tropical setting, retaining their own customs, traditions and way of life. Even as late as 1941, the urban population of Assam was less than four per cent.

From the above it is apparent that although Assam was undergoing rapid economic change in certain spheres, the general economic condition of the province merely shifted from the traditional pattern of indolence to backwardness. The partially modernised economy was completely geared to serve the colonial interests and as a result, the limited development that occurred transformed the province into a raw material producing and capital absorbing area. This led to stagnation of agriculture, repression of indigenous industry and foreign economic domination. It is true that the volume of trade did increased dramatically, but the important factor was not its volume but its pattern, the nature of the goods exchanged and its impact on domestic income, industry and employment. What developed with amazing speed was the British-owned and British-managed part of the economy with its labour and middlemen services almost entirely recruited from other Indian provinces. The induction of foreign capital in the industries of Assam did not represent an addition to the internal capital through import of foreign funds. They merely represented a portion of the profit drained out earlier to be reinvested for further gains. Foreign capital also created vested interests which gradually wielded an increasing and dominating influence on the administration.

The communication network which was set up to promote industrial interests in Assam, actually contributed towards the economic backwardness in the long run. They facilitated the growth of new trade centres and the active penetration of the local market by foreign consumer products, serving as a 'social overhead' not for Indian industries but British industries. As the local economy was restructured and the control of the government on the land and resources solidly entrenched, Assam was systematically grafted into the scheme of colonial extraction and domination where enclaves of prosperity existed amidst a stagnant economy. Like all developing countries, here also the fundamental problem lay not in the creation of wealth but in the creation of the capacity to create wealth.

NOTES AND REFERENCES

1. Refer Chapter 2 for details.
2. Shihabuddin Talish, who accompanied Mir Jumla to Assam during his expedition to Assam in 1662–63 wrote that the 'Ahoms cast excellent matchlocks and *bachadar* artillery and show great skill in this craft.' J. N. Sarkar 's translation of *Fathiya-i-ibria*, cited in J. N. Phukan's unpublished thesis *The Economic History of Assam under the Ahoms*', Gauhati University, 1973, p. 122.
3. There are numerous examples in India showing that the basic requirements in most cases ofsuccessful entrepreneurship has been membership of a particular caste or community .e.g., the Marwaris, the Seths, the Voras, the Komatis, etc.
4. The Ahom rulers were wary of foreign merchants and did not allow them to settle in Assam. They feared that as secret agents of some conspiring state, they might create disruption. The foreign traders, therefore, had to transact their business hurriedly and return. S. K. Bhuyan, *Anglo Assamese Relations 1771–1826*, Guwahati, 1949, (reprint 1974), p. 50.
5. W. Robinson, *A Descriptive Account of Assam*, Calcutta, 1841, pp. 293–94.

6. As a substitute for salt, people of Assam generally used a preparation of ash procured from the burnt barks of plantain trees.
7. R. B. Pemberton, *Report on the Eastern Frontier of British India*, Calcutta 1835, (Reprint), Guwahati, 1966, p. 82.
8. Local coinage had been introduced from the sixteenth century, but on a very limited scale.
   The standard coin of the Ahoms weighed one tola or 96 *ratis*. Instead of being circular, the coins were octagonal in accordance with the *sloka* in the *Yogini Tantra* which describes Assam as having 8 sides.
9. J. P. Singh, *Monetary Development in Early Assam*, Jorhat, 1989, p. 20.
10. Ibid.
11. Debdas Banerjee, *Colonialism in Action*, New Delhi, 1999, p. 7.
12. Rural poverty stemmed from the fact that production was at a low and very primitive level. The average holding was around 5 acres with an average yield of 18.6 maunds an acre of *sali* rice and 16.2 maunds of *ahu* rice
13. A. Guha, *Medieval and Early Colonial Assam: Society, Polity, Economy*, New Delhi, 1991, p. 48.
14. 1 acre = 3.25 bighas.
15. *Assam Secretariat Records*, File No. 388, 1861.
16. A. Guha, *Planter-Raj to Swaraj: Freedom Struggle and Electoral Politics in Assam1826–1947*, Delhi, 1977, p. 10.
17. A. S. R., (General Department) Revenue A, April 1902, No. 16–75–2.
18. A. S. R., Report on the Administration of the Province of Assam, 1891–2, Land Revenue Demand, p. 128.
19. Ibid., Report on the Administration of the Province of Assam, 1892–3, Land Revenue Demand, p. 142.
20. William Ward, *Assam Land Revenue Manual*, p. XXX.
21. *A. S. R.*, File no. 106, 1916, B. C. Allen, Agitation Against Grazing Tax. Initially, the tax was assessed and collected by the Forest Department. Later, the tax continued to be assessed by the Forest Department but the collection was entrusted to the *Mauzadars*.
22. Foreign Political Proceedings, 11 February 1835, No. 90.
23. Chapari is highland formed by silt deposits on the banks of a river. Basti is homestead land.
24. *Imperial Gazetteer of India (Eastern Bengal and Assam)*, 1908, p. 94.
25. H. K. Barpujari, *American Missionaries and North East India 1836–1900*, Guwahati, 1986, p. 180. Commenting on the serious situation, Miles Bronson wrote: 'Multitudes of people I daily see, going almost naked, and without any single comfort in life , who, if they get a *pice* or two, will immediately expend it on the noxious drug.'
26. *A. S. R.*, Assam Legislative Council Proceedings, 1913. Kali Prasad Chaliha, Kutubuddin Ahmed and Radhanath Phukan were the other members. The Committee submitted its Report in April 1913.
27. N. K. Sinha, *The Economic History of Bengal, 1773–1848*, Vol. II, Calcutta 1970, p. 13.

28. There were several reasons for this: (i). The dress of the Assamese women was peculiar to this region and was not procured from outside the province. (ii) Silk competed with cotton in supplying the apparel of the people. (iii) Weaving in Assam was not confined to a particular caste but was part of every woman's household duties. (iv) The sizing of English cotton goods was said to make them less durable.
29. E. Stack, *Silk in Assam 1884,* Shillong 1896.
30. For details, refer to Priyam Goswami, *Assam in the Nineteenth Century: Industrialization and Colonial Penetration,* Guwahati, 1999.
31. The Assam Company was formed in 1839 with a capital of half a million pound sterling in 10,000 shares of 50 pounds each. 8,000 shares were allotted in Britain and 2,000 in India. The Company was aware of the probable existence of lime, coal and oil in the region. As the extension of their activities into these fields in the near future was a distinct possibility, they decided to name the Company *Assam Company* rather than *Assam Tea Company* although tea was the main object of its enterprise.
32. Percival Griffiths, *The History of the Indian Tea Industry,* London, 1967, p. 53.
33. E. A. Gait, *The Assam Land Revenue Manual,* Calcutta, 1896, pp. XXXIX–XLII.
34. Ibid., pp. LXI–LXII.
35. E. A. Gait, *Land Revenue Manual,* Calcutta, 1884, p. LIII
36. G. M. Barker, *A Tea Planter's Life in Assam,* Calcutta, 1838, p. 77.
37. The first mention of a paid recruiter is in the Minutes of the Board of the Assam Company of 4 June 1839, when it agreed to offer Mr Campbell of Midnapore the job of going to Chota Nagpur or Bhagalpur to collect families of labourers willing to migrate to Assam. He was to be paid two rupees as commission for every able-bodied man who came to the site, one rupee for every woman and child and 150 rupees monthly for his expenses and travel.
38. *Report of the Assam Labour Enquiry Commission, 1906,* Shillong, 1907.
39. Apart from the daily task , known as *hazri,* there was overtime work usually at a higher rate of payment, known as *ticca.* In theory, the labourer was at liberty to accept or decline a ticca offered to him, but in practice, in most labour-short gardens, considerable pressure was exerted on him to undertake it. On the other hand, since the daily task was fixed at the planter's discretion, it was usually so heavy that for an average labourer additional *ticca* work was almost impossible.
40. G. M. Barker, *A Tea Planter's Life in Assam,* p. 168.
41. H. K.Barpujari, *Political History of Assam,* Vol. I, Guwahati, 1977, p. 51.
42. The travelling time from Calcutta was reduced by more than half resulting in a drastic decline in mortality rates.
43. F. R. Mallet, *Memoirs of the G.S.I.,* 1876, Vol. XII, Pt 2, p. 3.
44. Ibid.
45. *Report of the Coal Committee, 1838,* Calcutta 1845, p. 112.
46. The Assam Company, for instance, had been working on the coal mines near Jaypur since 1840.
47. T. E. Rogers, 'Coal Beds on Namsang Naga Hills', *J.S.A.B.,* June 1848, Vol. XVII, pp. 489–91.

48. H. B. Medlicott, 'The Coal of Assam', 1865, *Memoirs of the G. S. I.*, Vol. IV, p. 395.
49. W. R. Gawthrop, The Story of the Assam Railways and Trading Company, 1881–1951, London, 1951, p. 36.
50. *Assam Secretariat Records*, Revenue and Agriculture, August 1894, No. 327/3849 Engn.R.
51. Ibid., Prog. No. 110, August 1894.
52. Ibid., Prog. No.111, August 1894.
53. For details, refer to Gawthrop, *The Story of the Assam Railways and Trading Company, 1881–1951*, London, 1951, pp. 29–31.
54. The area of a single grant was not to exceed 640 acres; a surface rent of 6 annas but no royalty, was charged; the land was liable to redemption if operations were not commenced within three years or if work was suspended for five years or more.
55. *A. S. R.*, Revenue , Letter No. 704, dated 22 March 1879.
56. R.Wilcox, 'Memoir of a Survey of Assam and the Neighbouring Countries Executed in 1825–28', *Asiatic Researches*, 1832, Vol. XVII, pp. 314–469.
57. John Berry White, a civil surgeon, was closely connected with the oil industry of Assam, He had been a shareholder of the Assam Mineral oil Company and he realised that the most urgent requirement of Assam was an improvement in her transport and communication system, without which neither the coal deposits nor the oil springs could be profitably worked. In 1879 Dr White invited applications in London for shares in the proposed Assam Railways Company. The main object of the company was the construction of a railway line from the steamer ghat in Dibrugarh to the 51st mile on the Sadiya Road, together with three branch lines extending to the coal and oil areas. Initially, the response was not encouraging, but the idea soon picked up momentum and in 1881 the Assam Railways and Trading Company was incorporated.
58. In the early years, the method of extraction of oil was very crude. The first wells were plank-lined shafts that were five feet square. Once the shaft was completed, the oil diggers were lowered down the wells on a rope over a pulley. It took about 15 seconds to reach the bottom of a 250 feet deep well. After about half a minute of frantic digging and loading pots in an atmosphere saturated with gas, the digger was hauled up. He then required half an hour's rest before he recovered sufficiently to go down again. The light by which the digger worked was provided by a mirror at the mouth of the shaft. *Batori*, Silver Jubilee edition, Digboi, September 1978. Also Priyam Goswami, *Assam in the Nineteenth Century: Industrialization and Colonial Penetration*, p. 125.
59. W. Schlich, *Memorandum on Forest Operations in Assam*, A.S.R. File No. 38/45, 1873, 94C.
60. W. Jackson, *Monograph on the Iron and Steel Works of Assam*, Shillong, 1907.
61. Forbes, R, *Memorandum on the Production of Hemp and Rhea Fibre in India*, London, 1854; A.S.R. file no. 283/612, 1854–57.
62. G. N. Gupta, A *Survey of the Resources and Industries of Eastern Bengal and Assam, 1907–08*, Shillong , 1908, p. 108.
63. J. N. M'Cosh, *Topography of Assam*, Calcutta 1837, (Reprint), Delhi, 1975, p. 82.

64. There are references to small boats that cost around 250 rupees each. In the bigger stations like Calcutta and Dacca, the Assam Company is recorded to have started building its own fleet having to pay about 37 rupees a month as hire charges for a boat of 300 *maund* capacity and to take on the crew for a year's service at a time.
65. H. A. Antrobus, *A History of the Assam Company*, Edinburgh, 1957, p. 349.
66. B. C. Allen, *Gazetteer of Bengal and North East India*, Calcutta, 1905, p. 224.
67. A. J. M. Mills, *Report on the Province of Assam*, 1853, pp. 22–23.
68. A passenger ticket from Calcutta to Gauhati cost 150 rupees while cargo was charged at one rupee per cubic ft.
69. G. M. Barker, *A Tea Planter's Life in Assam*, p. 150.
70. S. Barkataki, (ed.) *India:The Land and People–Assam*, Delhi, 1969, p. 118.
71. *Foreign Political Consultations*, April 1836, No.4, Secretary, Government of India to Captain Jenkins.
72. H. A, Antrobus, *A History of the Jorehaut Tea Company 1859–1946*, London 1949, p. 72.
73. Ibid., p. 76.
74. (i) Dibrugarh to Nagahuli; (ii) Panitola to Hopwell on the Rangagora Road; (iii) Dumduma to the river Buridihing.
75. For the Dibru-Sadiya Railway, the government paid a total subsidy of 1.2 million rupees between 1884–1903; In the Tezpur-Balipara railway, half the share capital was owned by the tea companies and almost one-fourth of the paid up capital was invested by the Tezpur Local Board.
76. The tunneling was done by Cornish miners brought for the purpose by M/S Lewis and Jones, the contractors. Mortality among these miners was very high. H.A. Antrobus, *A History of the Jorehaut Tea Company, 1859–1946*, p. 79.
77. B. C. Allen, *Gazetteer of Bengal and North East India*, Calcutta, 1905, p. 89.
78. For details, refer to S. B. Medhi, *Transport System and Economic Development in Assam*, Guwahati 1978, Chapter 3. Also, A. K. Dutta, *Indian Railways: The Final Frontier*, New Delhi, 2002.

SUGGESTED READINGS

Bhattacharjee, J. B., (ed.), *Studies in the Economic History of North East India*, New Delhi, 1994.

———, *Trade and Colony: The British Colonization of North East India*, Shillong, 2000.

Goswami, P.C., *The Economic Development of Assam*, Bombay, 1963.

Goswami, Priyam, *Assam in the Nineteenth Century: Industrialization and Colonial Penetration*, New Delhi, 1999.

8

Social Transformation of Assam

Chapter Highlights

- Impact of British rule on society
- Education
- Establishment of institutes of higher learning
- Press and public associations
- Women's emancipation
- Opium use

Colonial rule in Assam triggered a series of sweeping changes, not only in its polity and economy, but in its society and culture as well. The British brought with them new institutions, knowledge, ideas, technology, beliefs and values. Within a few years of their occupation of Assam, they had laid the foundations of a modern state by surveying the land, settling revenue collection, creating a bureaucracy of officials, codifying the law and instituting law courts, introducing western education, establishing industries, and a communication network, thereby opening her up to the outside world.

IMPACT OF BRITISH RULE

The direct impact of the presence and activities of the American Baptist missionaries and the Bengal Renaissance were felt on Assamese society. The changes were distinctly visible by the 1850s. With improved means of communication and hope of greater employment opportunities, the youth went to Calcutta in search of higher education. There they came into contact with the liberal ideas of the west which they embraced enthusiastically and brought back with them when they returned home. These youth, educated in English and imbued with 'modern' ideas, started the process of change in Assam. A wide variety of important issues were discussed and debated upon by the emerging intelligentsia and in the process ideas and attitudes underwent a profound change. In course of time these ideas filtered down to the common man and although illiteracy was still rampant, the gradual infiltration of radical ideas instilled a spirit of rational enquiry in the minds of the people. There was a growing demand for social reforms and the eradication of certain social evils. A small section of the provincial population emerged to form the provincial elite, and it was this vocal group that took upon itself the task of organising public opinion. The emergence of the press and modern Assamese literature helped in the dissemination of ideas and information and this in turn resulted in the growth of a political awareness which found expression in the formation of a number of socio-political organisations.

Education

One of the most significant impact of British rule in India was the opening up of a new intellectual world for the people that resulted in a sea change in their outlook. Indeed, if we have to choose one single factor which helped more than others in bringing about a transformation in the country, we can, without any hesitation, choose the introduction of English education.

Education Prior to the Arrival of the British

Assam had remained, by and large, fairly isolated till British entry into the valley. But there was a system of education as is evident from a mass of literary and religious works that have survived but are yet to be fully catalogued. The survival of a number of *tols* till recently also unmistakably shows the existence of a system of education which was not very different from the rest of the country. It was also not unusual for some young boys to go to Nawadip or Benaras which were centres of classical learning at that time. However, the education that was imparted in these institutions was primarily religious in nature. During Ahom rule, education was confined to the priestly class, the *kakoties* (official scribes) and few others connected to the government. In any case, the running of the administration did not involve much paperwork and hence it was not essential for the official aristocracy to be literate. Gunnar Myrdal has observed that 'whenever education is considered from the point of view of development, its purpose must be to rationalise or modernise attitude as well as to impart knowledge and skills'.[1] Pre-colonial education in Assam did not conform to this idea and during the early years of the British occupation, most of the population was illiterate.

British Efforts at Introducing Modern Education

While setting up the new administration, David Scott had realised the practical necessity of preserving indigenous institutions and had retained many of the earlier officials in the revenue and judicial departments. But they were found to be completely unfit for the work that was expected of them and he had to recruit omlahs from Bengal to perform the official tasks. When Jenkins took over the administration of Assam he was appalled at the predominance of non-Assamese in all government offices. He strongly believed that the 'natives of the soil' must be relied upon and that it was imperative on the part of the government to educate and train them to take up positions of responsibility. Schools imparting English education were set up at each of the *sadar* stations of Gauhati, Darrang, Nowgong and Bishwanath. The general belief that knowledge of English was necessary for obtaining employment in the government sector led to the establishment of more than 600 such schools by 1841. Most of these were funded by the public. The quality of education that was imparted in these schools was very elementary. There was neither a fixed curriculum nor adequate textbooks. In fact, books were so scarce that teachers were compelled to devote much of their time in instructing students in letter writing, framing petitions, keeping simple accounts or engaging in religious discourses. The meagre monthly salary of 20 or 30 rupees that was offered did not attract qualified teachers from Bengal. In the circumstances, it is not surprising that William Robinson, Inspector of Schools, reported that 'even the most advanced students were able to read only a few pages of their text books without any comprehension whatsoever of their meaning...their handwriting was illegible, orthography much worse and of arithmetic they literally knew nothing'.[2] James Matthie, the Collector of Gauhati, was convinced that the solution lay in setting up anglo-vernacular schools. He put forward a set of proposals which became the foundation for primary education in Assam. Apart from primary schools, there were secondary and collegiate schools as well. Secondary schools were classed as high and middle schools. Middle schools were further categorised as middle English and middle vernacular schools. The results, however, were far from encouraging as is evident from Mills' Report of 1854[3] and subsequent government reports on education.

The Role of Missionaries

The Christian missionaries rendered invaluable service in spreading modern education in Assam. The American Baptist Mission was the most active among the missions in the Brahmaputra Valley. Their main aim was evangelisation. They realised that primary education was necessary so that people could read and understand the Bible. Within two months of their arrival at Sadiya, two Baptist missionaries, Nathan Brown and Oliver T. Cutter started a school with an initial enrolment of six students which soon rose to 20. In the following years they established several other schools in the vicinity and one each at Jaipur and Namsang. By 1844 they had set up 11 schools in Sibsagar district and five at Gauhati along with an orphanage at Nowgong for orphan and destitute children. The students were taught reading, writing, arithmetic and elements of geography apart from religious teachings. The Welsh Calvinistic Mission, which started work in the Khasi-Jayantia Hills and later spread to other areas, had about a dozen schools to their credit by 1858. There was a growing demand for these mission schools because the education imparted there opened up various avenues for employment. The missionaries learnt the regional dialects, wrote text books and usually imparted education in the vernacular language. They did not confine their teaching to the text books alone and succeeded in imparting a certain amount of informal education as well.

One of the most important focus of their activities was women in the region and their untiring effort in furthering the cause of women's education deserves special mention. Appalled by the 'degradation' of 'heathen' women suffering from the disabilities of widowhood, child marriage and polygamy, they considered it their sacred duty to try and improve their status through education and through women working for women. With this in mind, they started schools for girls where, besides imparting lessons on general education, they also taught sewing, knitting, embroidery and handicrafts. They soon realised that for a majority of girls, early marriage was the most formidable obstacle to getting formal education in schools. One of the solutions that they came up with was the concept of *zenana* education where women teachers went from home to home to teach women. These private efforts were socially more acceptable than formal education. They were progressive yet at the same time traditional, providing women with basic education while restricting them to the parameters of their homes.

Despite these commendable efforts, the progress of education in Assam in general was very slow. A major difficulty was the foreign medium of instruction which made it hard for students to grasp their lessons and inevitably resulted in large-scale failures in examinations. Although English was made optional in 1844, Bengali continued to be the language of the schools and courts of Assam till 1873. Apart from the difficulties of studying a foreign language, the general sense of frustration at the failure of many educated youth to find suitable employment, made the study of English less attractive. The initial euphoria over the study of English had, therefore, dwindled over the years although the elite still believed that knowledge of the English language was necessary.

Higher Education in Colonial Assam

The scope for quality higher education in Assam was limited and so students who wanted to pursue their studies had no alternative but to go to Calcutta. As an incentive to these students, the government awarded a few monthly scholarships of around ten rupees each, but this amount was not enough to meet their expenses. Moreover, caste restrictions and prejudices against life in a metropolis prevented many families from sending their children away from home for higher studies. Hence, few could aspire for college and not surprisingly, the scholarships remained under-utilised. Continued representations to the government for the establishment of a collegiate school at Gauhati eventually bore fruit in 1865 when the school at Gauhati was upgraded to a collegiate school with a grant of 12,000 rupees per annum. But the number of successful candidates at the entrance examination was so small that it was not economically viable to maintain the school and a few years later the collegiate section was abolished. This brought home the point which Mills had made back in 1853 when he had strongly recommended to the government the substitution of Bengali with Assamese with the remark that 'an English youth is not taught Latin until he is well grounded in English and in the same manner an Assamese should not be taught a foreign language until he knows his own'.[4]

The failure of the collegiate experiment reflected the state of education in Assam. Only a few schools had developed to the standard required for entrance in colleges and it was evident that unless the quality of the feeder schools improved, an institution of higher education would not succeed. The general level of education in Assam was so poor that apart from some minor clerical positions, the Assamese were unable to be part of the administrative set up. In a memorandum to the Chief Commissioner, Assam, the Jorhat Sarbajanik Sabha (founded by Jagannath Barua in 1884) raised this point and stated that the time had arrived 'when the main body of the service should be recruited from natives of the province, and the proportion should not be less than three-fourths of the whole'.[5]

Setting up of Colleges: It was only in the closing years of the nineteenth century that Assamese was gradually introduced in the primary and middle schools. There was also a rapid expansion of institutions for secondary education and a successful agitation culminating in the foundation of a college, the Cotton College in Gauhati in 1901. By the first quarter of the twentieth century, another college, the Murari Chand College that had been set up in Sylhet in 1892, was affiliated to a number of courses of Calcutta University. Cotton College also offered a variety of courses. Girl students were admitted into the college from the academic session of 1929–30 and their number rose from one in that session to 75 in 1940–1.

Law and Medical College: Colleges for other professional courses were also set up by the beginning of the twentieth century. The Earle Law College was established at Gauhati as a temporary one because the government was of the opinion that the legal profession was 'an overcrowded profession' and that it was in any case a burden on the exchequer. Medical education similarly made a slow and hesitant start. The John Berry White Medical School was set up in 1900 almost entirely on private initiative,[6] but in course of time much of the expenditure incurred was borne by the government. They also made an attempt to encourage the indigenous systems of medicine by awarding two scholarships, one to a member of a *kaviraj* family and the other to a member of a *unani hakim* family, annually tenable at the Berry White Medical School with the intention that the knowledge thus acquired would be used in the practice of indigenous systems.

Technical Education: The Indian Education Commission or Hunter Commission of 1882 had recommended the need for establishing indigenous schools. But technical and industrial education received little attention in Assam. The Assamese intelligentsia urged the government repeatedly to establish institutes for vocational training. Manik Chandra Baruah, strongly urged the government to set up technical schools and had suggested the utilisation of the Williamson Fund, which had been created for the establishment and maintenance of artisan schools, for the purpose. But the authorities conveniently believed that the Assamese were 'not anxious to have a trade involving scientific or quasi-scientific training',[7] and as such took little initiative in this regard. Even as late as 1929, there were only seven technical institutes[8] in the whole of the northeast imparting elementary training in skills such as weaving, woodwork, and metal work. The establishment of the Prince of Wales Technical School at Jorhat in 1927, initiated by a donation of 100,000 rupees by the family of Jagannath Barooah, was the first step in the direction of imparting some form of mechanical training.

Establishing a University: For a long time the only university in the entire eastern region was at Calcutta. This university catered to the needs of students not only from Bengal but also those from Bihar, Orissa and Assam. Therefore, seats for students from Assam were extremely limited and very often even meritorious students found themselves ousted from the fray. Over the years this caused resentment among the educated Assamese youth and the necessity of a separate university was acutely felt. Soon after the capital shifted from Calcutta to Delhi in 1911, Bihar and Orissa got their own universities. Assam, too, put forward her claim to the government for a separate university. The first public demand was made at the annual session of the Assam Association held at Sibsagar in 1917. From then till 1928, representations and petitions on the issue were presented to the government from time to time. However, serious agitation started only in 1928. It is worth mentioning here that the media played a very positive role in moulding public opinion in this regard. But Assam's ardent pleas fell on deaf years. The government pleaded that there was no fund to sustain a university in Assam and the number of local students was too small to justify the establishment of a separate university. These excuses failed to deter the Assamese from continuing with their agitation. In the backdrop of the growing nationalism in the country, the government was eventually forced to concede to the demand of the people and the Gauhati University was incorporated by an Act of 1947.[9]

The progress of modern western education in Assam was, thus, very slow. Much time had been initially wasted by imposing a foreign medium of instruction which in effect put the clock back by almost half a century. Had it not been for the efforts of the Christian missionaries, the progress of education would have been further stalled. Nevertheless, within a century of British occupation, a completely new system of education had been firmly established, although literacy, when the whole of the population was taken into account, continued to be negligible. Perhaps the most important outcome of the new education was the emergence and growth of an educated elite who developed radical ideas and looked beyond the provincial boundaries to establish a commonality of purpose with the mainstream Indian elite.

Press and Public Associations

The growth of the educated intelligentsia coincided with the emergence of new social and political ideas and in course of time these ideas filtered down to the masses through the new media of newspapers, journals etc. Thus, along with education, the press played an extremely vital role in the regeneration of Assamese society.

Newspapers, however, were not published from Assam until much later. The newspapers and periodicals in circulation in the period like *Samachar Darpan, Samachar Chandrika, Somprakash, Sanjivani, Digdarshan* and *Friend of India,* were all published from Bengal. These papers regularly reported on issues relating to Assam and were so popular that the *Samachar Darpan,* in its issue of 30 July 1831, observed:

> The distinguished persons in the province of Assam maintain contact with every affair in and about Bengal through the newspapers of this province. In no district of Bengal are found so many subscribers to our newspaper as are found among the people of Assam. Moreover, while from about half the districts of Bengal no letter is sent and appears in newspapers, hardly a week passes without a letter being sent from Assam to us or to other newspaper editors of this province.[10]

Orunodai

In Assam, the pioneers of the printing press were the American Baptist Missionaries who set up the Baptist Mission Press at Sibsagar primarily for the publication of Christian literature. In 1846, they published *Orunodoi*, the first news magazine in Assamese. Based on the model of the *Samachar Darpan* and edited by Nathan Brown, *Orunodoi* intended to serve the dual purpose of filling the vacuum in Assamese journalism and supplementary reading material in schools. The emphasis was on arousing a spirit of enquiry among the Assamese through the diffusion of 'useful knowledge'. Although the magazine contained articles on religion in every issue glorifying Christianity, it also included a variety of informative news items of general interest and educational, cultural and literary importance. There were articles on contemporary events, history, geography, botany, zoology, astronomy and the general sciences apart from stories and poems and even embroidery designs. The magazine also devoted considerable space to social issues like education, women, health and hygiene, language and literature. The *Orunodoi* was essentially non-political in character and scrupulously steered clear of controversial religious or political issues. It was profusely illustrated and throughout the entire period of its existence (1846–82), it maintained a uniformly high standard in the variety of its contents and in its usefulness.

By upholding the cause of modern scientific knowledge against ignorance and superstition, the *Orunodoi* firmly established the tradition of western liberal and secular ideas in Assamese literature. But perhaps one of its most important contributions was that it opened up knowledge to the masses and for the first time, reading material was accessible to the common man and not just the privileged classes. *Orunodoi* had such an impact on the Assamese mind that for a long time any newspaper published in the province was referred to as the *Orunodoi* by the common man.

Other Publications

Orunodoi set the trend and others followed. The close of the nineteenth century saw the 'appearance and disappearance' of over a dozen newspapers and journals, both in English and Assamese, in Assam. The *Assam Bilasini* was the first Assamese newspaper published by an Assamese. Printed at the Dharma Prakash Press in Majuli, *Assam*

Bilasini (1871–83) was the brainchild of Sri Sri Duttadev Goswami, the *satradhikar* of the *Auniati Satra,* who sought to counter the missionaries' activities through the promotion of Vaishnava culture and religion. Though religious in tone, it highlighted local problems and grievances and contained news and articles of general importance. *Assam Mihir* (1872–3), the first weekly published from Gauhati first in Bengali and then in English and Bengali, survived only for a year due to lack of support. *Assam Darpan, Goalpara Hitasadhini, Assam Dipika* and *Chandrodaya* were other publications that suffered a similar fate. However, some papers like *Assam News, Assam Bandhu* and *Mau,* though short lived, played a significant role in the dissemination of news and views.

***Assam News* and *Assam Bandhu*:** *Assam News* (1882–5), edited by Hem Chandra Barua, and published from Gauhati, was the first Anglo-Assamese weekly. During the three years of its existence, it succeeded in creating strong public opinion on issues of common interest, such as the problem of the coolies vis-à-vis the planters, high rates of assessments, employment of non-Assamese in the government services etc. It also considerably raised the standard of journalism in Assam. Its work was carried on by *Assam Bandhu* (1885–6), an Assamese monthly, edited by Gunabhiram Barua and published from Nowgong. Unfortunately, its publication stopped after 16 issues. Both these papers contributed immensely to the development of Assamese language and literature. Lakshminath Bezbarua, the great Assamese writer, described them as the two giants of Assamese language, which provided the groundwork for the creation of Assamese prose and poetry in modern form.

In 1886, appeared *Mau,* a monthly newspaper.[11] It published a large number of thought provoking articles on a variety of issues but the paper's radical views roused considerable opposition and ultimately it was forced out of circulation after its fourth issue.

The trend set by the papers mentioned above was continued by newspapers and periodicals like *Jonaki, Bijuli, Usha, Banti, Banhi, The Advocate of Assam* and *The Times of Assam. Jonaki*(1889–96), published and edited by Chandra Kumar Agarwala, brought about a literary awakening in the province giving the literature of the period the epithet *Jonaki* era. Several Bengali newspapers like *Srihatta Mihir,*

Paridarsak and *Silchar*, were published from the Surma Valley. Almost all the papers of the period were moderate in tone and non-political in nature, concentrating on social, scientific, historical, literary and other subjects of general interest. *Jonaki* aptly reflected this general view when it stated that 'a subject nation has no politics'.

The press in Assam played a vital role in creating awareness by not only highlighting the various problems of the province and suggesting remedies but also discussing contemporary issues in an all-India context. These were supplemented by regular discussions in papers like *Hindu Patriot* and the *Ananda Bazar Patrika*. One of the most important examples of the power of the press to mobilise public opinion was seen when Dwarka Nath Ganguly, one of the pioneering reformists, went to tea gardens to gather first-hand information on the working conditions of the tea garden labourers of Assam. His reports in the press raised much concern and the problems that labour in Assam faced figured prominently in the sessions of the Indian National Congress.

Public Assocaiations

Along with the press, public associations also made their appearance. One of the earliest public associations in the Brahmaputra Valley was the *Jnan Pradayani Sabha* of Anandaram Dhekial Phukan and Gunabhiram Barua. As its very name suggests, the objective was to spread knowledge among the Assamese people. In the process it hoped to instil a spirit of enquiry among the people and make them conscious of their rights. Several other organisations like the Assamese Literary Society (1872) and *Assamiya Bhasar Unnati Sadhini Sabha* (1888) followed. In the Surma Valley, the *Srihatta Sanmilan*, the *Swadeshi Sabha* and the Student Association were active public associations where leadership was provided by Kamini Kumar Chanda. A distinguished lawyer and social reformer, he was a staunch advocate of women's emancipation and fought relentlessly, along with others like Radha Binode Das, Girish Chandra Dutta and Tara Kishore Choudhury, against untouchability, the caste system and other social evils. Although most of these organisations were socio-cultural and literary in character, they served as important meeting places where contemporary issues were discussed and created a bond among the people. Political associations were few and far between but the birth of the Indian Association in 1876 and the Indian National Congress in 1885 had important effects on the organisations of Assam and subsequently they began to develop political overtones.

Questions of social reform were discussed and debated at length in the press and in these public associations. There were two different schools of thought that worked at reforming society. One strove to defend the indigenous traditions and culture while the other sought to 'modernise' society by importing ideas from the west. These two streams were particularly visible in the discussions relating to the emancipation of women. While one section of the Assamese intelligentsia stressed the need to redefine gender relations, another section firmly believed that gender relations were perfect as they were and as such needed no modification.

Emancipation of Women

The necessity for meaningful social reform in Assam was first articulated by Anandaram Dhekial Phukan, although his father, Haliram Dhekial Phukan, had identified certain prevailing evils. Anandaram's proximity to the American Baptist Missionaries and to the Bengali intelligentsia during his brief stint at the Hindu College, Calcutta, contributed immensely towards his liberal and advanced ideas. Anandaram had an unflinching faith in the efficacy of British rule and sincerely believed that Assam could be transformed through a series of liberal reforms. Although he was mainly concerned with the anomalies in the existing revenue and judicial systems, he did not overlook the 'women's question'. This was a burning issue in Bengal at that time and Anandaram could relate many of the problems to the women in his own family. He concluded that the subordinate status of women in Assam was primarily because they were looked upon as commodities that could be traded at will by men. He forcefully pleaded that unless this basic attitude was changed, and until the women were assured the security of a marriage, Assamese society would never prosper. Depicting a gloomy picture of the marital status and gross abuse of women, he urged the government to introduce a system of registration of marriages. His early demise at the age of 29 left no scope for pushing his views further and it was left to his kinsman, Gunabhiram, (1837–94) to carry on his work.

Widow Re-marriage

Gunabhiram Barua, exposed to liberal ideas from childhood under the influence of Anandaram, was deeply influenced by the Brahmo movement during his stay at Calcutta between 1851 and 1857. The impact of the Bengal Renaissance on Gunabhiram was so great that he began working for social reform at a very early age. He wrote extensively on issues which touched him most and he was fortunate to find a platform for his ideas. Between 1853 and 1854, the *Orunodoi* published a series of articles on various issues written by 'An Assamese in Calcutta'. These articles have been ascribed to Gunabhiram. He led by example and married a widow, Bishnupriya, after the death of his first wife, Brajasundari. This was after the Widow Re-marriage Act of 1856. His daughter, Swarnalata, also remarried after the death of her husband. Like Gunabhiram, Hemchandra Barua also wrote extensively on women's issues and his liberal attitude and tremendous zeal for social reform found reflection in his forceful writings. He championed the cause of widow remarriage as reasonable not only for the sake of equality of the genders but also on the ground that the system was already an accepted notion among the non-brahmin communities in Assam.

Both Gunabhiram and his contemporary, Hemchandra Barua, made use of both reason and ancient Hindu literature to uphold their arguments. They realised that they could never build up a convincing argument without referring to the *shastras* and that it was imperative to strike a balance between reason, custom and tradition if their views were to have any impact on the conservative Assamese mindset. Hence they substantiated their arguments with extensive references from ancient Sanskrit texts. They also attempted to impress upon society the need for social reform. Gunabhiram's *Ramnavami Natak* ,written in 1857 at the age of 20, was an endeavour to sensitise Assamese society on gender justice.

In an article published in *Orunodoi*, Gunabhiram expressed his views on marriage reforms which were both novel and daring in the context of the nineteenth century. He proposed that

- A period of courtship should precede marriage so as to enable the couple to get acquainted with one another.

- That the boy should be at least 23 years of age and the girl at least 18 years old at the time of marriage so that they were mature both physically and emotionally.
- That the difference in age between the husband and wife should be such that they could be more like friends rather than like a grandfather and a granddaughter.
- That girls should have the liberty of choosing their own partners.[12]

The article, however, raised a hue and cry among the conservative sections of Assamese society. Some of those who opposed it were Ratneswar Mahanta who argued that the age of the bride should ideally be one third that of the groom, that a girl ought to be married before she attained puberty so as to ensure her chastity and that on attaining puberty she should be immediately sent to her husband's home.[13] Purnakanta Sarma also emphatically stated that girls should be married off by the age of 11. But Kamal Chandra Sarma and Krishna Kumar Baruah, both members of the Assam Language Development Society, on the other hand, insisted that logic should govern human relations and argued that as societies underwent change, new norms needed to be introduced. Krishna Kumar Baruah also considered it his social responsibility to speak on behalf of change so as to prevent further deterioration of society. Unfortunately, these lone voices were subsumed in the clamour of the conservative majority.

Polygamy

Another issue that was raised was the question of polygamy which was widely prevalent in Assam. Writing under the pseudonym Sonar Chand, Hemchandra Barua strongly condemned polygamy by highlighting its evils and appealed to the youth to refrain from falling into the trap of polygamy if they aspired for marital happiness. [14] But at a time when polygamy was the order of the day, the majority preferred to listen to Ratneswar Mahanta who advocated *status quo,* and approvingly cited Kanna's advice to Sakuntala to treat co-wives as friends.[15]

Women's Education

Closely linked to the question of marriage was the issue of women's education. An early exponent of female education in Assam was

Anandaram Dhekial Phukan who emphasised the importance of imparting knowledge to girls and boys equally. Believing in practising what he preached, Anandaram made arrangements at home to educate the women in his family and initiated his daughter, Padmavati, to formal education at the age of five. His example was followed by Gunabhiram who made ardent pleas for equal educational opportunities for girls and boys. To prove his point, he himself got his daughter, Swarnalata, enrolled at Bethune School, Calcutta. Through the *Orunodoi*, he expressed his indignation at two sets of norms for the education of boys and girls. He pointed out that the shastras never discouraged female education and that the corrupt practices which had crept in at a later date had deprived Hindu women from acquiring education. Gunabhiram and his fellow reformers saw uneducated women as one of the principal obstacles to progress. They believed that the gap between educated men and uneducated women resulted in a communication gap between the husband and wife and prevented the wife from being an intellectual companion of the husband. Since both were interdependent, Gunabhiram concluded that the Assamese nation could never hope to prosper until and unless the womenfolk were emancipated, and this was possible only through education.

The liberal views of Gunabhiram and Hem Chandra were soon contested by a section of conservative men who argued that education was inherently de-feminising. According to them, domestic work was the sole objective of a woman's life. Education would foster in women an aversion to domestic duties, a love of luxury, and disrespect to traditional values. They argued that the identity of the woman rested on her role as a wife, mother and homemaker whereas the male identity was linked to productive work, public visibility and power. In an article in *Mau*, Bolinarayan Bora, the pioneer of Assamese satirical poems observed that these separate identities should be distinctly maintained and that educating the womenfolk was even more dangerous than the Burmese atrocities in Assam. Similar views were also expressed by Purnakanta Sarma. They found ample support from elderly ladies who not only believed that an educated woman was fated to become a widow but also that too much intellectual work would make her both unfeminine and irrelevant.[16]

Thus, in spite of liberal ideas of a small section and arguments in favour of female education, the majority were bitterly opposed to the idea of sending girls to school. They contended that there was nothing wrong in imparting education to girls, but it was not desirable for them to aspire for degrees and join the professions of doctors and lawyers because with education all the virtues in a woman would vanish. In the same vein Purnakanta Sarma wrote that the ideal age for female education was between five and ten years so that a girl could be married off by the time she was 11 years old. In any case, he believed that women's education would pollute this beautiful world and that it was god's wish that women should always be dependent on men.

Women's literacy was perceived as a challenge and an affront to feminine virtues and an invitation to masculine traits and even wickedness. The bias against female education was so marked that Ratneswar Mahanta presumed, among other things, that daughters-in law without formal education were much more suited to family life than those with education. Implicit in this preference was the desire to keep women where they were for centuries, playing second fiddle to men and with no identity of their own.

Opposition to Women's Reforms

The orthodox sections of society were very critical of missionary activities and the impact of western influence with regard to women. They said that women were no longer willing to spin their own thread and preferred to use imported thread. Under missionary influence the traditional art of weaving had been replaced by cutting, sewing, lace making, embroidery etc. An article in *Jonaki* elaborated how Assamese women had forgotten their traditional values under the influence of English culture. From hardworking housewives they had become idle and expected to be served by the men. There was continued hostility against women's education among the orthodox sections of society.

It is a generally accepted phenomenon that leadership in any social reform movement is usually provided by a handful of people who dare to defy the existing societal norms without fearing the consequences. In the case of Assam, this leadership was provided by Anandaram Dhekial Phukan, Gunabhiram Barua and Hem Chandra Barua. But unfortunately, they remained isolated and were unable to create a social circle of liberal intellectuals who could have given them unconditional support in their fight for the emancipation of women. Their appeals to the enlightened sections by and large, evoked little response. Even among the majority who advocated reform, the aim was not to make women independent or equal partners of men in the family or public life. Rather it was to make them better equipped to fulfil their conventional roles as mothers and wives. According to them, some education was necessary, but not such that would instil in women a desire or ambition to compete with men. This is evident even the writings of Lakshiminath Bezbarua whose views on women were those of a traditionalist rather than those of a radical reformist. Although the women's question frequently featured in the writings of Bezbarua, he opposed the emancipation of women on western lines. He repeatedly asserted that the primary sphere of a woman's activity was her home and that the education best suited to the Indian woman was one in which greater emphasis was laid on cooking, weaving and needlework rather than on science and mathematics.[17] Even women advocates of social reform like Padmavati Devi Phukanani (1853–1927) daughter of Anandaram Dhekial Phukan and Bishnupriya Devi, wife of Gunabhiram Barua, by and large conformed to the traditional notions of womanhood.

Achievements of the Reform Movement

The remarkable significance of the debates for women's emancipation was that it gave women a visibility which had been denied to them earlier. In the existing patriarchal set up, the subordinate position of women meant that their troubles were invisible. It was never discussed publicly. For centuries they had remained in the periphery of society and their problems had always been relegated to the background. In their plea for the creation of a just social order for women, the reformers now brought issues like polygamy, marriage reforms and women's education to the public space.

Nineteenth century Assam thus witnessed attempts by an enlightened section to create a just, non-discriminatory social order for women. Most of the advocates of social reform were from the upper caste, so it was natural that they were primarily concerned with the evils prevalent in upper caste Assamese society. Most drew inspiration from social reformers elsewhere in the country. The opening up of Assam from its relative isolation and exposure to modern ideas had provided the much needed sense of direction. Towards the end of the century, however, debates on women's issues gradually lost its centrality and focus, making way for the larger issues of political nationalism. Although a limited number of girls were able to avail of the opportunity of going to school, the mind-set of the society at large vis-à-vis women had not changed. The practice of child-marriage among the upper castes continued to be rampant; as a consequence, the number of child-widows also continued to be large. Despite *shastraic* and legal sanctions, there was no indication of the acceptance of widow re-marriage among the upper castes. Engulfed in an unfavourable social environment, widows continued to lead reclusive and degraded lives. Societal norms set for women continued to be based on age-old prejudices and not on reason or sympathy.

Opium

Another very important social concern was the widespread consumption of opium. The Assamese people had been introduced to the poppy plant and its use during the Mughal invasion in the seventeenth century, but for long its consumption had remained confined to the nobility only. With the influx of armed burgandazes and ex-sepoys of the Company from Bengal, its consumption had spread to the masses. When Captain Welsh came to Assam he observed that poppy was growing luxuriantly over extensive areas. The drug was obtained by saturating strips of coarse cotton cloth in the juice collected from incisions made into the poppy plant. These strips, known as *kanee*, were then dried and lightly rolled up to be sold in the market or were consumed by the producers themselves.

Campaigns against Opium

In due course addiction to opium was so widespread that even children were doped with the drug. Soon after his arrival in Assam, Miles Bronson, an American missionary, observed: '...multitudes of people I daily see, going almost naked, and without any single comfort in life, who, if they get a *pice* or two, will immediately expend it on the obnoxious drug'.[18] Though the *Orunodoi* repeatedly tried to create public awareness on the adverse effects of opium consumption by describing it as more dangerous than the Burmese, it appeared to have little impact.

The government's policy in this regard,[19] made matters worse. In his report to Mills, Anandaram Dhekial Phukan observed that the universal consumption of opium had 'converted the Assamese, once a hardy, enterprising and industrious race into an effeminate, weak, indolent and a degraded people' and that it was the 'sole cause of undermining the health and physical constitution of the whole population'.[20] He believed that unless the sale of government opium was discontinued and a tax on poppy cultivation progressively enhanced, the evil could never be eradicated. Interestingly, the planter community as a whole, supported the above view, not with any philanthropic intentions but for the simple reason that they believed that opium was a major reason for the non-availability of local labour for the plantations. The government eventually decided to ban poppy cultivation in 1860 but a brisk trade in government opium continued unhindered.[21] By the end of the nineteenth century, opium smoking had become a part of Hindu religious practices as a congregational ritual and long nocturnal sessions of opium smoking a regular feature of rural Assamese society.

Although there was no organised anti-opium campaign in the nineteenth century, the enlightened section of Assamese society consistently strove to create an awareness of the alarming situation. Apart from articles in the *Orunodoi* and the forceful memoranda presented to Mills by Anadaram Dhekial Phukan and Maniram Dewan, the *Assam Bilasini* and *Bijuli*, among others, wrote extensively on the evil consequences of the drug. In his satirical play, *Kaniyar Kirtan*, Hemchandra Barua showed how opium had permeated every section of Assamese society and the pathetic trap into which the addicts had fallen. Satyanath Bora, Trinayan Barkataki, Gunabhiram Barua and Radhanath Changkakoti were among the leading Assamese intellectuals who deposed before the Royal Commission on Opium (1893) pleading for the prohibition of the drug. The Commission's report revealed shocking statistics. Yet, the government preferred to advocate a policy of temperance rather than one of prohibition. From 1905 onwards, organised efforts to contain the opium menace took shape, but it was only under Gandhi's inspiration that the anti-opium agitation witnessed remarkable success in the second decade of the twentieth century.

Changes in Lifestyle

Changing attitudes in a changing environment also found expression in a new lifestyle. Western dresses and food habits slowly but gradually, seeped into Assamese society. Once again, the example was set by the western-educated youth. Anandaram Dhekial Phukan wore western attire whenever he visited his European friends; Lakshminath Bezbarua gave up the time-honoured custom of wearing a pig tail;

Jagyaram Khargharia Phukan and Govinda Bezbaruah freely dined with Europeans enjoying western delicacies and wine. More radical were the views of Kamalakanta Bhattacharya who denounced narrow casteism and social hypocrisy and deliberately defied caste taboos. In order to prove his point he tore apart his sacred thread and used the holy *saligram* stone, a symbol of Lord Vishnu, as a paperweight.[22] In further defiance of social conventions he publicly had food cooked by non-brahmins because he believed that what mattered was 'purity' in terms of cleanliness and hygiene and not in terms of caste. These were indeed radical attitudes and attracted strong criticism initially, but with the passage of time became accepted norms in a changing society.

IMPACT OF BRITISH RULE

Thus, it is apparent that modern education, a new scientific outlook and the doctrines of humanism and rationalism left a deep imprint on the Assamese intelligentsia. Through their powerful writings, the intelligentsia expressed their strong views on a wide variety of issues. Their almost unanimous condemnation of the hypocrisy and corruption prevalent in orthodox Assamese society was reflected in Hemchandra Barua's *Bahire Rongsong Bhitare Kowabhaturi.* Imbued with a critical outlook, they began questioning age old traditions and values and suggested radical changes through the medium of the press and by practising what they preached. The pace of change in Assam was indeed very slow. But social changes everywhere in the world have been shaped by forces that society does not always intentionally create. The ideas need to be persistently articulated for years before they are eventually accepted by the people at large. It is in this context that the work of the social reformers in nineteenth century Assam is so significant. Certain social conventions had been in existence for centuries. The very fact that they questioned the relevance of these conventions and their relentless struggle for the demolition of evil societal norms is perhaps their greatest contribution to Assamese society.

NOTES AND REFERENCES

1. Gunnar Myrdal, *Asian Drama,* London , 1972, p. 313.
2. *Report on Public Instruction, Bengal, 1845,* Appendix 4, Robinson to Jenkins.
3. Mills observed that not a single student from Assam had qualified for a government scholarship till the time of his filing the Report.

4. A. J. M. Mills, *Report on the Province of Assam,1854*, Guwahati (Reprint), 1984, Appendix J.
5. *A. S. R.* Home A, July1899, Nos. 123–4.
6. John Berry White, Civil Surgeon of Dibrugarh, tea planter and Director of the Assam Railways and Trading Company, bequeathed in his Will a sum of 50,000 rupees for the establishment of a Medical School in Assam for training Assamese students or one of whose parents had resided in Assam for ten years. The grant was conditional on the Government of Assam's acceptance to administer the fund and implement the scheme. Refer to *Will of Brigade Surgeon John Berry White*, 16 November 1896, A. S. R., Home A, Jan. 1898, Nos. 23–7.
7. A.S.R., Report on Public Instruction in Assam, 1916–17, p. 20.
8. Shillong Weaving School, Shillong Industrial School, Kohima Technical School, Tura Weaving School, Gauhati Weaving Institute, Sylhet Technical School, H. R. H. Prince of Wales Technical School, Jorhat.
9. For details, refer to Priyam Goswami, 'Gauhati University in Retrospect', in Gauhati University Journal of Arts, Vol XLI, Guwahati, 2010.
10. A. Guha, 'Impact of Bengal Renaissance in Assam, 1826–1875', cited in H. K. Barpujari (ed.) *Comprehensive History of Assam*, Vol. V, p. 230.
11. The proprietor and publisher of *Mau* was actually Bolinarayan Bora, an Assistant engineer at Nowgong. But since he was a government employee, the paper was published under the editorship of his brother, Haranarayan Bora.
12. 'Bibahar Samayat Ji Sakal Niyam Prati Palan Kora Kartobya Tar Kotha, *Orunodoi*, December 1853, (edited version), Guwahati 1983, pp. 10–66.
13. 'Bibah', *Jonaki*, Ahar, Bhada Ahin, Saka 1811.
14. 'Anek Biya Kora Ajugut, *Orunodoi*, April 1856, Nowgong, pp. 192–3.
15. *Assam Bandhu*, Sraban, Saka 1807.
16. V. Geetha, *Gender*, Calcutta, 2006, p. 17.
17. T. Misra, *Literature and Society in Assam*, Guwahati 1987, pp. 126–8.
18. H. K. Barpujari, *The American Missionaries and North East India (1836–1900)*, Guwahati, 1986, p. 180.
19. See Chapter 7 for details.
20. A. J. M. Mills, *Report on the Province of Assam*, 1854, Reprint, 1984, p. 110.
21. For details, refer to A. Guha, *Medieval and Early Colonial Assam; Society, Polity, Economy*, Calcutta, 1991, pp. 283–8.
22. Prafulladutta Goswami (ed.), *Kamalakanta BhattacharyarRasanavali*, Guwahati, 1982, p. 8

SUGGESTED READINGS

Barpujari, H. K., (ed.), *The Comprehensive History of Assam*, Vol. V, Guwahati, 1993.

Downs, F. S., *Christianity in North East India*, Guwahati, 1983.

Misra, T., *Literature and Society in Assam*, Guwahati, 1987.

9

Growth of Political Awareness

Chapter Highlights

- Language issue—Bengali vs Assamese
- Agrarian unrest
- Increase in number of migrants
- Public associations and popular protests

The annexation of Assam by the British bound her fate to that of the other parts of the Company's dominions in India. The sweeping administrative changes and the accompanying political, economic and social changes had enormous and far reaching consequences. Under the impact of British rule, numerous forces developed within the Assamese society and in course of time, the increasingly growing feeling of being exploited by the colonial government resulted in the emergence of a strong political consciousness in the province.

CAUSES FOR GROWTH OF POLITICAL AWARENESS

For almost a generation, British rule had been regarded as inevitable and people expected material progress within that framework. The Assamese intelligentsia was able to create a common bond among the Assamese on the basis of personal material aspirations. It was different from the earlier personal loyalty to the Ahom rulers. Although there was a strong regional identity, no voice was raised for Assam's identity as wholly independent of the Indian identity. Late nineteenth century Assamese literature had already created a framework alluding to the rightful place of Assam within India and *Sonar Asom* was never conceived as being outside *Bharat Varsha*.[1] But the focal point of intellectual discussions of the time was about the existence of Assam as a distinctive cultural, religious and linguistic entity, and until the beginning of the twentieth century, the predominant concerns of the people were those relating to regional issues.

Discontentment among the Aristocracy

Peasant cultivators formed the bulk of the population in the province. Their loyalty had been towards rulers who could ensure two square meals a day and they were not really concerned as to who was at the helm of affairs so long as they had enough to live on. The change in government did not matter much to them. The nobility, on the other hand, had a vested interest in the preservation of the *status quo*. Those who had been deprived of the benefits and munificence of Ahom rule, were therefore, the first to resist the alteration of the *status quo* that followed British occupation. But their resistance was confined to isolated and localised uprisings. The new administrative structure, which made the former nobility completely irrelevant, evoked a growing sense of deprivation. A large section of the nobility, and a still greater section of their dependents, had been virtually thrown out of employment. This feeling of being deprived increased with the influx of omlahs from Bengal, and, for the first time created a sense of common purpose and loyalty. In course of time, the earlier loyalty reserved for the rulers came to be replaced by a loyalty to the cause of the restoration of the Assamese language.

The Language Issue

The imposition of Bengali as the official language and as the medium of instruction in Assam in 1836 did not meet with any protest initially. Commenting on this, Jenkins in a letter to Grey, Secretary to the Government of Bengal wrote: 'I do not recollect that there was a single proposition made to retain Assamese, or that any difficulty was alleged as to the introduction of Bengali as the language of the Courts.'[2] On the contrary, the Assamese elite used the language in their writings and often even in their conversations. Haliram Dhekial Phukan wrote the *Assam Buranji* in Bengali while Maniram Barua's *Buranji Vivek Ratna* was also in a corrupt form of the language. Hence, for almost a decade, the language policy of the government remained unquestioned. But as recruitment of Bengalis in government services increased resulting in greater unemployment among the Assamese, strong feelings of resentment began to grow amongst the people. It was not the linguistic or cultural domination alone, though these were important factors, but their virtual monopoly of all offices that made these immigrants from Bengal irritants in the eyes of the local people.

A feeling of being subjugated not only by the British but also by the Bengalis gained ground.

Protests against use of Bengali

Role of the Missionaries: Initial protests against the government's language policy came from the American Baptist Missionaries and the educated Assamese elite. Soon after their arrival in Assam, the missionaries realised that they needed to use the vernacular medium to spread Christianity. They saw that books and pamphlets written in Bengali were received with little enthusiasm because they made little sense to the common man. Hence, they began to strongly espouse the cause of the Assamese language as the rightful medium of instruction. Apart from printing all their religious material in Assamese, they made fervent pleas in defence of the Assamese language through the *Orunodoi.* Reverend Danforth of the American Mission at Gauhati was among the first to submit a memorandum to the government on this issue. Significantly, the missionaries, who usually supported the government in matters of social legislation, differed on the government's language policy in Assam. They raised three crucial points.

1. They pointed out that the government's language policy was based on misconceptions about the Assamese language which in reality had a distinct identity.
2. The policy of replacing the vernacular with a foreign language was responsible for the slow progress of education in Assam.
3. They also argued that Assamese was the common medium of intercourse between the people of the plains and those of the hills and that by imposing Bengali, the government was attempting to dislodge Assamese from its rightful place.

The untiring efforts of the missionaries in asserting the separate identity of the Assamese language was indeed commendable. They received whole hearted support from the Assamese intelligentsia, whose chief spokesperson on the issue was Anandaram Dhekial Phukan.

The Role of Anandaram Dhekial Phukan: Anandaram wrote a pamphlet using the pseudonym 'A Native', where he strongly defended the Assamese language refuting every argument put forth by the government, and even appended a catalogue of books in Assamese to substantiate his point. The initiative taken by the American missionaries and Anandaram Dhekial Phukan was followed by a number of petitions and memoranda to the government and to a large extent the views of Moffat Mills on the government's language policy in Assam were based on these memoranda. Eventually, in 1873, a few months before the creation of Assam as a separate province under a chief commissioner in February 1874[3], the government revised its earlier language policy and decided to adopt Assamese as the official language of the courts and schools.

The debates on the language issue resulted in an increasing awareness about the distinctive linguistic, cultural and political existence of Assam among the educated people of the province. It instilled in them confidence and a sense of pride which went a long way in generating a regional consciousness in the second half of the nineteenth century.

Agrarian Unrest

The bulk of the Assamese population or the peasantry was hardly concerned with issues of language and cultural dominance. What concerned them was the progressive increase in land revenue and the numerous other taxes that were levied on them. We have seen in earlier chapters how the government's economic policies had adversely affected the people and how the peasantry had been reduced to penury. In course of time rural poverty became so acute that every assessment of land revenue raised a storm of protest.

Dissatisfaction among the Peasantry

The peasants made attempts at the grassroot level to collectively resist the government's increase of revenue. The ryots convened *mels* to ventilate their discontent. The *mels,* under the leadership of gosains, dolois or other influential people, were originally constituted as authorities on socio-religious matters. But their base was gradually broadened and converted to raijmels or popular assemblies, for the redressal of all grievances. In these raijmels, the ryots engaged in active discussions on their growing economic burden. Apart from the high land revenue, a considerable portion of their income was also spent on procuring opium which was a government monopoly. As a result, they fell prey to money lenders who lent money at exorbitant rates of income. It was a vicious circle.

The Phulaguri Uprising: The Phulaguri uprising of 1861 was the first instance of determined resistance by the ryots through the institution of the raijmel. In 1860 the government banned the cultivation of poppy and this prohibitory order shattered the domestic economy of the tribal areas where the consumption of opium was estimated to be the highest in the province. Moreover, the ban was looked upon as an infringement on the social habits and customs of the people. Around the same time, the government was finalising the scheme for the introduction of the licence tax and although this tax was not originally proposed to be extended to Assam, the ryots were alarmed at the prospect of another impending tariff. Matters worsened when rumours were rife among the Tiwa and Kachari communities of Phulaguri, near Nowgong, that the government intended to levy additional taxes on houses, baris (gardens) and betel leaf cultivation. Although the government dismissed these as 'unfounded apprehension', the people were convinced that they were seriously contemplating these additional taxes. Around 1,000 ryots gathered at the sadar court at Nowgong on 17 September 1861 to register their protest.

When the Deputy Commissioner, Sconce, failed to address the gathering, some ryots forced their way into his office. Sconce had the trespassers arrested for their 'riotous and disorderly conduct' and imposed a fine on them. About four weeks later, the ryots made another representation against the prohibition of opium cultivation and the proposed new taxes. But when they failed to receive a satisfactory reply, they decided not to pay the taxes when they were levied and convened a mel to discuss the future course of action. In order to enable the ryots from distant villages to take part in the deliberations of the mel, it was decided to hold the meetings over a period of five days. On the first day of the meeting, the deputy commissioner sent a police force to arrest the leaders and disperse the crowd of around 1,000 people who had assembled. When the ryots defied the orders, the daroga returned with reinforcements the following day, but the situation remained unchanged. Thereupon, the deputy commissioner dispatched Lieutenant Singer who was the assistant commissioner, to deal sternly with the situation. The crowd had by then swollen to over 3,000 and many of them were armed with clubs and sticks. In the scuffle that followed Singer's orders to disperse, Singer was beaten to death and thrown into the Kalang river. In was only after the arrival of the deputy commissioner that the situation was brought under control.

The Phulaguri uprising was neither a premeditated, organised peasant uprising nor an ordinary riot caused by a few disgruntled Tiwa and Kachari peasants. It was the culmination of a large number of deep rooted grievances accentuated by several acts of omission and commission on the part of the deputy commissioner. Had he explained the government's position clearly to the ryots, the unfortunate events that followed could probably have been averted. Nevertheless, the uprising is of immense significance primarily because it inaugurated a new era of peasant awakening in Assam and paved the way for the later agrarian uprisings in Rangia, Lachima and Patharughat.

Aftermath of the Uprising

Despite the growing discontent among the ryots, land revenue assessments continued to increase. Matters reached a breaking point when the Chief Commissioner, William Ward, raised the rates of land revenue in 1892 by around 70 per cent and in some cases, by even 100 per cent. A vigorous no-tax campaign was launched by the ryots of Patharughat in Darrang, and Rangia and Lachima in Kamrup.[4] The people resolved in their respective mels to not yield to the government demands and to boycott anyone who paid the revenue. The government, however, was not a silent spectator, and ordered the forceful collection of the revenue or confiscation of property. The ryot suddenly found himself in a precarious position. If he paid the revenue he faced ostracism, while if he did not pay his dues, his property was liable to be confiscated. Passions ran high and the atmosphere was charged with emotion. When petitions failed to have any impact on the government, simultaneous uprisings occurred at several places where the focus of attack was invariably the government official. Agitated crowds, armed with clubs, sticks and clods of earth, were fired upon by the police leaving many wounded and dead. But the ryots had been successful in making their point. Eventually, the government reduced the land revenue rates, but as a contemporary newspaper reported, 'it is a pity that the order of abatement did not reach sooner, in which case there would in all probability have been no riots'.[5]

These riots were so severe that they evoked considerable coverage in the national press. In the Imperial Legislature, the protest of the people found expression in a speech of Rash Behari Bose. *The Indian Nation* described the grievance of the people as 'real and not sentimental'. The paper further commented that the people complained not of loss of rights and privileges, or of lowering of status but of a material wrong in the shape of the enhancement of revenue and that when force was used to cow them down, they resisted. The riots were crushed with a heavy hand but they proved that the ground for public expression had been prepared. One far reaching consequence of these peasant uprisings, although unintended, was the establishment of a commonality of purpose among the masses on the basis of the consciousness that colonialism was inherently exploitative and that its victims had an innate mandate to resist it.

Immigration

Closely allied to the agrarian problem was the question of immigration. The magnitude of immigration into Assam, especially the tea districts, was so high that by the beginning of the twentieth century, a distinct demographic change had taken place.[6] The expansion of industries had also opened up new avenues for enterprising businessmen, an opportunity that was seized mainly by traders from Rajasthan. With the improvement and development of the communication network, they entered the province in large numbers and within a few decades, displaced the local petty traders. Other immigrants included Punjabi carpenters, cobblers from Bihar and the United Provinces, people from Afghanistan and graziers from Nepal. A major group of immigrants was that of the educated Bengalis who were employed as clerks and mohururs in the tea gardens. At the official level, the Bengali omlahs replaced the erstwhile aristocracy. Less permanent than the above immigrants, but nonetheless an important segment, was the European population. Forming their own social island, a miniature England in a tropical setting, this group was constantly aware of being the 'master race'. Thus, the last three decades of the nineteenth century saw the population of Assam increase by almost seven lakhs.[7] As the growth of the indigenous population had remained more or less static during 1881–8, and had actually decreased by around six per cent between 1899 and 1901 (because of the *kala azar* epidemic), the rise was obviously due to the immigrants.

In any agriculture-based economy, it is generally expected that an increase in demand for food crops would automatically lead to greater production. In Assam, however, this was not the case and the increase in population did not result in increased production. The Assamese ryot cultivated only as much land as he needed for his own subsistence and, under stress, this subsistence economy eroded resulting in growing dependence on imported food grains, the bulk of which came from Bengal. In the circumstance, the price of rice in Assam was abnormally high.[8]

Agriculture and Immigration

A major problem that exercised the minds of the British administration in Assam towards the close of the nineteenth century, was the urgent need to use the vast stretches of fallow land for the production of food crops. The revenue administration had only looked to enhance the revenue but had taken no steps to increase the acreage under cultivation. There were several reasons for this and they were:

- The government's systematic discouragement of sub-letting and the induction of middlemen had been strong obstacles.[9]
- Another factor that had determined government policy to a large extent was the influence of the tea lobby. The Tea Association of London had warned the government against any proposals for the extension of cultivation which might lead to an exodus of the tea garden labour force. Similar concerns had also been expressed by the Assam Branch of the Indian Tea Association in its memorandum to the chief commissioner of Assam in 1897.

The government decided to go ahead with its scheme of expanding cultivation but they stressed that it would not be at the expense of the tea industry. They formulated new Waste Land Rules in an effort to attract colonists to open up the waste lands for the cultivation of rice. Special efforts were made to colonise the Nambor forest and the areas around the railway tracks. They lured immigrants from East Bengal with easy terms to come and cultivate the fallow lands. But the influx of the immigrants from East Bengal only added to the problems rather than solving them.

The continuing imbalance between the modern industrial sector and the traditional agricultural sector, along with the high rates of assessments, had other repercussions as well. The growing interest in cash crops together with the introduction of abkari opium and the liberal issue of licenses to liquor shops, led to an increasing importance of money in the new economy. An important consequence of this was the growing indebtedness of the Assamese peasants which drew swarms of money lenders into the province. In fact, the *keya* and the *mahajan* assumed a prominent place in the economy of the region.

The demographic and economic changes that gradually swept over Assam inevitably resulted in popular discontent. As early as 1828–30, resistance to British rule had found expression in a number of anti-British resistance movements led by the disgruntled nobility. When reform and reorganisation under David Scott and Robertson failed to improve the situation, popular discontent found expression in the memorandums of Maniram Dewan and Anandaram Dhekial Phukan to Mills. Had steps been taken to rectify the situation, Maniram probably would not have taken the path he took in 1857.

The transfer of power from the Company to the Crown and the Queen's Proclamation had come along with pledges to work for the people, but in reality it had little impact on Assam. In fact, after 1857, the economic situation deteriorated. Rural poverty was so acute that every assessment raised a storm of protest. Economic discontent aroused political awareness and both in turn paved the way for an organised challenge to British rule. This lead, as we have observed, was taken by the ryots who were determined not to yield to government demands. The emerging intelligentsia made common cause with them and helped them to keep alive their newborn spirit of resistance.

Public Associations and Popular Protests

The popular raijmels were soon converted into more representative and more broad-based organisations called ryot sabhas. They were formed with the active support of the Assamese intelligentsia. When the land revenue was enhanced in 1893, a very well argued memorandum was sent not only to the chief commissioner of Assam but also to the viceroy urging the government to lower the assessment. The peasants would not have been able to write such petitions and it is therefore obvious that they received the support of the educated section of society. The emerging intelligentsia, however, was not in favour of the aggressive policy hitherto followed by the raijmels. Instead it advocated constitutional agitation through prayers, petitions, memorials and public meetings and believed that only through such means could political awareness among the people be aroused. Thus, the ryot sabhas which followed were more leadership oriented unlike the raijmels where popular sentiment dominated.

Newspapers and public associations also made their appearance nearly simultaneously. We have observed earlier[10] that although initially most of the organisations were literary and cultural in character, they were able to create a common bond among the Assamese people and raise their aspirations. These organisations advocated social reform, inspired the youth of the province to qualify themselves for higher positions, and worked for the all round progress of the society. The scope of their activities was broadened by the creation of the enlarged province of Assam under a chief commissioner in 1874 and soon thereafter, they began to develop political overtones.

Jorhat Sarbajanik Sabha

Jorhat emerged as the centre of activity. The Jorhat Sarbajanik Sabha was founded in 1884 under the initiative of Jagannath Barua. He was the son of a tea planter and was educated at Presidency College, Kolkata. He was deeply influenced by the new social and political ideas of the time. He was inspired by the work of associations like the *Atmiya Sabha*, Bengal British Indian Society, Patriots' Association, Indian Association, *Sadharan Janaparjika* and others in Bengal. He wanted to create a similar platform in Assam through which the aspirations and grievances of the people could be voiced and could take up government issues relating to the socio-economic development of the province. With this in mind, he set up the Jorhat Sarbajanik Sabha. The objectives of the Sabha were three-fold:

1. To represent the wishes and aspirations of the people to the government.
2. To explain the policies of the government to the people.
3. To ameliorate the condition of the people.

The founder-president of the Sabha was Raja Naranarayan Singha while Jagannath Barua was the Secretary.

Like most other organisations of the time, the Sabha did not believe in direct confrontation with the government, but nevertheless espoused the cause of the people even at the risk of displeasing the government at times. It protested against various unfair measures of the government and also spoke for the welfare of the people of the region:

- In 1886 it protested against the arbitrary introduction of the Assam Land and Revenue Regulations by the government.
- In 1892–3 it expressed its solidarity with the ryots who were protesting against increased and forcefully condemned the government's financial policy.
- It reiterated its demand for long-term land settlements with the right of sub-letting without any further enhancement of revenue.[11]
- In 1893 it submitted a memorandum to the Royal Commission on Opium.
- It was critical of the government's policy towards education and demanded adequate employment opportunities for the youth.
- It also demanded improved salaries and prospects and aroused public awareness to a large extent.

The Sabha took its lead from the Indian National Congress and strongly opposed the partition of Bengal in 1905. It disagreed with the governments view that partition was necessary for the speedy completion of the Assam-Bengal Railway and that a common province of Eastern Bengal and Assam was necessary for the development of the port of Chittagong. The Sabha argued that when the government was not separating Orissa from Bengal, which had been politically associated only for a century, there was little reason to break up Bengal into two. 'The people of both portions having been not only politically associated from the earliest historical times, but also forming one people both by language and race.'[12]

Commenting on the proposed changes, Jagannath Barua observed, Assam proper will secure only a small fraction of the chief commissioner's attention , his very seat will be removed and the people will have to meet a keen and unequal competition of highly educated, enterprising and advantageously situated districts, for which they are not yet prepared.[13]

However, realising that the government was determined to go ahead with the partition scheme despite countrywide protests, Jagannath Baruah demanded that at least the interests of the Assamese people should be protected and that a certain number of jobs be reserved for them in the newly created province.

Impact of the Sabha: The Sabha contributed significantly to the social and political awakening in Assam and paved the way for democratic and popular movements in the province. While focusing on the particular needs of the province, it had established strong links with pan-Indian aspirations. In fact, many of its members, including Debicharan Barua and Lakshminath Bezbaruah, attended the annual sessions of the Indian National Congress as delegates. Jagannath Baruah died in April 1907. Even during his lifetime a schism had occurred among the members of the organisation and differences of opinion that increased between the members after his death put an end to its activities.

Assam Association

The Assamese intelligentsia, led by Manik Chandra Baruah, one of the leading figures of the time, had increasingly felt the necessity of a more broad-based provincial organisation to communicate the wishes, grievances and aspirations of the Assamese people. The idea took definite form in 1903 when a group of 40 leading personages from Assam gathered in Gauhati to meet Denzil Ibetson, a member of the Viceroy's Executive Council. It was here that the Assam Association was founded along the lines of the Indian Association of Calcutta. It started as a temporary executive committee in which Prabhat Chandra Barua, Jagannath Baruah and Manik Chandra Baruah were president, vice-president and general secretary respectively. They were formally elected to these positions during the first session of the Association held at Dibrugarh in 1905. The headquarters of the Association was at Gauhati but it had several branches in the district and sub-divisional headquarters of the Brahmaputra Valley.

Role of the Association: The Association played a significant role in serving as the mouthpiece of the people of the Brahmaputra Valley during the first two decades of the twentieth century. Like the Jorhat Sarbajanik Sabha, the Assam Association too was extremely critical of the government's scheme to partition Bengal. It feared that the, 'historic name of Assam (would) be obliterated forever, her language (would) suffer'. It also felt that the shift of the seat of government to Dacca would result in 'loss of care and attention' which Assam had so long received from the government.[14] Some of the Association's leading members[15] were also members of the Legislative Council, and were, therefore, able to draw the attention of the government, through their speeches and debates on the floor of the House, to the demands and resolutions of the Association from time to time.

The Association'sAgenda:

- It was critical of the predominance of government officers in the Municipal Committees and of planters in the Local Boards. It demanded democratisation of these self-governing institutions.
- It condemned the excise policy of the government, opposed enhancement of taxes and insisted on the total prohibition of opium.
- The Association was also very concerned about the development of education in the province. It successfully negotiated for the representation of Assam in the Calcutta University Syndicate, the appointment of Assamese teachers in Cotton College, the establishment of an institution of technical education and the proper utilisation of the Williamson Fund which had been created for the establishment and maintenance of artisan schools.[16]

Although the Association had been initially formed to focus on regional issues and to press for regional demands, it gradually merged into India's mainstream politics. Over the years, a greater number of delegates from Assam had started attending the annual Congress sessions and under the leadership of people like Nabin Chandra Bardoloi, Chandranath Sarma, Prasanna Kumar Barua and Tarun Ram Phukan, the organisation became more and more assertive. Eventually it identified itself with the aims and aspirations of the rest of India as shown by the Indian National Congress. This was symbolically reflected in the merger of the Assam Association with the Assam Provincial Congress Committee in 1921.

The Growth of Political Awareness in other Areas

Like the Brahmaputra Valley, the Surma Valley, comprising of the districts of Cachar and Sylhet, was also active politically. Close ties with Bengal had resulted in a strong Bengali influence in the valley and nationalist ideas and sentiments that had filtered into the region over the years had paved the way for the establishment of several public organisations. Most of these were moderate in nature but a few, like the *Suhrid Samiti, Anusilan Samiti and Suhrid Sevak Samiti,* were more radical in their ideas and were often instruments for terrorist activities.

Curzon's plan to partition Bengal evoked spontaneous and widespread protests. The people held public meetings and the press too wrote strong articles opposing the move. The people realised that not only would they be forcibly separated from their kith and kin in Bengal, but that in the new province of Eastern Bengal and Assam, the educated Hindu Bengalis would be overshadowed by the educated Muslim Bengalis from Dhaka, Rajshahi and Mymensingh so far as employment opportunities were concerned. Hence, the call for swadeshi and boycott, spearheaded by the *Cachar Swadeshi Sabha* and the *Sribatta Swadeshi Sevak Samiti,* got enthusiastic response and in no time the *Swadeshi* Movement in the Surma Valley assumed the character of a mass movement. They also increasingly began feeling the need for a more broad-based association that would serve as a common forum for both the districts. The *Sribatta Swadeshi Sevak Samiti,* therefore, decided to organise a conference of political leaders, zamindars, merchants and traders of both the districts to promote the ideas of swadeshi and boycott. Accordingly, the first Surma Valley Political Conference was held in August 1906. The two-day conference, which was presided over by Kamini Kumar Chanda, and addressed by distinguished speakers including Bipin Chandra Pal, was attended by over a thousand people.[17] It resolved to;

- Form the Surma Valley Association to strengthen the swadeshi movement.
- To promote the general welfare of the people by taking practical steps to improve the condition of the masses in matters such as sanitation and agriculture.[18]

Both the Cachar Swadeshi Sabha and the Srihatta Swadeshi Sevak Samiti, merged themselves into the new organisation to facilitate the formation of this Association.

In its second session held at Karimganj in 1908, the objectives of the Association were outlined in more definite terms. It was declared that the political goal of the Association was the attainment of swaraj as put forward by Dadabhai Naoroji. Thereafter, the Association followed the line of the Congress and actively participated in the Swadeshi, *Khilafat* and Non-cooperation movements but significantly it retained its identity in the Surma Valley even after the formation of the District Congress Committees. It was only in 1924 that the Association decided to work as a Congress organisation and passed a formal resolution expressing its confidence in the leadership of Mahatma Gandhi.

Political Awakening

The close of the nineteenth century and the beginning of the next thus saw a new awakening in the province. The common bonds established by the British rule, common sufferings with other fellow Indians, common inspirations from the epics and the shastras, a uniform administrative set up, improved means of communication, the impact of western thoughts and ideas and above all, shared discrimination and frustration at every step, induced the people of the region to look beyond the provincial boundaries and establish a commonality of purpose with mainstream India. The Indian National Congress provided the common forum. Thus, it was in this backdrop that Assamese nationalism merged with mainstream Indian nationalism even while maintaining a distinct Assamese identity.

NOTES AND REFERENCES

1. For an early exposition that all major languages of *Bharat Varsha* originated from Sanskri, and that the merit of learning Sanskrit was that it enabled one to know the religion and customs of the ancient Hindus, see Maheswar Neog, (compiled and re-edited) *Orunodoi*, Guwahati, 1983, 'Ejon Asomiya Lok' (pseud. Gunabhiram Barua), 'Asomiya Bhasha', pp. 1095–6. The pan-Indian tenor could be perceived in another article of Gunabhiram Barua. He described Bengali as a *bideshi* (literally foreign) language and Assam as *amar desh* (literally our country). However, the terms *desh* and *bidesh* were not intended to mean sovereign independent countries. They were used in a loose provincial sense.

2. Jenkins to Grey, 7 December 1854, cited in H. K. Barpujari, *The American Missionaries and North East India*, Delhi 1986, p. 146.
3. For details of the adminstrative systems under the chief commissioners, refer to K. K. Bhattacharjee, *North East India: Political and Administrative History*, New Delhi, 1983, Chapter 7
4. For details, refer to A. Guha, *Planter Raj to Swaraj Freedom Struggle and Electoral Politics in Assam 1826–1947*,New Delhi, 1977, pp. 47–54.
5. Editorial, *The Indian Nation*, Calcutta, 21 April 1894.
6. Although the immigrant labour force of the Brahmaputra Valley taken as a whole in 1901 was 13 per cent, in Lakhimpur District, which had the largest concentration of tea plantations, it was 41 per cent . The trend was similar throughout the industrial belt of Assam.
7. *Census of India*, 1901, Vol. IV, Pt. 2, p. 2.
8. The quantity of rice available per rupee in a few important places in Assam in 1897 was as follows: Gauhati–11 seers; Tezpur–9 seers; Nowgong–8 seers; Sibsagar–10 seers; Dibrugarh–9 seers.
9. For details see Priyam Goswami, *Question of Subletting: Henry Cotton and Public Associations of Assam*, NEIHA Proceedings, Twenty-Second Session, Tezpur, 2001.
10. Chapter 8.
11. Priyam Goswami, *Question of Subletting: Henry Cotton and Public Associations of Assam*, Tezpur, 2001, pp. 256–63.
12. H. K. Barpujari (ed.), *Political History of Assam*, Vol. I, Guwahati (Second edition), 1999, pp. 180–1.
13. H. K. Barpujari (ed.), *The Comprehensive History of Assam*, Vol. V, 1993, Guwahati p. 252.
14. Proceedings of the Assam Association, 14 February 1904, Appendix E.
15. M. C. Baruah, Ghanashyam Baruah, Phanidhar Chaliha, Tarun Ram Phukan, Nabin Chandra Bardoloi, among others.
16. Assam Sectt. Records, Education (A), April 1917, Nos. 1–11.
17. Other distinguished personalities included Sundarimohan Das, Radhabenode Das, Saradacharan Shyam, Kalicharan Pare, Rajkumar Banerjee, Harish Chandras Roy, Idris Ali Choudhury, BankaBehari Das and Mafuz Ali Choudhury.
18. The Weekly Chronicle, 22 April 1908, cited in H. K. Barpujari (ed.), *Political History of Assam* Vol. 1, Guwahati, 1999, p.169.

SUGGESTED READINGS

Barpujari, H. K., Barpujari, *Political History of Assam*, Vol I, Guwahati, 1999.
Bhuyan, A. C., (ed.), *Nationalist Upsurge in Assam*, Guwahati, 2000.
Guha, Amalendu, *Planter-Raj to Swaraj: Freedom Struggle and Electoral Politics in Assam 1826–1947*, New Delhi, 1977.

10

Assam and the National Movement (1905–34)

Chapter Highlights

- Partition of Bengal and the *Swadeshi* Movement
- Response in the Brahmaputra and Surma valleys
- Politics during World War I
- Nature and extent of Non-cooperation Movement – Swarajists – Reaction to Simon Commission
- Nature and extent of Civil Disobedience Movement

Bengal was partitioned on 16 October 1905 despite widespread protests. The new province of Eastern Bengal and Assam, comprising 106,540 square miles, was placed under J. B. Fuller (the Chief Commissioner of Assam) who assumed charge as Lieutenant Governor of the new province at Dacca. He was assisted in his duties by a legislative council consisting of 15 members and a two member board of revenue. Judicial authority rested with the Calcutta High Court. Soon after assuming office, Fuller visited Assam in order to win over the confidence of the people. He assured them that the proposed administrative changes would neither hamper their employment prospects nor affect their privileges, like student scholarships, that had been earmarked for them. Although he conceded that Assam would lose her individuality in the new set up, he believed that the changes would be beneficial[1] to her in the long run.

ANTI-PARTITION AGITATION

These assurances failed to impress the people at large and apart from the tea planters and a section of Muslims in Eastern Bengal and the Surma Valley, Assam responded enthusiastically to the call for agitation against the partition. Protest meetings were held at Tezpur, Barpeta, Dhubri, Gauripur, Gauhati, Goalpara, Dibrugarh, Silchar, Habiganj, Maulvibazar and Karimganj among others. People of all communities attended these meetings and in some places they conducted mass prayers and performed *rakhi bandhan* as symbols of unity and solidarity among the various communities. In most places the people took out massive processions, accompanied by slogans of *Vande Mataram* and the singing of national songs. The movement, which started with meetings and demonstrations, soon took on a broader view with the boycott of foreign goods and educational institutions, use of indigenous commodities and the establishment of national schools. They called for *atma shakti* or self-reliance.

Swadeshi and Boycott

In the Brahmaputra Valley of Assam, however, the anti-partition movement was largely confined to the urban and semi-urban areas, unlike in Bengal where it had penetrated deep into the rural areas as well. The people were asked to use goods produced in the country or swadeshi and boycott foreign made goods. In the towns of Assam, people started using *khaar* instead of salt from Liverpool in England, sugar from Benares instead of foreign sugar and indigenously woven cloth instead of the mill produced cloths of Europe. At a time when religious heads wielded considerable influence on society, the head priest of the Kamakhya temple appealed to the *pandas* and grocers not to purchase or sell foreign items. To fill in the vacuum, indigenous shops, selling swadeshi goods were set up.[1] On an intellectual plane, Ambikagiri Raychoudhury, a poet and nationalist along with Govinda Lahiri, took the lead in instilling the concept of swadeshi in the minds of the students. The swadeshi songs and drama of Mukunda Das, the playwright and lyricist who, along with his troupe, visited Gauhati in 1905, left a strong imprint on the cultural scene of Assam.

By and large, the movement in the Surma Valley was more widespread with the leadership being taken up by the Surma Valley Association. The stirring speeches of Bipin Chandra Pal, a son of the soil, had tremendous impact on the people. National schools which were set up at Sylhet, Habibganj, Srimangal, Baniachang, Lakhai, Karimganj, Silchar and other places became nerve centres for spreading the ideas of swadeshi and boycott.

Government Response

The government was not a silent spectator to these activities. It reacted to the situation harshly.

- It issued the Carlyle and Risly Circulars which ordered the management of educational institutions to make sure that students did not participate in any protest against the government. Disciplinary actions were taken against those teachers and students who defied these orders.
- Meetings and processions were banned and political leaders jailed.
- The press was heavily censored.
- Many agitators were fined, jailed or even deported.

These repressive measures provoked a section of the youth to take to revolutionary activities and inspired by their counterparts in Bengal, they began to set up secret societies in Assam, often as branches of the organisations of Bengal. The *Tarun Sangha, Suhrid Samiti,* and *Arunachal Ashram* were very active in the Surma Valley, while in the Brahmaputra Valley, the Seva Sangha, founded by Ambikagiri Raychoudhury, developed into a terrorist organisation on the lines of the Anusilan Samiti. These organisations, however, were inherently weak and did not command mass support. Organised as small, secret groups, they were moreover, unable to withstand the all-out suppression by the colonial state. But despite their eventual failure, it cannot be denied that they succeeded in unsettling the mind of the government.

Some of the protests took a more formal method. Some of the Assamese settled in Calcutta led by Raja Prabhat Chandra Baruah, president of the Assam Association, submitted a memorandum to the Secretary of State in 1907 deploring the fact that instead of progress and development, partition had resulted in the underdevelopment of Assam. Moreover, Assam was barely represented in the Council. In fact, until the election of Manik Chandra Barua, the general secretary of the Assam Association in 1908, the Brahmaputra Valley had remained unrepresented in the Legislative Council of Eastern Bengal and Assam. The following year Manik Chandra Baruah was joined by Bhuban Ram Das, Prabhat Chandra Baruah and Abdul Majid. Together they fought for the cause of Assam as forcefully as they could in the given circumstances, but were unable to make much impact. Hence, they pleaded for the annulment of the partition.

Morley-Minto Reforms and its Consequences

A change in government in England had brought the Liberals to power. Lord Curzon's successor, Lord Minto, realised that repression alone would not solve the problem. He believed that what was needed was 'a skilful division of the enemy forces and a dexterous combination of ruthlessness and affability'.[2] Minto believed that an effective way of counteracting the growing menace of Indian nationalism was to appease the Muslim community. The government had already lent its support to the Muslim League which was formed in 1906. It now sought to strengthen this policy through the Government of India Act 1909 (also known as the Morley-Minto Reforms). The Act granted:

- Separate electorates to the Muslims and,
- Also additional membership not warranted by their numerical strength.

Map 10.1: India in 1909

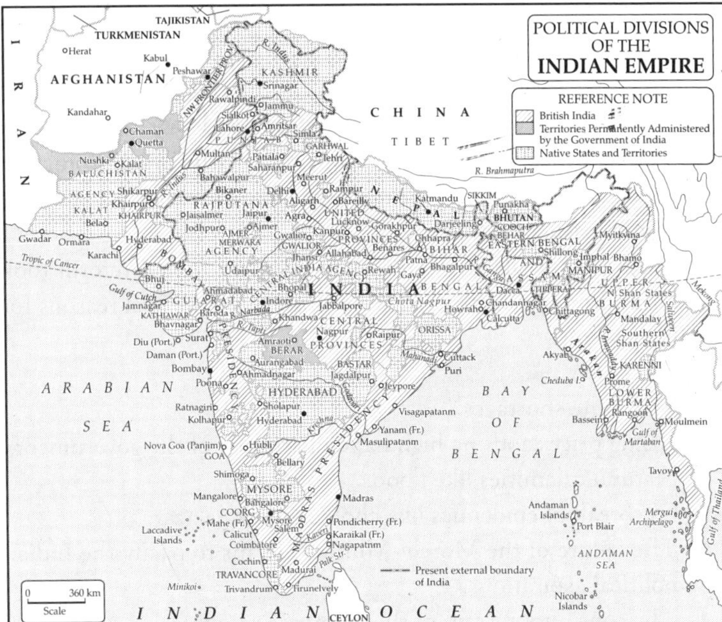

Source: Wikimedia Commons.

The Act failed to resolve the political problems in India. While the Extremists rejected the reforms outright, the Moderates were wary of the dangerous consequences of the government's policy of 'Divide and Rule'. Lord Hardinge, the Viceroy, informed the Secretary of State that 'if there was to be peace in the two Bengals, it was absolutely necessary to do something to remove what was regarded by all Bengalis as an act of flagrant injustice without justification'.[3] He proposed that the province of Eastern Bengal and Assam be reconstituted and that the capital be shifted to Delhi. Accordingly, by a Royal Proclamation at a durbar held at Delhi in December 1911, the partition of Bengal was annulled and Assam, including Cachar, Sylhet, Goalpara and the Hills, reverted to its old status as the chief commissioner's province with a legislative council[4] of its own at Shillong.

The Act of 1909 reduced the Council to the position of a mere advisory body. It was subordinated to the executive and the powers and responsibilities of the members were heavily curtailed. As the nominated members were in the majority, every government decision was easily carried through. The debates and discussions that took place in the House on the working of the self-governing institutions, sanitation, education, grazing taxes, local rates etc., were pointless exercises, because the elected members, being in the minority, were in no position to prevail upon the government to bring about the desired changes. There was therefore a general demand that the Councils should be reformed and enlarged, for as Sita Nath Roy, a prominent nationalist very aptly put it, 'the tax payer, like the man who plays the pipe, should have a voice in the tune'.[5]

With the outbreak of World War I, constitutional reform took a back seat. Popular discontent grew. There were several reasons for this. They were:

- War time shortages.
- Rising prices and the high handed attitude of the government.
- Natural calamities like floods.
- Outbreak of epidemics like cholera and kala azar.
- The failure of the Morely-Minto Reforms to pacify the Indian political aspirations.
- The continuous drain of the country's resources.

Montague-Chelmsford Reforms and its Consequences

In the face of mounting public pressure, the government was compelled to take measures to justify the declaration that they had made earlier to the effect that the basic objectives of the war 'was to make the world safe for democracy' and to ensure the 'liberty, self determination and the development of the people'. E. S. Montague, the secretary of state, visited India to make a personal assessment of the political situation. Along with the Viceroy, Lord Chelmsford, he toured the country and received a large number of delegations. But the Montague-Chelmsford Report that proposed several reforms including the gradual introduction of self-governing institutions, was received with mixed feelings. While one section of the Congress welcomed the proposed reforms, another section rejected them as being far short of their demand for self-government.

Assam and the Montague-Chelmsford Reforms

Assam's position in the context of the Montague-Chelmsford Report was not clear as it did not mention whether it would be included in the reform scheme. The situation was made worse by the chief commissioner of Assam, Beatson Bell, and the European community who opposed the inclusion of Assam as they felt that it could not administer itself.[6] On the other hand, several groups and organisations, like the Surma Valley Mohammedan Association, Ahom Association, *Mahishya Samiti*, Zamindari Association and the Assam Mohammedan Association put forth their sectional claims for representation in case Assam was included in the new reform scheme. The Assam Association staunchly opposed these divisive forces and deputed Nabin Chandra Bardoloi, a lawyer and leading political figure, to present Assam's case to the Parliamentary Committee at Calcutta. The proposed Bill for reforms was introduced in the British Parliament for scrutiny in May 1919. The Indian delegation that went to present their views for consideration included Nabin Chandra Bardoloi and Prassanna Kumar Baruah who represented Assam's case. Although the demand for self-government for India remained unfulfilled, the persistent endeavours of the Assam Association in general and that of the delegation in particular, ultimately resulted in the inclusion of Assam in the reform scheme.

The Swadeshi agitation, the Home Rule Movement, revolutionary activities, contemporary world events and the stirring speeches of national leaders like Gokhale, Tilak and Bipin Chandra Pal, all combined to create a new awareness among the youth. Students in Assam translated this awareness into action by creating a platform for concerted action on matters of regional and national interest. The Assam Students' Conference, founded in 1916, (later renamed as *Assam Chatra Sanmelan*)[7], although not a political association, helped to create a cadre of student leaders like Chandranath Sarma, Omeo Kumar Das, Hem Chandra Barua, Padmadhar Chaliha, Bimala Kanta Barua, Kanak Chandra Barua, among many others, who actively participated in the national movement that followed.

NON-COOPERATION MOVEMENT

The closing years of the second decade of the twentieth century witnessed a highly discontented India. The War had taken a big toll on her economy and people resented having to pay heavily in men and resources for a war that did not concern them directly. While generous war time promises had raised expectations, the results did not match expectations. There were several reasons for the Non-cooperation Movement. Some of them are:

- The Montague-Chelmsford Reforms, announced towards the end of 1919 were disappointing.
- The Indian Muslims had launched the Khilafat Movement to ensure British protection for the Ottoman Empire in Turkey. They were unhappy about the plan to partition the Empire after the end of the World War I.
- The Rowlatt Act of 1919 gave the authorities the right to imprison anyone suspected of terrorism for two years without a trial. This led to widespread protests and national leaders including Gandhi, were extremely critical of it.
- One of the protests against the Act held at the Jallianwala Bagh in Amritsar led to the infamous Jallianwalla Bagh massacre and the imposition of martial law in Punjab.

All these added fuel to the already raging fire. The leaders of the national movement realised that there would be no redressal for their grievances through constitutional means. The Indian National Congress at a special session held at Calcutta in 1920, decided to launch the Non-cooperation Movement under the leadership of Gandhi.

Assam and the Non-cooperation Movement

The Assam Association had been observing the political developments in the rest of the country but for most people the concept of swaraj or self-rule was still vague and incomprehensible. Hence, when the call for non-cooperation was given, one section, led by Ganga Gobinda Barua, Tara Prasad Chaliha, Ghanashyam Barua and Chandradhar Barua, felt that the Assam Association had to maintain its separate identity if they had to fight for local issues with the British. The majority, however, felt the necessity of joining mainstream politics. After considerable debate, the seventeenth session of the Assam Association held at Tezpur in December 1920, endorsed the resolution on non-cooperation which stated that 'the object of the Assam Association is to work for the attainment of swaraj by all legitimate means and to educate the people towards this object'.[8] The Association also decided to follow the directives of the Congress on all matters regarding the movement. This meant that the Assam Association lost its independent identity. The movement in Assam merged with the national one when the Congress decided to constitute provincial committees based on linguistic divisions. Accordingly, Assam, which had till then been a part of the Bengal Congress Committee, was given an independent identity with the formation of the Assam Provincial Congress Committee in June 1921. The jurisdiction of the Committee was limited to the Brahmaputra Valley districts of the province.[9] Kuladhar Chaliha and Nabin Chandra Bardoloi were elected as President and Secretary, respectively. This marked the *de facto* end of the Assam Association and the complete merger of Assam with mainstream Indian politics.

Impact of the Movement on Assam

The Non-cooperation Movement had a tremendous impact on Assam. Gandhi's visit to Assam in August 1921 was a catalyst for arousing public consciousness. Despite official opposition, all the meetings that Gandhi addressed in the major towns of Assam were attended by all sections of society. Pledges in favour of boycott were invariably accompanied by huge bonfires of British goods. Energetic and vocal leaders like Chandranath Sarma, Hemchandra Baruah, Omeo Kumar Das, Triguna Charan Barua and Muhibuddin Ahmed took the lead in organising the youth many of whom boycotted government educational institutions. National schools were set up at Gauhati, Nalbari, Jorhat, Tezpur, Sibsagar, Nowgong, Karimganj, Rajnagar and Maulvibazar. These served not only as study centres but also as publicity and training centres for Congress volunteers. Lawyers like Nabin Chandra Bardoloi, Kuladhar Chaliha, Tarunram Phukan, Kamini Kumar Chanda and Mahendra Chandra Biswas suspended their legal practice and joined active politics. Many lawyers and teachers, along with government officials resigned from their jobs and took up organisational work at various levels. As the agitation gained momentum, panchayats were instituted at the village level to settle local disputes.

Fall in opium consumption: Of the various areas of the constructive programme, the temperance movement and the propagation of khadi were among the most successful in Assam. Significantly, the virtual non-existence of the salt trade during this period was even officially recorded.[10] Opium consumption in Assam had become a cause of great concern because addiction to the drug had reached immense proportions and was consumed irrespective of the price demanded. Gandhi's fervent appeal to the Congress workers 'to make Assam free from opium' had a stirring effect. The vigorous anti-opium drive by Congress workers saw a fall in the consumption of abkari opium from 1615 maunds in 1902–21 to 993 maunds in 1922–3. In 1925, the Assam Opium Enquiry Committee reported that consumption of liquor had fallen by 49.8 per cent, opium by 35.8 per cent and ganja by 24.4 per cent. The decline in terms of revenue was 19 lakh rupees.[11]

Khadi: The concept of khadi was received with equal enthusiasm in Assam where the tradition of spinning and weaving was already strongly entrenched. But since cotton production in the region was limited to individual households, cotton growers, especially in Kamrup and Darrang, were given subsidies by the Congress to encourage production on a large scale.[12] The Assam Khadi Board was established with its headquarters at Jorhat in order to facilitate more effective networking,

Impact on the tea gardens: Congress volunteers had meanwhile, penetrated deep into the tea districts and had been very successful in propagating the messages of swadeshi and non-cooperation. Many former tea garden labourers who had settled down as cultivators often acted as intermediaries between the Congress workers and the labourers. The large population of tea garden labourers found this as an opportunity to express their long felt grievances. Exasperated by the atrocities and ill-treatment meted out to them by the planters, they resorted to sporadic strikes and disturbances. In May 1921, Congress workers organised a protest around 8,000 labourers of thirteen tea gardens of the Chargola and Longai valley of Karimganj subdivision were organised by the Congress workers. Demanding a huge wage increase and accompanied by slogans of '*Gandhi Maharaj Ki Jai*', they resolved to leave the gardens en masse as they were told that it was Gandhi's order. The labourers had heard rumours that under Gandhi-Raj they would be given land in their villages from where they had been lured away with false promises. This sudden exodus of the labourers completely unnerved the planters who pressurised the district administration to use force to bring them back. But the labourers were determined not to return. Hundreds of them lost their lives in the turmoil that followed. While some escaped, the majority were forced back into the gardens. As a mark of protest against the Chargola tragedy, the railway and steamer workers of Assam struck work for six weeks. The continuous spate of strikes, especially in the tea districts throughout 1921–2, caused considerable anxiety to the authorities who had to deal with protests on many fronts.

Women's role in the movement: The induction of women in the movement had created additional problems for them. Gandhi's call to women had an immediate liberating effect and he was able to draw large numbers of women into the struggle. He was aware of women's potential for passive resistance and projected them as symbols of courage, intelligence, perseverance, robust independence and power and not as stereotypes of submission, subservience, self effacement, helplessness and patience. The fact that there was no material weaponry involved in the Gandhian programme, made women equal, or perhaps even better fighters and they participated wholeheartedly in the campaigns, protests, fasts and donated generously to the cause of freedom. As Geraldine Forbes has observed, 'the nature of their work influenced how women saw themselves and how others saw their potential contribution to national development'.[13]

In the beginning, the conservative society in Assam stood in the way of the participation of women in the movement and active participation was limited to a small section of women like Bidyutprova Devi, Girija Devi (sister of Tarun Ram Phukan), Hemanta Kumari Devi,

Dharmada Devi, Nalinibala Devi (wife, sister and daughter respectively of Nabin Chandra Bardoloi), Pushpalata Das, Guneswari Nath and Chandraprova Saikiani, among others. All of them belonged to or had connections with families of Congress leaders. They organised meetings, both in rural and urban areas, to spread the message of non-cooperation, swadeshi and constructive work. But their task was not easy. They often had to confront hostile situations, especially in remote rural areas, but the fact that they persisted despite threats to their lives on several occasions, is testimony to their commitment to the cause.[14]

Gandhi's visit to Assam in 1921 provided the much needed impetus to their work. His appeal went beyond the so-called 'respectable' women to even those women marginalised by middle class society. One of the foremost examples of this was Mongri, who was a labourer in a tea garden. She was also an alcoholic. She was so influenced by Gandhi that she not only gave up drinking but also actively participated in the anti-liquor drive. Mongri died in a clash that occurred during the picketing of liquor shops and was the first woman in Assam to be killed for participation in the Non-cooperation Movement. In Godebori, a remote village in Kamrup district, Bhanumati Talukdar, a mother of three children, enrolled herself as a full time worker of the Congress. Referred to as *Volunteerani bai* by the local people, Gandhi called her the Sarojini of Assam. Pramila Medak, of the Mising community of Golaghat, remained an active worker despite being excommunicated by her community for defying social restrictions and joining the Movement.[15] Mongri, Bhanumati and Pramila are just three examples. There were hundreds of others like them who came out in large numbers in support of the Movement and in course of time became an integral part of the struggle for independence. While many participated directly in the form of joining protest processions, attending meetings, taking up spinning and weaving, propagating the use of khadi and the *charkha* and boycotting foreign goods, others contributed indirectly by supporting the male members of the family and shouldering their responsibilities while the men actively participated in the struggle.

Visit by the Prince of Wales

While the Non-cooperation Movement had spread like wildfire, the Prince of Wales decided to visit India despite the opposition of the Congress. The Congress had earlier affirmed that '...it is the duty of everyone to refrain from participating in or assisting any welcome to his Royal Highness or any function organised officially or otherwise in connection with the visit'.[16] Like the rest of India, Assam also organised *hartals*, meetings and other forms of demonstrations on 17 November 1921 as a mark of protest. The Congress then decided to launch the second phase of the Movement by paralysing the civil administration. In Assam, they formed the Assam National Volunteer Corps, comprising around 70,000 enthusiastic youth who pledged to work for the movement through non-violent means. The party also launched a vigorous no-tax campaign and anti-liquor drive and official records show that during 1921–2 excise revenue as well as land revenue fell drastically.

Government Response

Initially, the government had refrained from taking any action because it felt that repression would only fan the spirit of revolt and make martyrs of the nationalists. But as the movement progressed, the authorities realised that they needed to change their policy and they could no longer remain silent spectators. The Government of India was also under tremendous pressure from the provincial governments to take action. The boycott of the Prince of Wales, moreover, had been extremely humiliating and had affected the prestige of the government. In the circumstances, the Viceroy, Lord Reading, came up with a three-pronged policy to tackle the situation.

1. First, to try to win over some influential leaders by showering favours and honours on them.
2. Second, to suppress the movement using force.
3. Third, to break up the unity of the people by exploiting communal differences.

At a time when the commitment of the people to the cause of swaraj was so strong, it was futile to expect many to be tempted with titles and favours. In any case, the movement had become too deep rooted and widespread to be affected by a minority leaving it. It was apparent that repression alone was the most effective measure. The authorities made use of several measures. They:

- Made extensive use of the Indian Criminal Law Amendment Act (1908) and the Prevention of Seditious Meetings Act (1911) to arrest and imprison leaders and workers, to beat up crowds for gathering together at meetings and to arrest volunteers engaged in picketing schools, colleges, and shops selling foreign cloths and liquor.

- The Volunteer Corps was declared illegal and all the members were promptly arrested.
- The army was deployed to ensure collection of punitive taxes that were imposed at many places.
- The Press Act (1920) ensured a virtual censorship of the print media. Several pamphlets like *Swaraj* by Purnakanta Gogoi and *Mahatma Gandhir Kabita* by Chandranath Das were banned while defamation cases were lodged against those papers who defied the government directives in any way.
- The jails in Assam were swiftly filled up with more than 4,000 political prisoners.
- The government had to set up prison camps to accommodate more prisoners. Once a place of fear and humiliation, the jail now turned into a place of pride.

Despite the ban on civil liberties and large-scale arrests, the movement gained in strength and momentum.

However, Gandhi's decision to withdraw the movement abruptly following the Chauri Chaura incident in 1922[17] came as a rude shock to most people. Gandhi's promise in 1920 of swaraj within a year had aroused soaring expectations and people now felt let down. Like many other nationalists, Chandranath Sarma, who had led the movement in Assam, regretted Gandhi's decision and believed that the political movement should continue till the goal of swaraj was reached. But the majority decided to abide by Gandhi's decision. The AICC Working Committee which met at Bardoli endorsed Gandhi's decision and agreed to suspend the programme of civil disobedience and concentrate instead on constructive programmes.[18] For Gandhi, the end of the Non-cooperation Movement was not the end of the struggle. It had just begun.

THE SWARAJISTS

The withdrawal of the Non-cooperation Movement was followed by Gandhi's arrest, followed by his conviction and imprisonment for six years on the charge of spreading disaffection against the government.

This resulted in demoralisation in the nationalist ranks. Many even questioned the wisdom of the Gandhian strategy. In order to keep the political spirit alive, a new line of political activity was suggested by C. R. Das and Motilal Nehru, both towering national leaders. They proposed to end the boycott of the legislative councils and instead asked members to obstruct all work of the councils from within. After considerable debate, Das and Nehru announced the formation of the Swaraj Party on 1 January 1923. Apart from the question of council entry, the Swarajists accepted all the other aspects of the Congress programme. Their idea was to stall the functioning of the colonial administration by wreaking the councils from within by creating deadlocks on every issue. They believed that work in the councils was essential in order to fill the temporary political void and to keep up the morale of the people. Their opponents, however, felt that rural reconstruction was the only form of political activity that ought to be pursued during the movement's non-active phases.

The Swaraj Party in Assam

The situation in Assam was a reflection of the general state of affairs in the country. A branch of the Swaraj party was formed with Tarun Ram Phukan as President, Rohini Kumar Choudhury as Secretary and Gopinath Bardoloi as Assistant Secretary. Others like Nabin Chandra Bardoloi and Kuladhar Chaliha believed that the priority should be trying to revitalise the Congress by working at the grassroot level, on intensifying politicisation and on keeping up the recruitment, training and morale of the cadres.

It did seem like the Congress was heading for a split. But with the split of 1907 between the Extremists and Moderates still fresh in their minds, both groups realised the necessity for unity within the nationalist ranks. They were also aware that the real force that would compel the government to concede to nationalist demands lay in a mass movement. Moreover, there was also recognition of the central role played by Gandhi's leadership. Hence, at a special session of the Congress held at Delhi in 1923, it was decided to accommodate the Swarajists by allowing Congressmen to contest the elections to the legislative councils.

Swarajists in the Legislative Councils

Elections to the legislative council were held in November 1923 in Assam. The Swarajya Party contested almost all the seats but it failed to secure a majority. Hence, it decided to collaborate with the independent councillors to form a solid opposition to the government. The Assam Nationalist Party which was subsequently set up, elected Faiznur Ali, Brojendranarayan Choudhury and Kamakhyaram Barua as Leader, Deputy Leader and Secretary, respectively. With remarkable determination, grit, discipline and cohesion, the councillors intervened on every issue and often outvoted the government. They raised important issues like:

- The abolition of the unpopular grazing tax.
- The prohibition of opium.
- The reduction of land revenue.
- Restriction of migrants from East Bengal.

Most of the proposals, however, could not be passed because they were in no position to prevail upon the government to bring about the desired changes. Nevertheless, they were successful in keeping alive the spirit of nationalism.

Congress Party's Work among the People

While the Swarajists carried out their struggle in the council, the Congress workers worked at the grassroots levels on rural reconstruction with emphasis on the promotion of khadi, national education, communal harmony, boycott of foreign cloths and anti-liquor and anti-opium propagation. Ambikagiri Raychoudhury founded the *Sangrakshini Sabha* through which he voiced the demands of the Assamese people within the framework of the larger Congress demands. Swaraj, for him, meant religious, cultural and linguistic freedom for all regions in India and the demolition of all vested interests that ran counter to the interests of the Assamese people. Ambikagiri's ideology attracted many leading public figures like Padmanath Gohain Barua and Nilmoni Phukan. Several ryot sabhas also sprang up in different parts of the province during this period. All these served as major channels for the recruitment of the youth into the Congress.

The 41st annual session of the Congress was held at Pandu, at the foot of the Kamakhya Hills in December 1926. It was a tremendous morale booster for the people of Assam. Gandhi's participation was an additional incentive. The township that was erected to accommodate all the delegates was built with bamboo and mud and adorned with *khadi*. It won widespread admiration. One of the most important events for Assam was the election of Tarun Ram Phukan as a member of the All India Congress Working Committee for the term 1926–27. Commenting on this session, Gandhi wrote:

> I felt that Assam was too far away, too unorganised and too poor to shoulder the heavy burden of holding a Congress session. Gauhati has a population of only 16,000. No place with such a small population... had the temerity to invite the Congress. Gauhati, however, beat all previous records, and in an incredibly short space of time erected, in the midst of surroundings of great natural beauty on the banks of the great Brahmaputra, a city under *khadi* canvas.[19]

Assam's prestige had risen in the eyes of the rest of the country. The session, however, had involved a lot of expenditure, the brunt of which was felt by the AICC for years to come. Nevertheless, the enthusiastic involvement of all sections of society in the session, including large numbers of youth and women, had clearly demonstrated the popularity of the Congress and faith in Gandhi's leadership. Gandhi believed that the country was almost ready for the next phase of active struggle.

THE SIMON COMMISSION

The opportunity to rejuvenate the Congress presented itself in the form of the all-white Simon Commission appointed in 1927 to review the working of the Government of India Act of 1919 and to recommend whether India was ready for further constitutional reform. The immediate reaction to this announcement in India was one of profound resentment and indignation. The Indians felt humiliated that the British government did not consider any Indian fit enough to be included in the Commission that was appointed to decide on the political future of the country. Cutting across party and organisational affiliations, a call was given to boycott the Commission. The Indian National Congress turned the call for boycott into a popular movement.

Protests against the Commission in Assam

In Assam, the first manifestation of public anger was expressed at a public meeting at Sylhet in November 1927. Subsequently, a meeting at Jorhat not only condemned the Commission but also suggested the appointment of a parallel commission comprising of Indians. The Muslims, however, were divided on the issue. The *Anjuman-i-Islamia* decided to welcome the Commission while the pro-Jinnah faction, led by Abdul Matin Choudhury, called upon both Hindus and Muslims to make the boycott a success. In Assam too most of the towns observed hartal on 3 February 1928, the day the Simon Commission reached India. But despite vigorous protests, the Commission set about its work of visiting different provinces. The visit to Assam was scheduled for January 1929 and in preparation for the visit the government constituted a seven member committee of the Assam Legislative Council 'for the purpose of cooperating with the Statutory Commission'.[20] This proposal met with strong protests from most quarters.

The movement for the boycott of the Simon Commission provided a taste of political action to a new generation of youth who dominated urban demonstrations. In fact, the Assam Chatra Sammelan, which had remained non-political till then, made political resolutions for the first time in 1928. The government looked upon this with grave disfavour and Small, the European Director of Public Instruction, warned the students' body that any discussion on politics in its forums would result in the suspension of all government help and sympathy in future.[21] In spite of these warnings, student participation in the anti-Commission movements continued, thereby, paving the way for a greater involvement of students and youth in the political activities that followed in the subsequent years.

Lahore Session of the Congress—1929

The failure of the British government to accept the demand for full 'Dominion Status' for India by 31 December 1929, and the Congress resolution that it would not only adopt *Poorna Swaraj* or 'complete independence' as its goal but also launch a civil disobedience movement to attain that goal, raised popular expectations to new heights. The Congress met at Lahore in December 1929 amidst mounting political tension. At midnight on 30 December 1929, the Indian tricolour was raised for the first time with a pledge to fight until the attainment of Poorna Swaraj. The Congress further resolved to completely boycott the Central as well as all Provincial Legislatures and called upon all Congressmen, including the Swarajists, to resign their seats and refrain from participating in elections in the future. Twenty-sixth January was declared as Independence Day and a pledge was to be taken denouncing the British who had 'ruined India economically, politically, culturally and spiritually', asserting that it was 'a crime against man and God' to submit any longer to such a rule and to 'prepare for civil disobedience including non-payment of taxes'.[22]

Impact of Lahore Session on Assam

The Congress decision to boycott the Legislative Councils was received with mixed feelings among the leaders in Assam. Tarun Ram Phukan, Gopinath Bardoloi and R. K. Choudhury were initially hesitant to implement the Congress directive for they felt that the time was not opportune for such a drastic policy. Instead, they believed that the presence of a strong opposition in the Council was necessary to stall the government's repressive measures especially in the context of the decision to fight for Poorna Swaraj. The decision to celebrate 26 January 1930 as the first Independence Day, however, was spontaneous throughout the province. After deliberations with senior colleagues, Phukan resigned from the Central Legislative Council, along with 14 others who resigned from the Assam Legislative Council. Subsequently, however, he resigned from the AICC as well and together with Bardoloi and Choudhury, formed a new party called the Assam Swaraj Party and decided to contest the elections. In the absence of the main leaders, the Congress in Assam was directionless and was overcome by feelings of despondency and frustration on the eve of the Civil Disobedience Movement.

CIVIL DISOBEDIENCE MOVEMENT

Gandhi's 11 point ultimatum of 31 January 1930 to the Viceroy, Lord Irwin, had been ignored and this set the stage for the next phase of the struggle. The Working Committee of the Congress Party that met in February invested Gandhi with full powers to launch the Civil Disobedience Movement. Gandhi had already made up his mind that he would take up an issue that even the poorest could identify themselves with and link it to the ideal of swaraj. Explaining his decision to make salt tax the central issue, he stated: 'There is no article like salt outside water by taxing which the State can reach even the starving millions, the sick, the maimed, and the utterly helpless. The tax constitutes therefore the most inhuman poll tax the ingenuity of man can devise.'[23] To many sceptics, the choice of salt appeared somewhat eccentric when it was first announced. But subsequent events proved otherwise and even Irwin was constrained to admit later that Gandhi had 'planned a fine strategy around the issue of salt'.

Dandi March

Gandhi's Dandi March (12 March–6 April 1930) from Sabarmati Ashram near Ahmedabad to Dandi, a village on the coast attracted enormous publicity within the country and even abroad. The Congress in the meanwhile sent guidelines to all the provincial committees to hasten preparations for the Civil Disobedience Movement. The call for salt *satyagraha* came along with a call to boycott foreign cloth and liquor and the authorisation of a 'free hand' in political activities subject to pledges of non-violence and truth. Salt was thus just the catalyst for the wave of struggle that followed.

The Movement in Assam

The people of Assam also responded to Gandhi's call and were ready to launch the campaign. But at this critical juncture, the Congress leadership in the province announced, to the utter disappointment of the people, that Assam was not ready for a mass movement. The most serious handicap was the absence of an effective leadership. Tarun Ram Phukan was hostile to Civil Disobedience while R. K. Choudhury and Nabin Chandra Bardoloi were unenthusiastic. The Congress Party in Assam seemed rudderless. There were indeed many committed workers like Bishnuram Medhi, Hem Chandra Baruah, Siddhinath Sarma, Mohammedd Tayebullah and Ambikagiri Raychoudhury; but apart from being directionless, they had to face the additional challenge of carrying out organisational work amidst extreme financial constraints. The Congress session at Gauhati in 1926 had involved a huge expenditure and the Party had been reeling under debt since then. They could not even train volunteers in adequate numbers as they did not have adequate funds. There were initial problems in implementing the national programme as well. As there were no salt brines in the province, the salt law could not be violated. Even the non-payment of the *chowkidari* tax was applicable only in the Goalpara district. The government was jubilant and proudly commented on the 'peaceful situation' in the province.

Revival of the Congress Party and the Movement in Assam

At a time when the entire country was in flames, it was not easy to restrain the Assamese who refused to remain on the sidelines. In the circumstances, the immediate tasks at hand were to reorganise and rejuvenate the Congress in Assam as quickly as possible. At this crucial hour Bishnuram Medhi who had been the joint-secretary of the reception committee of the Indian National Congress session in 1926, came forward to take charge as president. The new Working Committee included members like Siddhinath Sarma, Mohammed Tayebullah and Ambikagiri Roy Choudhury. The new leadership took several steps to revitalise the party.

- They formed committees and sub-committees to look into various aspects of the Movement under the leadership of persons like Harekrishna Das, Debeswar Sarma, Bhubaneswar Baruah, Omeo Kumar Das, Harendra Chandra Chowdhury, Rajanikanta Goswami and Rajendra Nath Baruah.
- They created five Congress circles at Gauhati, Chaygaon, Nalbari, Tihu and Rangia to facilitate the implementation of the programmes.
- Their focus was fund raising, defiance of repressive laws and ordinances, boycott of British goods and vigorous anti-opium/anti-liquor drives.
- Bishnuram Medhi and Hem Chandra Baruah toured the province extensively addressing public meetings at numerous places.
- They made earnest attempts to revitalise the ryot sabhas, especially in the districts of Kamrup, Nowgong and Darrang in the Brahmaputra Valley to involve the rural peasantry in the struggle.
- In Sylhet, Congress workers led by Harendra Choudhury agitated for the abolition of the zamindari system. They also formed a District Peasants' and Ryots' Conference.

Student participation

Young leaders like Omeo Kumar Das and Hem Chandra Baruah appealed to the students to get involved in the movement but as most of the educational institutions were closed and the students away on vacation, they were unable to make much headway. Apart from a hartal to protest against Gandhi's arrest, there was little political activity. But the situation changed when J. R. Cunningham, the Director of Public Instruction, issued a circular on May 1930 requiring students and their parents or guardians to give a written undertaking guaranteeing that their wards would refrain from participating in any kind of political activity. He thought that the hartal was the beginning of political agitation by the youth. The circular declared that the punishment for participation in strikes, hartals, or other demonstrations of a political nature, or the defiance of the school authorities would result in the imposition of fines and the loss of privileges like scholarships and hostel seats. Those found guilty of greater crimes would be expelled. It provoked sharp reactions in both the Brahmaputra and Surma Valleys and students refused to be humiliated by such a diktat. The dormant fire now burst into flames.

The Assam Chatra Sanmelan held a special session at Gauhati to evolve a new programme of action. They decided to picket government institutions and according to official records, 3,117 of 15,186 students left their institutions between July and August 1930. [24] Picketing was soon extended to liquor and opium shops as well. The students were supported by peasants who demanded a 50 per cent reduction in land revenue, thus lending the agitation the colour of a mass movement.

Inspired by the activities of the students and the stirring speeches of their leaders, the Congress committees in each of the districts saw no reason to hold back any longer and plunged headlong into the movement. Forest laws were violated in certain areas in Chapapur and Bijni and demonstrations and public meetings held in defiance of government orders. Similar student unrest occurred in the Surma Valley as well. During July and August several government institutions like the Jogendrakishore High School at Habiganj, Government High School at Maulvi Bazar and the Girishchandra High School at Sylhet were razed to the ground.[25] They also launched campaigns for non-payment of the chowkidari tax in Sylhet district. The Cunningham Circular had indeed sparked off the Civil Disobedience Movement in Assam.

Participation of Women

In 1930, Pushpalata Das, a young *satyagrahi* who had joined the *Banar Sena* to propagate khadi at the age of six, along with Sarla Saxena,

Punyaprava Barua and Jyotsna Majumdar, organised the Mukti Sangha to mobilise girls in the national movement. Their fiery speeches electrified young minds who pledged to fight for Poorna Swaraj. The rapidly increasing membership and the activities of the Sangha, caused grave concern to the government and Pushpalata, who was then the Union Secretary, Panbazar Girls' High School, was expelled from the institution. The government agreed to reinstate her on condition that her mother signed a bond guaranteeing her 'good behaviour'. Swarnalata, Pushpalata's mother, refused to give this undertaking. The support of her family emboldened her further and rather than defusing her spirit, the incident ignited the spark in Pushpalata's into a flame.[26] Inspired by her courage and commitment to the cause, several student committees started imparting training in martial arts for girls in order 'to meet exigencies' in the ensuing Civil Disobedience Movement[27].

With a large number of men behind the bars, women came out in thousands defying prohibitory orders to demonstrate their solidarity with the programme of the Salt Satyagraha. Women's power had been strengthened by the organisational activities carried out during the years before of the movement and the formation of the mahila samities. The main thrust of their activity during this period was their anti-opium campaign, which gained momentum as the days passed. The Assam Pradesh Congress Committee (APCC) Report of 1930 records with appreciation the tremendous participation of rural women, along with their urban counterparts, during this phase of the Movement.

Government Response to the Movement in Assam

The government's attitude was initially ambivalent. It had underestimated the strength of the Gandhian programme and had hoped that it would fizzle out. The decision to arrest Gandhi itself had come after much wavering. But once the movement gained momentum, especially after Gandhi's arrest, the government responded with a heavy hand.

- They issued ordinances curbing the civil liberties of the people and provincial governments were given the freedom to ban the Civil Disobedience organisations.
- The government put pressure on the civil authorities at Gauhati to arrest and convict picketers because the authorities felt that

any show of weakness there was bound to have repercussions throughout the Assam Valley.

- They banned the Working Committee of the APCC, the District Congress Committees of Dibrugarh and Barpeta and the Assam Youth League in Kamrup district on the ground that they had 'used as their agents school boys and youth'[28]in August 1930.
- Those arrested under the Criminal Law Amendment Act were subjected to inhuman torture and hundreds of people languished in jail.

Despite these stringent measures, Congress activity continued with many leaders going underground. The ruthless oppression failed to deter others who were determined to paralyse the administrative machinery through continuous boycott and defiance of government ordinances. Several national schools were set up with public contributions at different places in the province[29] in order to accommodate those students who had left government institutions.

THE ROUND TABLE CONFERENCES

The publication of the Simon Commission's report in 1930, which contained no mention of Dominion Status, added fuel to the fire. The Viceroy Lord Irwin, however, reiterated the goal of Dominion Status and suggested a Round Table Conference. The First Round Table Conference, held at London in November 1930, was attended by a handful of Indians who in no way represented the majority in the sub-continent.[30] It was clear that any talk of constitutional advance without the Congress was an entirely futile exercise. As a conciliatory gesture, therefore, the Viceroy released Gandhi and other members of the Congress Working Committee from jail.

The Gandhi-Irwin Pact

The Gandhi-Irwin Pact that was signed in May 1931[31] has been variously described as a 'truce' and a 'provisional settlement'. Gandhi's critics have accused him of 'having tea with treason' especially because he was unsuccessful in getting the death sentences of Bhagat Singh, Rajguru and Sukhdev commuted. But Gandhi was aware of the limitations of mass movements and knew that he could not stretch it too far. The Pact had several salient points like:

1. Gandhi agreed to call off the Civil Disobedience Movement and assured the participation of the Congress in the next Round Table Conference.
2. The government agreed to release all political prisoners not convicted for violence.
3. To return all confiscated land that had not been sold off to other parties.
4. To remit all fines not yet collected.
5. To treat leniently those government employees who had resigned.
6. To concede the right of peaceful picketing.
7. To allow the manufacture of salt on the sea coast by people for their personal consumption.

Reaction to the Pact in Assam

In Assam, the Pact was received with mixed reactions. The radical nationalists believed that amnesty was meaningless if it was not granted to all, including the revolutionaries, but others were more realistic. They realised that the very fact that the British government had signed a pact with Gandhi as an equal was a reflection of the strength of the masses and the recognition of Gandhi as a leader. They felt the need for space was necessary to recuperate, consolidate and gather strength for the next round of the struggle. The Congressmen in Assam therefore, devoted their energies to invigorate the Party and to work at the grassroot level to politicise all social groups when they were released from jail.

Second Round Table Conference and its Repercussions

Gandhi attended the Second Round Table Congress in September 1931 as the sole representative of the Congress. The general attitude in England was one of pessimism. The imperialist financial and political forces opposed any political and economic concessions which would lead to the loosening of their control on India. Winston Churchill strongly objected to the British government's decision to negotiate on equal terms with a 'seditious fakir' and demanded instead a strong government in India. Given this background, it is not surprising that the British government refused to concede to the Indian demand for swaraj. Gandhi returned home empty handed to a charged political atmosphere.

The British had arrested Jawaharlal Nehru and Khan Abdul Ghaffar Khan and implemented repressive measures in many parts of the country. Gandhi stated that this was contrary to the spirit of the Pact, and requested an interview with the Viceroy, Lord Willingdon. But the request was rudely turned down, leaving the Congress with no option but to resume the Civil Disobedience Movement. The government retaliated with a series of ordinances[32] giving the authorities unlimited powers and curbing the civil liberties of the people. The Congress and its allied organisations were declared illegal. Within the first week of the second wave of the Movement, most of the Congress leaders were in jail.

As in other provinces, in Assam too the popular response to the repressive measures was massive. The ordinances were defied openly and people successfully participated in the picketing, boycott and swadeshi programmes in Gauhati, Tezpur, Dhubri, Mangaldai, Nowgong, Goalpara and Badarpur. The people also campaigned for the non-payment of the chowkidari tax all over Goalpara, and a no-revenue campaign in many areas. The government unleashed a virtual reign of terror. Picketers and those who took part in the processions were beaten, awarded rigorous sentences and their property confiscated. The press was also heavily censored. Armed with liberal licenses, the police committed innumerable atrocities. Excesses continued even within the jails where women and children too were subjected to strenuous labour. Though they had to face brutal repression, the satyagrahis persevered till Gandhi decided to withdraw it in April 1934.

The Communal Award of 1932

The British government announced certain constitutional changes in the form of the Communal Award in 1932. This Award allocated seats to various communities in the central and provincial legislatures on the assumption that India was not a nation but an assortment of diverse racial, religious and cultural groups each with their own castes and other vested interests. They incorporated an Additional Explanatory Memorandum for Assam where reservations were made for a number of categories.[33] Gandhi, then in jail, undertook a fast to secure a modification of the Communal Award so as to keep the depressed classes, to whom a separate electorate had been conceded in the Award, within the Hindu fold. The result was the Poona Pact between Gandhi and Ambedkar, the leader of the depressed classes, in 1932.[34] Gandhi gave up all other preoccupations and carried out an extensive campaign against untouchability for nearly two years. His visit to Assam in 1934 in this connection provided the much needed impetus to the constructive programme which filled a vacuum at a time when political activity was negligible.

Within the Congress, the Congress Nationalist Party was established by Pandit Madan Mohan Malaviya and a few others with the objective of entering the Councils and obstructing them from within. Tarun Ram Phukan and R. K. Choudhury joined this party. Elections to the Central Legislative Assembly were held in 1934. Of the 75 elected seats for Indians, the Congress captured 45. Nabin Chandra Bardoloi and Basanta Kumar Das, both official Congress candidates from Assam, won sweeping victories demonstrating once again people's faith in the Congress leadership.

The government had successfully suppressed the Civil Disobedience Movement and hoped to throw the Congress organisation into confusion. They hailed with satisfaction all internal disputes within the Congress as indicated by the emergence of the Congress Nationalist Party and the Congress Socialist Party. The fond hopes of the government, however, were soon shattered. Despite differences of opinion, everyone realised that in the anti-imperialist struggle, unity around the Congress was indispensable. Certain changes in the Congress constitution and the reorganisation of its Executive Committee, the inauguration of the All India Industries Association and Gandhi's resignation from the Congress to enable him 'to serve it better in thought, word and deed' raised new fears in the mind of the colonial government. It realised that a resurgence of another powerful mass movement was perhaps just a matter of time. At this stage therefore, it was essential for it to prevent the nationalist movement from gathering force and consolidating itself in rural areas. More importantly, Gandhi's attempts to build up the tempo for another protracted mass movement had to be thwarted by all means. Hence, conforming to the carrot and stick policy, the colonial government decided on another dose of constitutional reforms in the form of the Government of India Act 1935, details of which will be discussed in the following chapter.

NOTES AND REFERENCES

1. In Gauhati there were four such enterprises which functioned very successfully. They were, Munshi Taibali, B. N. Dey & Company, Brajanath Pandit and the Assam Valley Trading Company.
2. H. K. Barpujari (ed.), *Political History of Assam*, Vol I, Guwahati, 1999, p. 199.
3. Tarachand, *History of the Freedom Movement in India*, Vol III, Delhi, 1972, p. 434.
4. In the newly reconstituted Council of 25 members, the government was in the majority with 14 nominated members, including the chief commissioner as ex-officio President. There were 11 elected members.
5. H. K. Barpujari (ed.), *Political History of Assam*, p. 211.
6. Ibid., pp. 217–18.
7. For a historical background of the Assam Chatra Sanmelan *refer to* Shiela Bora, *Student Revolution in Assam, 1917–47 (A Historical Survey)*, New Delhi, 1992, Chapter 1.
8. A. C. Bhuyan, S. De (eds.), *Political History of Assam*, Vol II, Guwahati , 1999, p. 14.
9. The Surma Valley districts remained under the Bengal Congress Committee.
10. *Report on the Administration of Assam for the year 1921–22*, para 26.
11. Report of the Assam 0pium Enquiry Committee, Shillong, 1925.
12. In 1921, the AICC gave 25,000 rupees to the Assam Congress for the *khadi* programme. A. C. Bhuyan, S. De (eds), *Political History of Assam*, p. 219.
13. Geraldine Forbes, *Women in Modern India*, Cambridge, (Reprint), p. 122.
14. Dipti Sharma, *Assamese Women in the Freedom Struggle*, Calcutta 1993, p. 66.
15. Ibid.
16. R. C. Majumdar, *History of the Freedom Movement in India*, Vol. III, Calcutta, 1963, pp. 125–6.
17. Congress volunteers were fired at by the police at Chauri Chaura in Gorakhpur district in UP. In retaliation, an infuriated mob set fire to the police station and killed 21 policemen. This incident shocked Gandhi and he immediately suspended the Non-cooperation Movement.
18. Gandhi had definite ideas about socio-economic reforms or ameliorative activities which he characterised as the constructive programme. For him this was as important as the political campaigns. The list of his constructive programmes included eighteen items of which the most important were Hindu-Muslim unity, removal of untouchability, temple entry, *swadeshi* and boycott and prohibition of liquor/opium.
19. *Young India*, 6 January, 1927, cited in A. C. Bhuyan, S. De (eds), *Political History of Assam*, p. 114.
20. *Assam Legislative Council Proceedings*, Vol VIII, 3 April 1928, p. 260. W. D. Smiles was the Chairman while Arjan Ali Majumdar, Mukundanarayan Baruah, Keramat Ali, Sadananda Dowerah, Munawwar Ali and Amarnath Ray were members of the committee.
21. For details, refer to Shiela Bora, 'Role of Students in the Nationalist Upsurge' in A. Bhuyan (ed.) *Nationalist Upsurge in Assam*, Guwahati , 2000.

22. D. G. Tendulkar, *Mahatma, Life of Mohandas Karamchand Gandhi*, New Delhi, 1969 reprint, Vol III, pp. 8–9.
23. Cited in Bipan Chandra, *India's Struggle for Independence*, New Delhi, 1989, p. 270.
24. *Assam Legislative Council Proceedings*, 8 September 1930, Vol X, p. 730.
25. *National Archives of India*, Home Pol. File Nos. 14/13/1931; 18-8 F. R. first half of July 1930; 18-9, F. R., first half of August 1930.
26. Dipti Sharma, *Assamese Women in the Freedom Struggle*, p. 136.
27. *Asomiya*, 10 May 1931, cited in Dipti Sharma, *Assamese Women in the Freedom Struggle*, p. 147.
28. *Assam Sectt. Records*, Home (Pol), File No. 254/11 of 1930.
29. Among others, Kamrup Academy in Gauhati, Barpeta Vidyapith, Tezpur Academy, Sibsagar Vidyapith , High Schools at Dibrugarh ,Karimganj, Silchar and national schools at Habiganj and Maulavi Bazar.
30. Assam was represented by Chandradhar Baruah, but he appears to have made no impact at all at the conference.
31. The fact that the Pact, (signed by Gandhi on behalf of the Congress and Irwin on behalf of the Government) placed Gandhi on an equal footing with the government was disliked by most officials.
32. Emergency Powers Act, Unlawful Association Act, Unlawful Instigation Act, Molestation and Boycotting Act.
33. The allocation of seats were as follows: Non-Muhammedan–46; Muhammedan–34; Khasi and Jayantiya Hills–2; Garo Hills–2; Mikir Hills–1; Backward Plains Tribes–4; Depressed Classes (Surma Valley)–3; Depressed Classes (Brahmaputra Valley)–1; Planting Community (European)–8; Planting Community (Indian)–2; Commerce and Industry (Indian)–1; Labour (Tea Garden areas)–4. **Total 108 seats.**
34. According to this Agreement, the idea of separate electorates for the Depressed Classes was given up but the seats reserved for them in the provincial legislatures were increased from 71 in the Award to 147 and in the Central Legislature to 18 per cent of the total.

SUGGESTED READINGS

Bora, Shiela, *Student Revolution in Assam, 1917–47(A Historical Survey)*, New Delhi, 1992.

Bhuyan, C., (ed.), *Nationalist Upsurge in Assam* , Guwahati , 2000.

———, and S. De (eds), *Political History of Assam*, Vol II, Guwahati, 1999.

Geraldine Forbes, *Women in Modern India*, Cambridge, (Third reprint), 2004.

11

Struggle for Independence (1935–47)

Chapter Highlights

- Saadullah's coalition ministry
- Congress coalition ministry
- Saadullah's second ministry
- Governor's rule
- Quit India Movement and Assam
- Second Bardoloi ministry
- Cabinet Mission Plan
- Formation of Interim Government
- Mountbatten Plan
- Partition and Independence

In August 1935, the British Parliament passed the Government of India Act 1935. It was the culmination of the process that started with the appointment of the Simon Commission in 1928. The salient features of the Act were:

- The Act provided for the establishment of an all India federation based on the union of the British Indian provinces and the princely states.
- The franchise was restricted to around one-sixth of the adults.
- While representatives from the provinces were to be elected, those from the princely states were to be nominated by the respective rulers. It was believed that the nominated members could be used to counter the nationalists.
- Defence and Foreign Affairs remained directly under the control of the viceroy and the powers of the elected ministers were limited.
- Provincial autonomy was granted in theory but in practice, the governors of the provinces, appointed by the British govern-

ment, wielded immense authority. They could veto legislative and administrative measures and could even takeover the administration of a province if deemed necessary. The ministers could give advice but their views could be rejected.

Thus, for all practical purposes, political and economic authority remained in British hands. It was further hoped that provincial autonomy would gradually produce strong provincial leaders and that in course of time the authority of the central leadership would be at least weakened if not destroyed.

The Congress Party rejected the Act completely. It instead, demanded the formation of a constituent assembly, elected on the basis of adult franchise, to frame a constitution for an independent India. Despite protests, the government announced its decision to hold elections to the provincial legislatures in 1937. In the circumstances, the Congress decided that an effective way of deepening the anti-imperialist consciousness would be to contest the elections on the basis of a detailed political and economic agenda. Although this was a unanimous decision, differences of opinion arose on the issue of acceptance of office. While certain sections were totally opposed to accepting office on the ground that it would result in co-option by the colonial government, others believed that the Congress should combine mass action with effective work. At the Congress sessions held at Lucknow and Faizpur in 1936, the leaders decided to fight the elections and to defer the question of acceptance of office till the elections were over.[1]

THE ACT OF 1935 AND ASSAM

The Government of India Act 1935 provided for a bicameral legislature in Assam, consisting of an Upper House (the Legislative Council) and the Lower House (the Legislative Assembly). The Council's membership was fixed at 22, of which 18 were to be elected and 4 nominated. The Assembly was to have 108 seats with representations to various communities.[2] In the elections, the Congress emerged as the largest single party with 33 seats. Gopinath Bardoloi was elected as the leader of the Congress Assembly Party. The Congress could have formed a coalition ministry, but Bardoloi believed that forming a solid opposition instead would be more expedient at this stage. In the circumstances, Syed Mohammed Saadullah, the leader of the Muslim group in the Brahmaputra Valley, formed a ministry with the help of some Europeans and other groups.

Saadullah's Coalition Ministry: 1 April 1937–18 September 1938

On 1 April 1937, Saadullah took office as the chief minister and formed a coalition ministry comprising Muhammad Waheed (United Muslim Party), J. J. M. Nichols Roy (Progressive Nationalist Party), R. K. Choudhury (United Peoples' Party) and Ali Hyder Khan (United Muslim Party). Basanta Kumar Das, a Congress nominee, was elected Speaker. Saadullah had to depend heavily on pacts and compromises with various groups in the Legislative Assembly which placed him at a disadvantage from the start. The first budget session showed the weakness of his government which suffered as many as 11 defeats through cut motions and resolutions.[3] The ministry's policy with regard to nominations to the local boards had also aroused considerable displeasure. The Congress functioned as an effective opposition and was very forthright in its views on issues such as the Line System,[4] prohibition of opium, reduction of land revenue and abolition of the legislative council. Saadullah turned to the Muslim members of the Surma Valley, who constituted an overwhelming majority among the Muslim members in the Assembly, for support and to consolidate his position. With this goal in mind, he joined the Muslim League in 1937. In the circumstances, a reshuffling of the ministry was inevitable. He dropped Muhammad Waheed and Ali Hyder Khan and inducted Munawwar Ali and Abdul Matin Choudhury (both from the Muslim League) and Akshay Kumar Das (Constitutionalist Party) into his cabinet in February 1938.

Despite these changes, the government was unpopular and was criticised for being incompetent and having no definite policy. On 21 February a no-confidence motion against the ministry was defeated by just a single vote, showing its precarious nature of its existence. Subsequent defeats on the floor of the House, escalating labour unrest in the oil fields of Digboi, the collieries of Upper Assam and in several tea gardens, and the general belief that local aspirations were being neglected by the government, resulted in growing discontentment among the people. Many of Saadullah's supporters even joined hands with the opposition. To avoid facing another unpleasant no-confidence n, Saadullah submitted his resignation to the governor on 13 mber 1938. It was accepted by the governor who asked the leader ne opposition, Gopinath Bardoloi, to form the new government.

Congress Coalition Ministry: 19 September 1938–17 November 1939

task of forming a coalition government was not easy. The Congress ssam was short of a majority by 22 members and had to garner support of the Tribal League, independent members and Muslim embers who were not part of the Muslim League. Moreover, there vere differences of opinion among Congressmen themselves regarding he composition of the ministry. Eventually, after skilful mediation by Subhas Chandra, Bose, (the then AICC President), Abul Kalam Azad and Tarun Ram Phukan, the differences were ironed out and the formalities regarding the formation of the ministry were finalised. Bose and Azad issued a joint statement to the media:

> After consultations with the leaders of the Assam Congress Parliamentary Party, it was decided to have a cabinet of eight members—five Hindus and three Muslims. It was further decided to select the Hindu personnel immediately, but to postpone the selection of the Muslim personnel with a view to giving those Muslim groups who have not joined the Congress coalition an opportunity of doing so by accepting the Congress policy and programme and Congress discipline. After considering the response from these Muslim groups, the Muslim personnel of the cabinet will be finally selected.[5]

The formation of the first Congress coalition ministry headed by Gopinath Bardoloi as Premier, was announced on 19 September 1938. It comprised Gopinath Bardoloi (Congress), Akshaya Kumar Das (Constitutionalist), Ram Nath Das (Independent), Kamini Kumar Sen (Independent) and Rupnath Brahma (Independent). A few weeks later Fakhruddin Ali Ahmed (Independent), Mahmud Ali (Congress) and Ali Hyder Khan (Independent) were inducted into the cabinet.[6] Bardoloi and Mahmud Ali were the only two Congressmen in the ministry. But Bardoloi's commitment, sincerity and personal qualities enabled him to build a cohesive team.

Despite many difficulties, the ministry tried to implement certain measures that were promised in the election manifesto like:

- The progressive eradication of opium.
- Reduction of land revenue and restoration of land confiscated by the previous government for failure to pay revenue because of poverty.
- Safeguarding the interests of the indigenous people and restriction of immigration into Assam.
- More attention to primary, technical and higher education, public health and sanitation. They introduced basic education with an emphasis on manual and productive work.

An important but contentious measure was the Assam Agricultural Income Tax Bill which was strongly opposed not only by the planters, both European and Indian, but also by some rich peasant cultivators. Maulana Bhasani, the provincial leader of the Muslim League, opposed the Bill on the ground that the high taxes would siphon away the surplus capital which would otherwise have been invested in agriculture. The Bill was initially defeated in the Upper House but was eventually passed in a joint session of both the Houses.

Within the framework of provincial autonomy, the growing labour unrest[7] and the immigrant problem arising out of the Line System[8] had no solutions. The indecision of the ministry on these issues evoked severe criticism even from its own ranks. The Congress ministry had sincerely attempted to make the parliamentary system of government a success but often sectarian interests prevented the smooth functioning of the government. World War II broke out in September 1939. The Congress Party decided to not co-operate with the British government's war efforts. The Bardoloi ministry resigned on 17 November 1939 as part of this Congress decision. The Muslim League was jubilant and observed the day as one of 'deliverance'.

Saadullah's Second Ministry: 17 November 1939–24 December 1941

When Saadullah took over as the chief minister after Bardoloi resigned, he gave a commitment to support the war efforts and the Defence of India Rules. He actively cooperated with the British in this regard. The Assam government set up a Provincial War Aid Committee[9] with branches at the district headquarters. Both Saadullah and his colleague, R. K. Choudhury, were also closely associated with the National War Front and the National Defence Council. Immediately after taking office Saadullah implemented a proposal to create an Assam Regiment to enable Assamese youth to join the armed forces. The government contributed one lakh rupees to the War Fund and despite strong protests by Congress members, most local boards and town committees also resolved to contribute 3,000 rupees each to this Fund. Although Congress members in most of the local boards complied despite resentments, 11 members of the Tezpur local board, led by Jyoti Prasad Agarwala, resigned in protest.[10]

While Saadullah was busy garnering support for his war efforts, the Congress launched its anti-war programme stating that it was wrong to help the British war effort with men and money. The Working Committee of the Congress Party in Assam virtually became the provincial satyagraha committee. It did the groundwork for launching individual satyagraha programmes. Bardoloi offered the first individual satyagraha at Gauhati on 9 December 1940. During the next five months, 334 satyagrahis were arrested and imprisoned.

Resentment against Saadullah's Ministry

After the Congress coalition ministry resigned, the Congress legislators had stopped attending the Assembly sessions. Taking advantage of the situation, Saadullah announced the Land Development Scheme which envisaged opening particular areas for settlement only to indigenous landless people and immigrants who had come to Assam before 1938. Eligible migrants were to receive wasteland in specified development areas that were segregated according to different communities, on payment of a stipulated premium. The scheme raised a storm of protest and it was increasingly felt by most people that unless Congress legislators participated in the Assembly sessions and renewed parliamentary activities, Saadullah would have a free hand in going ahead with the proposed scheme. The Congress, therefore, decided to re-enter the legislature and move a no-confidence motion against the Saadullah ministry.

They soon had an opportunity when there was student unrest. A student of Cotton College was manhandled by a member of the managing committee of that institution for boycotting a science exhibition organised to raise money for the War Fund. The infuriated students held a protest meeting and took out a large procession through the city. The police brutally broke up the procession causing severe injuries to a large number of students. This led to spontaneous student strikes and a wave of hartals throughout the province. 'Gauhati Day' was observed for anti-war demonstrations all over the country at the initiative of the All India Students' Federation.[11] Dissatisfied with the functioning of the government, R. K. Choudhury, the minister of education, resigned from the ministry. Immediately thereafter, he formed the Nationalist Coalition Party and started negotiations with the Congress legislators with the intention of forming a ministry. In the wake of the several no-confidence motions that were tabled, Saadullah submitted his resignation to the governor on 12 December 1941.

The governor then formally invited Bardoloi, the leader of the single largest party, to form a ministry. He refused but stated that the Congress would extend general support to R. K. Choudhury, if he formed a ministry, except in matters relating to the war effort. With such an important precondition, it was clear that Choudhury would be unlikely to form a stable government. Hence, Assam was placed under Section 93 of the Government of India Act 1935 which gave the governor the right to govern the province himself without the advice of ministers and the legislature if he felt that the situation warranted such an action. The legislature was suspended and the administration was taken over by the governor on 25 December 1941.

Governor's Rule: 25 December 1941—24 August 1942

One of the first steps of the governor Robert Neil Reid was to scrap the controversial Land Development Scheme. This was obviously calculated to appease the Hindu and Assamese public opinion at a critical juncture when the War was fast approaching the eastern frontier of India. The Congress had been under considerable pressure to launch an all-out struggle against British imperialism. The pressure was intensified after the failure of the Cripps Mission in April 1942 which did not offer any concrete proposals for self-rule for India. It revealed that the British were in no mood to concede to Indian demands. The situation became more serious after mid-1942. As lakhs of refugees from Singapore and Burma started entering Assam, there was a growing feeling of imminent British collapse. Popular discontent mounted especially when the government discriminated in the treatment of European and Asian refugees. The Assam Congress made arrangements to strengthen the *Shanti Sena* or 'Peace Army' to maintain peace and order in the rural areas and to provide help to the refugees. The organisation grew so rapidly that it virtually 'swallowed' the parallel official bodies. The governor's attempt to build a National War Front and set up village defence forces to counter the Shanti Sena proved futile. The high handed attitude of the government, wartime shortages and rising prices intensified the feelings of resentment among the people. In the face of escalating frustration and discontentment, the next phase of a mass struggle was inevitable.

QUIT INDIA MOVEMENT AND ASSAM

At a special session of the AICC held at Bombay on 7 and 8 August 1942, the historic 'Quit India' resolution was adopted. The Congress sanctioned an indefinite non-violent mass struggle 'on the widest possible scale' under Gandhi's leadership. In the absence of leaders, every participant was to act for himself within the limits of the general instructions issued.[12] Gandhi's message was simple: 'Do or die. We shall either free India or die in the attempt; we shall not live to see the perpetuation of our slavery.' In Assam, the government arrested all the major Congress leaders in the next few days.[13] The Assam Pradesh Congress Committee, the district congress committees, Shanti Sena and all other subsidiary bodies were declared unlawful bodies. All forms of meetings, gatherings, processions and hartals were banned.

The detention of the Congress legislators meant that it was now favourable for the return of Saadullah to power. The government was happy to revoke Section 93 so that public resistance could be confronted by a 'popular' ministry. It was also expected that Saadullah would remain loyal to the British. Hence, on 25 August 1942, Saadullah was invited to form the government. His ministry was at the helm of affairs during the Quit India Movement.

In Assam, the Quit India Movement started with Gandhian non-violent methods of protest like hartals, processions, demonstrations, picketing and hoisting of the Congress flag on government buildings. As the movement progressed and police violence increased, there was a general atmosphere of rebellion. The people attacked government buildings, damaged railway tracks and sabotaged military supply lines. The chief secretary appraised the situation and noted that Nowgong and Darrang were the two most disturbed districts where officers were assaulted, shops gutted and government buildings regularly attacked. There were cases of sabotage on railways near Shahajibazar in Habiganj, Barpathar in Golaghat, at Panbari and Rangiya in Kamrup and Suffrai in Sivasagar.[14] The government tightened the noose on the people. Kushal Konwar was hanged in connection with the derailment of a train at Barpathar. He was the only martyr to be hanged in the whole country during the Quit India Movement. There were brutal firings at Patacharkuchi (Barpeta subdivision), Fakiragram (Goalpara), Gohpur and Dhekiajuli (both in Darrang district) leaving several, including a 15 year old girl, Kanaklata, dead. Volunteers of the village defence committees, organised by the Saadullah government to assist the police, terrorised the people in the rural areas.[15]

Government Repression

In a desperate attempt to contain the increasing disturbances, the government let loose a virtual reign of terror. It enforced a number of special ordinances[16] curbing the civil liberties of the people. The authorities' exacted forced labour from the villagers to guard vital installations, imposed punitive taxes and collective fines on villagers, and assaulted, arrested, convicted and imprisoned people on mere suspicion. The brutal all-out repression succeeded in bringing about an end to the mass phase of the struggle. But underground networks had been consolidated. Most of the prominent leaders were in jail. Those who were out, like Sankar Chandra Barua, Mahendra Hazarika, Jyotiprasad Agarwala, Gahan Chandra Goswami and Lakshmi Goswami went underground to sustain the movement. Influenced by the revolutionary activities elsewhere in India, they took to militancy and justified their actions in the context of spiralling police atrocities on non violent crowds. By 1943 there were as many as 32 underground volunteer camps at Bajali alone.[17] Similar camps were also organised at different places of Kamrup, Darrang, Nowgong and Sibsagar districts. As in other parts of the country, in Assam, too, the main activity of the underground movement was the disruption of the communication network by blowing up bridges, derailing trains and cutting telephone and telegraph wires. Though the underground resistance movement only made a limited headway in Assam; but it did help to keep the spirit of defiance alive.

The leaders of the struggle also attempted to form parallel governments in a few rural areas. They established village panchayats and schemes for panchayat administration drawn up and implemented at various places such as Bajali, Hatisung, Dhakuakhana, Raha, Jamuguri and Bahjani. A vigorous no-revenue campaign was also carried out.

Though the intensity of the campaign varied from mauza to mauza, it created a deep sense of insecurity among the mauzadars. At many places the traders attempted to stop supplies to the army, police and government. They boycotted and picketed government haats and in their place Congress set up their own haats, though with limited success, as part of the civil disobedience programme.

Participation of Students

The movement had a strong popular base. As in the earlier mass struggles the youth were at the forefront of the struggle. Students from colleges and even schools were the most visible element, especially during the early phase of the movement. They not only took the lead in organising protest meetings, demonstrations, hartals, picketing and processions, but also organised the Shanti Sena squads. As the movement progressed, they became actively involved in sabotage activities as well. Under their leadership the rural masses were motivated to participate actively in the movement in all possible ways.

Women and the Movement

Women came out in large numbers. But despite their massive involvement in the movement, they often found themselves sidelined in the organisational work. Women leaders of the struggle campaigned for separate women's wings. It was only in 1940 that women's wings were made an integral part of the Congress at both the national and provincial levels. In Assam, the women's wing was set up in September 1940 with Pushpalata Das and Amalprova Das as joint secretaries. The following year, the All Assam Girl Students' Committee was formed at Shillong.

Female activism was very visible during this period. In the face of unprecedented police repression and with large numbers of men in prison, prominent women leaders took upon themselves the task of coordinating the activities. Chandraprova Saikiani was one of the main guiding forces among women. While the majority of the women concentrated on programmes of reconstruction and, as Congress volunteers, also enrolled themselves as members of the Shanti Sena, a small but determined section was much more radical in their activities. Violence and sabotage were their weapons of choice. In 1942, the *Mrityu Bahini*[18] (Suicide Squad) was formed to carry out subversive activities in a more organised manner. Women members no doubt pledged allegiance to the male leaders like Hem Chandra Barua and Sankar Chandra Barua, but a new image of female militancy presented itself. Kanaklata, Ratnabala Phukan, Buddheswari Hazarika, Khahuli Nath and Damayanti Bora were all active members of the Mrityu Bahini and were acclaimed as exemplary women among radical circles. But there were hundreds of others, ordinary women who, from behind the scenes, made immense contributions in hiding weapons, sheltering fugitives and encouraging men, using their domestic role to cover subversive and revolutionary activities. Many others worked as spies, money raisers, conspirators and saboteurs.

Saadullah's Ministry

Saadullah was in power during these troubled times. In spite of the heroic actions of a leaderless people, the Quit India Movement was snuffed out in eight weeks. Pockets of resistance continued but could not hold out for long. Inflation was high, essential commodities scarce and hoarding, black marketing, profiteering and corruption rampant. Yet, despite untold sufferings, people did not lose hope. News of the activities of Subhash Chandra Bose and the INA and the gradual release of political prisoners aroused new expectations. Political energies surfaced after almost three years of repression and the popular assumption was that it would mark the beginning of rapid political progress. This caused fresh apprehensions to the government.

SECOND BARDOLOI MINISTRY: 10 FEBRUARY 1946–50

When the War ended in 1945, everyone heaved a sigh of relief. The Labour Party, under Attlee which had come to power in England after the War, was anxious to settle the Indian problem. They lifted the ban on Congress and announced elections. In the elections that followed, the Congress secured 58 seats in a House of 108 in Assam[19]. Along with a few independent members, Gopinath Bardoloi formed a government on 10 February 1946 with an absolute majority in the legislature.[20] The new ministry faced numerous problems of reconstruction after the war but one of its first tasks was to deal with the problem of immigration. Saadullah had revived the Land Development Scheme which had been squashed earlier by the governor. His policy of letting in streams of migrants from East Bengal and allowing them to settle in the Grazing and Forest Reserves of Assam had resulted in numerous clashes between the migrants and the local people. The Congress ministry's decision to evict the migrants evoked strong protests from the Muslim League which organised a civil disobedience programme against it. This led to further clashes at several places.

Meanwhile, Muslim League politics in the country had generally centred round the issue of Pakistan. In Assam, too, the popular agitation against the eviction policy had been channelised towards that end. When Jinnah visited Assam in 1946 he reiterated the demand that Assam should be included in the Eastern Pakistan zone.

THE CABINET MISSION

By early 1946 the British realised the need for a graceful withdrawal from India. Accordingly, the Cabinet Mission, comprising Pethick-Lawrence (the Secretary of State for India), Stafford Cripps (the President of the Board of Trade) and A. V. Alexander (First Lord of Admiralty) was sent to India in March 1946 to establish a national government and work out a constitutional arrangement for the transfer of power. British policy in 1946, however, contradicted their earlier policy of divide and rule. British authorities were now of the opinion that a united India, friendly to Britain, would be an active partner in the defence of the Commonwealth while a divided India would hamper the defence plans. Conforming to this view, the Cabinet Mission declared that Pakistan would not be viable as a separate entity. Instead, it drew up a plan to safeguard the interests of the Muslim minority within the overall framework of the unity of the country. The Cabinet Mission Plan conceived of three sections:

1. Section A comprising Madras, Bombay, United Provinces, Bihar, Central Provinces and Orissa.
2. Section B comprising Punjab, North West Frontier Province and Sind.
3. Section C comprising Bengal and Assam.

Each section would meet separately to work out their constitutions. There would be a common centre to look after defence, foreign affairs and communication. A province could leave the group to which it was assigned after the first general elections. After ten years it could demand a modification of both the group and union constitutions.

But disagreements arose between the Congress and the League over the issue of grouping.[21] Keeping in mind the Congress ruled provinces of Assam and North West Frontier Province which had been placed in sections C and B, Congress demanded that a province should have the option of not joining the group in the first place. The League accepted the Plan so far as the basis of Pakistan was implied by the compulsory grouping but demanded that the provinces be given the right to question the Union Constitution immediately and not after ten years. It was obvious that both the Congress and the League interpreted the Plan to suit their own stand. The basic problem lay in the fact that the Cabinet Mission Plan was not clear whether grouping was compulsory or optional. Nehru explained in his speech to the AICC that Congress had only decided to participate in the Constituent Assembly. Since the Assembly was a sovereign body, it would formulate the rules of procedure. Jinnah took advantage of Nehru's speech and withdrew its acceptance of the Mission Plan.

Assam and the Cabinet Mission

The Assam Provincial Congress protested strongly against the grouping plan as soon as it was announced. It was feared that if Assam was tagged to Bengal, she would lose her distinctive identity and would be a mere pawn in the chessboard of Muslim politics. This aspect had been repeatedly emphasised by the Congress leadership and Bijoy Chandra Bhagawati and Mahendra Mohan Choudhury had in fact gone to Srirampur to apprise Gandhi of the situation. Amidst protests and public agitation, another group of leaders comprising of Hareswar Goswami, Debakanta Baruah, Kamakhya Prasad Tripathi, Harendranath Barua, F. A. Ahmed, O. K. Das and Pushpalata Das met AICC leaders at Calcutta, Delhi and Patna with the same objective. The Assam Legislative Assembly adopted a resolution moved by Gopinath Bardoloi himself expressing strong disapproval of the Plan. Bardoloi even directed the ten representatives from Assam in the Constituent Assembly not to sit in any Section with any other province for the settlement of any issue relating to Assam.

FORMATION OF THE INTERIM GOVERNMENT

The British Government was in a dilemma. It realised the need for cooperation of the Congress and invited the Party on 2 September

1946, to form an interim government with Jawaharlal Nehru as the *de facto* head. Jinnah retaliated by a call for Direct Action with a new slogan, *Larke lenge Pakistan* (We will fight and get Pakistan). The communal frenzy that followed saw more than 5,000 people killed and many more wounded in what came to be known as the 'Great Calcutta killings'. Trouble in Noakhali, in East Bengal, soon spread to other parts of the country. Jinnah's action had led to a virtual civil war. In the circumstances, the British authorities decided to revert to their old policy of placating the Muslims. On 26 October 1946, the League was brought into the interim government although it had neither accepted the short and long-term provisions of the Cabinet Mission Plan nor given up Direct Action.

The Leagues's entry into the interim government did not end the conflict. Jinnah merely viewed it as another step towards its goal of Pakistan and refused to cooperate with the government. The Congress members demanded that the League either give up Direct Action or leave the government. The breaking point came when the League demanded that the Constituent Assembly be dissolved because it was unrepresentative. Congress members of the interim government then demanded the resignation of the League members. A crisis was imminent. However, the situation was saved by Attlee's announcement in Parliament that the British would withdraw from India by 30 June 1948 and that Lord Mountbatten would replace Lord Wavell as the Viceroy. The statement was enthusiastically received in Congress circles as a final proof of British sincerity to finally quit. Jinnah's reaction was entirely different. He was now more confident than ever of achieving his goal of Pakistan.

When Mountbatten arrived in India, the situation was far from favourable. The Muslim League was adamant that he would accept nothing less than a sovereign Pakistan. The Cabinet Mission Plan had clearly become defunct and there was no point persisting with it. Unity required positive intervention which included dealing with communal elements with a strong hand. Attlee later claimed that he would have preferred a united India and they were unable to achieve it though they tried hard. The truth was that the British chose to play safe without exercising any restraint even when the situation demanded the assertion of authority.

THE MOUNTBATTEN PLAN (3 JUNE PLAN)

Mountbatten's formula was to divide India but to retain as much unity as possible.[22] This was done by making concessions to both the Congress and the League. The Plan proposed the division of Punjab and Bengal. In the case of Assam, a referendum was to be held in Sylhet district so that the people could decide for themselves whether to remain in Assam or opt to join East Pakistan. Thus the League's demand was accommodated by creating Pakistan, though it was made as small as possible to accommodate the Congress stand on unity. Mountbatten also supported the Congress stand that the princely states must not be given the option of independence. He realised that it was essential for Britain to retain the goodwill of the Congress if he hoped to persuade India to remain within the Commonwealth. Dominion Status offered a chance of keeping India within the Commonwealth. The 3 June Plan thus declared that power would be handed over by 15 August 1947 on the basis of Dominion Status to India and Pakistan. Mountbatten's plan was approved by the British Parliament and also accepted by both the Congress and the Muslim League. The India Independence Bill 1947, received royal assent on 18 July 1947.

With the acceptance of the Mountbatten Plan, the anti-grouping movement in Assam came to an end. The focus of political activity now shifted to Sylhet where the referendum was held on 6 and 7 July 1947. Although public opinion in general welcomed the decision as it anticipated the termination of an 'artificial union' between the two sections of people, several leaders, including Bardoloi, favoured the retention of the district.[23] The referendum results were as expected. Of the valid votes cast, 56 per cent were in favour of Sylhet's inclusion in Pakistan and 43.4 per cent for an undivided Assam within India. The votes practically reflected the communal composition of the district's population. Thereafter, the Boundary Commission, under Cyril Radcliffe, was entrusted with the task of demarcating the Muslim and non-Muslim majority areas. According to the Award, the thanas of Patharkandi, Ratabari, Badarpur and half of Karimganj were to be retained by Assam. The rest were to be amalgamated with East Pakistan.

Map11.1: Northeast India Post-1947

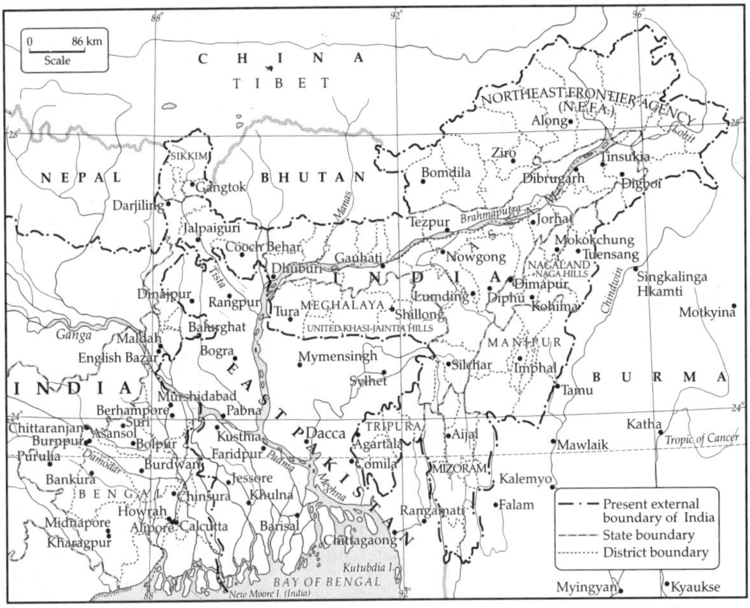

Source: Adapted from map in Wikimedia Commons.

PARTITION AND INDEPENDENCE

On 15 August 1947, India became independent. A glorious struggle, hard fought, had at last been won; but at the cost of partition. The speed with which the country was partitioned and power transferred aggravated the tragedy of partition. Delays in the announcement of the Boundary Commission's Award created confusion for ordinary citizens many of whom stayed on in their homes in the belief that they were on the right side of the border. Frenzied migrations often culminated in massacres. Yet, despite the sorrow in their hearts, people all over the country celebrated. The pledge of Poorna Swaraj had finally been redeemed.

Assam, however, connected by the Siliguri Corridor with the rest of India, now became virtually isolated. The creation of East Pakistan between the Indian provinces of West Bengal and Assam, constricted Assam's communication links. The old railway network and shorter land routes to Bengal were disrupted while the utility of the Brahmaputra River as an effective waterway to the Bay of Bengal was considerably undermined. The situation was aggravated when river communication via East Pakistan was completely discontinued after the Indo-Pakistan War of 1965. The continuing influx of refugees from East Pakistan, (present Bangladesh) has seriously affected Assam's economy and has changed her demographic profile significantly. Partition set in motion forces whose impact is being felt even today.

NOTES AND REFERENCES

1. In the elections to the provincial assemblies which were held in February 1937, the Congress won 716 seats out of 1,161seats that it contested. It had a majority in all provinces except Assam, Bengal, the North West Frontier Provinces, Punjab and Sind. In Assam, Bengal and the North West Frontier Province, the Congress was the single largest party. After a few months of vacillation, the AICC decided to accept office.
2. Representation was as follows: General, including Scheduled Castes–7; Muhammedan–34: Women–1; Indian Christian–1; European–1; Backward Plains Tribes–4; Backward hill areas–5; European Planters–7; Indian Planters–2; Commerce and Industry (European)–1; Commerce and Industry (Indian)–1; Tea Garden Labour– 4.
3. *Indian Annual Register*, Vo.l II, (July–December 1937), Calcutta 1937, pp. 242–3.
4. Since the second decade of the twentieth century, immigrants (mainly Muslims) from the overpopulated districts of East Bengal had been streaming into the Brahmaputra Valley. Very often they encroached upon the grazing grounds and vacant lands in and around villages. In order to contain the influx of immigrants from East Bengal and the resultant conflicts of interests which arose, the government formulated the Line System in 1920. Under this system, a line was drawn in the districts under pressure to settle the migrants in segregated areas specified for their exclusive settlement. This obviously restricted the mobility of the migrants which they objected to. Despite the fact that the indigenous Assamese population supported the Line System, the influx of immigrants continued with the support of the Assam Provincial Muslim League. For details, refer to A. Guha, *Planter Raj to Swaraj Freedom Struggle and Electoral Politics in Assam*, Delhi, 1977, pp. 206–8.
5. *Indian Annual Register*, Vol. II, (July–December 1938), Calcutta 1938, pp. 191–2.
6. The allocation of portfolios was as follows: Gopinath Bardoloi–Premier: Home and Education; A. K. Das–Excise and Agriculture; R. N. Das–Medical and Public Health; K. K. Sen–Legislative, Judicial, General Department and Local Self Government; R. Brahma–Forest and Registration; F. A .Ahmed– Finance and Revenue; M. Ali–Cooperatives and Industry; A. H. Khan–Public Works; A. C. Bhuyan and S. De (eds.), *Political History of Assam*, Vol. II, Guwahati, 1999 (Second edition), p. 356.

7. The Digboi labour strike of 1939, involving around 10,000 labourers, was a cause of immense concern to the government. A Conciliation Board was appointed to settle the disputes between the Assam Oil Company and the A. O. C. Labour Union, but before any settlement could be arrived at, World War II broke out and Digboi and Tinsukia were declared 'protected areas' under the War Ordinance.
8. The magnitude of this influx was so serious that the Muslim population in the Assam Valley districts (including the Garo Hills) increased from 355,320 in 1911 to 1,303, 962 in 1941 (Home Political File No. 119/46, Pol. i). During 1939–41, the Saadullah Government allotted one lakh bighas of land in the Brahmaputra Valley to East Bengal immigrants. This raised a hue and cry in the province.
9. This Committee, headed by Saadullah, included R. K. Choudhury, Abdul Matin Choudhury , Hirendra Chandra Chakravarty and Rup Nath Brahma.
10. *The Assam Tribune,* 25 April 1941.
11. A. Guha, *Planter Raj to Swaraj Freedom Struggle and Electoral Politics in Assam,* p. 268.
12. Tarachand, *History of the Freedom Movement in India,* Vol. IV, Delhi, 1972, pp. 375–6.
13. These included M. Tayyebulla, Siddhinath Sarma, Liladhar Barua, B. R. Medhi, F. A. Ahmed, O. K. DAs, Padmadhar Chaliha, Laksheswar Barua, Harekrishna Das, G. N. Bardoloi, Debeswar Sarma, A. K. Chanda, Kedarnath Bhattacharya, Purnendukishor Sengupta, Chanchal Kumar Sarma and Achitya Kumar Bhattacharya.
14. K. N. Dutta, *Landmarks in the Freedom Struggle in Assam,* Guwahati 1969, p. 102.
15. Bebejia, Raha, Dhalpur, Bihpuria, Panigaon, Ranga Ali, Chatia, Jamuguri, Sorbhog, Dhupdhara, Teok, Kharikatia, Nitaipukhurighat, Goalpara and Chaygaon are some places which bore the brunt of police atrocities.
16. Like the Subversive Activities Ordinance, Special Criminal Courts ordinance, Penalties (Enhancement) Ordinance and Defence of India Rules.
17. Brajanath Sarma was one of the main underground leaders in Bajali during the Quit India Movement. He was responsible for the destruction of the Barnagar Aerodrome and the Sarbhog Police station.
18. Membership to the Mrityu Bahini was conditional. Both men and women between 18 and 50 years who were physically fit were eligible, but only those with total commitment to the cause were inducted under an oath of secrecy.
19. The election results were as follows; Congress–58; Muslim League–31; *Jamiat–ul-Ulema*–3 ,European–9; Others–7.
20. Bardoloi's seven member cabinet comprised the following ministers: G. N. Bardoloi–Appointment, Education and Publicity; B. K. Das–Home, Judicial, Legislative, Registration and General Department; B. R. Medhi–Finance and Revenue; R. N. Das–Excise, Medical, Public Health, Labour; J. J. M. Nichols Roy–Public Works, Forests, Industry, Cooperatives; B. Mukherjee–Supply Reconstruction, Jails; A. M. Majumdar–Local Self Government, Veterinary, Agriculture.

21. For details, refer to V. P. Menon, *The Transfer of Power in India*, Chennai, 1997, Chapter 11. For Assam, also refer to Ranju Bezbaruah, *The Cabinet Mission: Grouping and the Congress*, Azad Institute Paper 21.
22. In accordance with the 3 June Plan, it was decided to set up two Boundary Commissions, both under the Chairmanship of Radcliffe. One was set up to deal with the partition of Bengal, (also the separation of Sylhet from Assam), and the other to deal with the partition of Punjab. Each Boundary Commission consisted of a Chairman and four members, two nominated by the Congress and two by the Muslim league. For details, see Menon, *The Transfer of Power in India*, pp. 401–3.
23. A.C.Bhuyan and S.De (eds), *Political History of Assam*, pp. 389–93.

SUGGESTED READINGS

Bhuyan, C., (ed.), *Nationalist Upsurge in Assam*, Guwahati , 2000.
Dutta, K. N., *Landmarks in the Freedom Struggle in Assam*, Guwahati, 1969.
Sharma, Dipti, *Assamese Women in the Freedom Struggle*, Calcutta, 1993.

Glossary

Abkari	Excise duty on drugs and liquor
Anna	One-sixteenth of a rupee
Arkatti	Recruiting agent
Bailung	Ahom priest
Barangani	Subscription
Bari	Garden land
Bar Panchayat	Tribunal for trial of major offences
Barphukan	Ahom viceroy at Gauhati
Bar Senapati	Literally, commander-in-chief, title conferred on the ruler of the Muttock territory
Basti	Homestead land
Bepari	Merchant
Bharat Varsha	Greater India as referred to in the *Puranic* literature and Mahabharata
Bigha	One-third of an acre
Brahmottar	Rent-free land grants for supporting brahmins
Buragohain	Chief of the three ministers in the Ahom monarch's cabinet
Buranji	A chronicle
Burgandazes	Armed raiders
Chapori	Highland formed by silt deposits on the banks of rivers
Chaukidari tax	A local tax collected in permanently settled areas to maintain a village watchman
Charukar	Hearth tax
Chirap	Courts in Manipur which tried both civil and criminal cases
Chokey	Frontier outpost
Choudhury	Revenue officer in charge of a *pargana*
Company Bahadur	East India Company's government
Coolie	Labourer
Daroga	Superintendent of police
Dangoria	A title of the Ahom nobility
Debottar	Rent-free land grants for the upkeep of temples
Dewani Adalat	Civil Court
Dharmottar	Rent-free land grants for religious and charitable purposes
Dola	Palanquin

Doloi	A priest; also, chief of an administrative division in the Jayantia Hills
Duar	Mountain pass
Faringati/Pharingati	Dry land
Gadhan	A poll tax
Gamati	Land allotted to a *paik* by the Ahom government
Ghat	Landing place on the banks of a river
Gaum	Tribal chief
Gossain	A brahmin preceptor
Haat	Periodical market
Hengdang	Sword
Jagir	Estate
Jamadar	Junior commissioned police officer
Jhum	Shifting or slash and burn system of cultivation.
Jumadhan	Total revenue assessment
Juma mati	Another name for *gamati*
Kala azar	Black fever
Kani	Opium
Kaviraj	Practitioner of Ayurvedic medicine
Kharikatana	Poll tax
Keya	Marwari trader / merchant
Kheddah	Enclosure into which elephants are driven to be captured
Khel	A division or unit of Assamese subjects having to perform specific services to the state and presided over by a Phukan or Baruah and commanded by a gradation of officers
Kheldar	Person in charge of a *khel*
Khidmatgar	Servant
Khiraj	Land paying full revenue
Kutchery	Court
Kulbah	Measurement of land in Cachar equivalent to 4.82 acres
Lakhiraj	Rent-free tenure
Lallup	Compulsory unpaid labour in Manipur for construction of roads, bridges and repair of public buildings
Lyngskor	Officer who acted as the Syiem's deputy in the Khasi administrative set up
Mahajan	Trader
Mahila Samiti	Women's Association
Manmati	Rent-free grants of land granted as remuneration for one's services.

Matharakha	A security tax levied by the Garos in the hills on the villages at The border
Mauza	Revenue circle
Mauzadar	Revenue officer in charge of a *mauza*
Mel	A tribunal or assembly
Moffusil	Rural
Moffusil Panchayat	Rural tribunal
Mohurur	Clerk
Narayani	This coin was originally introduced by Maharaja Nara Narayan (1540–84) in Cooch Behar. The rate of exchange was: 100 sicca rupees = 126. 74 narayani rupees.
Navis	Subordinate fiscal officer
Nizamat Adalat	Criminal Court
Nisf Khiraj	Tenures paying revenue at half the rate.
Omlah	Clerk
Opar mati	Surplus land
Paik	An enrolled adult subject of the Ahom Government having specific duties to render to the state for fixed periods of the year
Palki	Palanquin
Panchayat	Village assembly
Panda	A temple priest
Pargana	Revenue division
Pathsala	Primary school
Patwari	Accountant
Perakagaz	Register of survey
Peshkar	Minor revenue officer
Phukan	Superintendent of a *khel* comprising of 6,000 paiks
Posa	System of payment to hill people
Pothang	In Manipur, state officials could get food and their luggage also transported for free when they visited villages on duty
Pura	Three-fourth an acre of land (approx.)
Pundit	Learned man
Qanungo/Kanungo	An officer in charge of revenue records, village maps, statistics.
Raijmel	Popular assembly
Rubakar	Minor revenue officer
Rupit	Arable land or land on which winter crops or transplanted paddy is grown
Ryot	Peasant cultivator

Ryot Sabhas	Association of ryots
Ryotwari	System of land tenure where the settlement was made directly with the ryots
Sadiya Khowa Gohain	Khamti chief
Sabha	An association
Satra	Vaisnavite monastery
Satradhikar	Head of a satra
Saroo	Cooking pot
Sezwal	Officer appointed to collect taxes
Sherishtadar	Keeper of records
Sicca rupee	Coin issued by the East India Company's government and valued at approximately 2 shillings
Sirdar	Khasi village headman
Surasree Panchayat	Tribunal for disposal of minor offences
Subahdar	Officer in charge of a *subah*
Swadeshi	indigenous
Swaraj	independence
Syiem	Khasi chief
Thakuria	subordinate collector
Tongso Penlop	Governor of eastern Bhutan
Tol	An institution where emphasis is on the teaching of Sanskrit
Tola	11.66gms
Unani Hakim	*Unani* refers to a tradition of Graeco-Arabic medicine; Hakim is a physician practicing this form of medicine.
Zenana	Apartments for the ladies
Zimmadar	A custodian; an officer responsible for the arrest of offenders in a particular area.

Select Bibliography

REPORTS/ARCHIVAL MATERIAL

Jackson, W., *Monograph on the Iron and Steel Works of Assam*, Shillong, 1907.

Report of the Assam Opium Enquiry Committee, Shillong, 1925.

Report of the Assam Labour Enquiry Commission, 1906, Shillong, 1907.

Report of the Coal Committee, 1838, Calcutta, 1845.

Royale, Forbes, *Memorandum on the Production of Hemp and Rhea Fibre in India*, London, 1854.

Schlich,W., *Memorandum on Forest Operations in Assam*, A.S.R. File No.38/45, 1873, 94C.

Reports on the Administration of Assam (relevant years).

Reports on Public Instruction (relevant years).

Reports on the Revenue Administration of Assam (relevant years).

Select Files (Assam State Archives).

——— Assam Commissioner's Office,

——— Files of the Dacca Commissioner's Office.

——— Board of Revenue Papers.

——— Papers relating to the Government of Bengal.

——— Letters from miscellaneous sources.

Select Files (National Archives of India).

——— Foreign Proceedings.

——— Home Department Proceedings (Public, Political, General, Judicial Forests).

——— Land Revenue Records.

——— Finance and Commerce Department.

——— Despatches to the Secretary of State (Revenue).

DOCUMENTS/ACCOUNTS/MEMOIRS

Aitchison, C. U., 1983, *A Collection of Treaties, Engagements, and Sanads*, Vol XII, Reprint, Delhi, Mittal Publications.

Allen, B. C., 1906, *Gazetteer of Bengal and North East India*, Calcutta: Baptist Mission Press.

Allen, B. C., 1968, *Assam Land Revenue Manual*, Shillong: Assam Revenue Department.

Barker, G. M., 1884, *A Tea Planter's Life in Assam*, Calcutta, Thacker, Spink & Co.

Fox, C. S., 1947, *The Economic Mineral Resources of Assam*, Shillong: Assam Government Press.

Gait, E. A., 1896, *The Assam Land Revenue Manual*, Calcutta: Superintendent of Government Press, India.

Gupta, G. N., 1908, A *Survey of the Resources and Industries of Eastern Bengal and Assam 1907–08*, Shillong: Secreteriat Press.

Hunter, W. W., 1879, *A Statistical Account of Assam*, Vols I & II, London: Trubner & Co.

M'Cosh, J. N., 1975, *Topography of Assam*, Delhi: Sanskaran Prakashak.

Mallet, F. R., *Memoirs of the G.S.I.*, Vol. XII, pt 2, Calcutta, 1876.

Michell J. F., 1883, *The North-East Frontier of India*, Calcutta: Superintendent of Government Printing, India.

Mills, A. J. M., 1984, *Report on the Province of Assam*, (Reprint), Guwahati: Assam Publication Board.

Mills, A. J. M., 1985, *Report of the Khasi and Jaintia Hills*, edited version, NEHU.

Pemberton, R. B., 1839, *Report on Bootan*, Calcutta: Bengal Military Orphan Press. 1966.

Pemberton, R. B., 1835, *Report on the Eastern Frontier of British India*, Calcutta: Baptist Mission Press.

Stack, E., 1896, *Silk in Assam, 1884*, Shillong: Assam Agricultural Department.

Wade, J. P., 1927, *An Account of Assam*, (ed.) Benudhar Sarma, Sibsagar: R. Sarmah.

Ward, William, 1917, *Assam Land Revenue Manual*, Shillong: Assam Secretariat Press.

White, A., 1832, *A Memoir of the Late David Scott*, Calcutta: Baptist Mission Press. 1988

Wilson, H. H., 1827, *Documents Illustrative of the Burmese War*, No.25, Calcutta: Government Gazette Press.

BOOKS

Antrobus, H. A., 1948, *A History of the Jorehaut Tea Company, 1859–1946*, London: Tea and Rubber Mail.

Antrobus, H. A., 1957, *A History of the Assam Company*, Edinburgh; T and A Constable.

Ashworth, W., 1960, *An Economic History of England1870–1939*, London: Metheune & Co.

Awasthi, R. C., 1975, *Economics of the Tea Industry in India*, Gauhati: United Publishers.

Banerjee, A. C., 1964, *The Eastern Frontier of British India*, (Third edition), Calcutta: A. Mukherjee.

Banerjee, Debdas, 1999, *Colonialism in Action*, New Delhi: Orient Longman.

Barkataki, S. (ed.), 1969, *India: The Land and People–Assam*, Delhi: National Book Trust.

Barman, Santo, 1994, *Zamindari System in Assam during British Rule (A Case Study of Goalpara District)*, Guwahati: Spectrum Publications.

Barooah, N. K., 1970, *David Scott in North East India*. Delhi: Munshiram Manoharlal.

Barpujari, H. K., (ed.), 1992, *The Comprehensive History of Assam*, Vol. IV, Guwahati: Assam Publication Board.

——— (ed.),1993, *The Comprehensive History of Assam*, Vol. V, Guwahati: Assam Publication Board.

——— (ed.), 1993, *The Comprehensive History of Assam*, Vol. III, Guwahati: Assam Publication Board.

——— (ed.), *An Account of Assam and Her Administration*, Guwahati, 1988.

Barpujari, H. K., 1977, Political History of Assam, Vol. I, Guwahati: Government of Assam.

———, 1976, Problem of the Hill Tribes: North East Frontier, Vol. II, Guwahati: United Publishers.

———, 1988, *Problem of the Hill Tribes North East Frontier*, Vol. I, (Reprint), NEHU.

———, 1963, *Assam in the Days of the Company: 1826–58*, Guwahati: Lawyers Book Stall.

———,1986, *American Missionaries and North East India 1836–1900*, Guwahati: Spectrum Publishers.

Barpujari, S. K., (ed.), 1997, *History of the Dimasas*, Guwahati: Autonomous Council, N.C. Hills District

Bezbaruah, Ranju, Priyam Goswami & Dipankar Banerjee, (eds.), 2008, *North East India: Interpreting the Sources of its History*, New Delhi: Indian Council for Historical Research.

Bezbaruah, Ranju, 2003, *The Cabinet Mission: Grouping and the Congress*, Kolkata, Azad Institute Paper 21.

———, 2008, 'Dr. Fraser's Crusade and Bawi Correspondences 1909–1923', in Bezbaruah, Ranju et al (ed.), *North East India: Interpreting the Sources of its History*, New Delhi.

———, 2010, *The Pursuit of Colonial Interests in India's North East*, Guwahati: EBH Publishers.

Bhattacharjee J.B. (ed.), 1986, *Studies in the History of North East India*, Shillong: NEHU.

——— (ed.), 1994, *Studies in the Economic History of North East India*, New Delhi: Har-Anand Publications.

Bhattacharjee, J. B., 1977, *Cachar under British Rule in North East India*, New Delhi: Radiant Publishers.

———, 1978, *The Garos and the English*, New Delhi: South Asia Books.

———, 1991, *Social and Polity Formations in Pre-Colonial North East India*, New Delhi: Har-Anand Publications in association with Vikas Publishing House.

Bhattacharjee, J. B., 2000, *Trade and Colony: The British Colonization of North East India*, Shillong: North East India History Association.

———, 2008, *Making of British Assam*, Kolkata: Institute of Historical Studies.

———, 2010, *State and Wealth: Early States in Northeast India*, Guwahati: DVS Publishers.

Bhattacharjee, K. K., 1983, *North East India: Political and Administrative History*, New Delhi: Cosmo Publications.

Bhuyan S. K., 1949, *Early British Relations with Assam*, Shillong: Assam Government Press.

———, 1949, *Anglo-Assamese Relations 1771–1826*, Guwahati: Department of Historical and Antiquarian Studies.

Bhuyan A. C. (ed.), 2000, *Nationalist Upsurge in Assam*, Guwahati: Government of Assam.

Bhuyan, A. C., and S. De (eds.), 1978, *Political History of Assam*, Vol. II, Guwahati: Government of Assam.

Bora, Shiela, 1992, *Student Revolution in Assam, 1917–47 (A Historical Survey)*, New Delhi: Mittal Publications.

Chakravorty, B. C., 1981, *British Relations with the Hill Tribes of Assam since 1858*, Calcutta: Firma KLM.

Bose, M. L., 1997, *History of Arunachal Pradesh*, Delhi: Concept Publishing Company.

Chakravarty, L. N., 1973, *Glimpses of the Early History of Arunachal Pradesh*, Shillong: Arunachal Pradesh Administration.

Chandra, Bipan, 1989, *India's Struggle for Independence*, New Delhi: Penguin.

Chatterjee, Subid, 1991, *Comprehensive History of Arunachal Pradesh*, Calcutta: Rina Chatterjee.

Chatterjee, Suhas, 1985, *Mizoram Under British Rule*, Delhi: Mittal Publications.

Chattopadhya, K. L. (ed.), 1972, *Slavery in British Dominion*, Calcutta: Jijnasa.

Clarke, R., 1854, *The Regulations of the Government of Fort William in Bengal 1793–1853*, London: J & H Cox.

Downs, F. S., 1983, *Christianity in North East India*, Guwahati: Indian Society for Promoting Christian Knowledge.

Downs, F. S., 1971, *The Mighty Works of God*, Guwahati: Christian Literature Centre.

Dutta, A. K., 2002, *Indian Railways The Final Frontier*, New Delhi: North East Frontier Railway.

Dutta, K. N., 1969, *Landmarks in the Freedom Struggle in Assam*, Guwahati: Lawyers Book Stall.

Forbes, Geraldine, 2004, *Women in Modern India*, (Third reprint), Cambridge: Cambridge University Press.

Gait, E. A., 1963, *A History of Assam*, (Third edition), Calcutta: Thacker, Spink and Co.

Ganguly, J. B., 2006, *An Economic History of North East India*, New Delhi: Akansha Publishing House.

Gawthrop, W. R., 1951, *The Story of the Assam Railways and Trading Company, 1881–1951*, London: Harley Publishing Co.

Geetha, V., 2002, *Gender*, Calcutta: Stree.

Goswami Prafulladutta (ed.), 1982, *Kamalakanta Bhattacharyar Rasanavali*, Guwahati: Gauhati University.

Goswami, P. C., 1963, *The Economic Development of Assam*, Bombay: Asia Publishing House.

Goswami, Priyam, 1999, *Assam in the Nineteenth Century: Industrialization and Colonial Penetration*, Guwahati: Spectrum Publications.

Goswami, Priyam, 2003, *Nationalism in the Brahmaputra Valley: Economic Background*, Kolkata: Azad Institute Paper 20.

Goswami, S., 1987, *Aspects of Revenue Administration in Assam*, Delhi: Mittal Publications.

Griffiths, Percival, 1967, *The History of the Indian Tea Industry*, London: Weidenfeld & Nicholson.

Guha, Amalendu, 1977, *Planter-Raj to Swaraj: Freedom Struggle and Electoral Politics in Assam 1826–1947*, New Delhi: People's Publishing House.

Guha, Amalendu, 1991, *Medieval and Early Colonial Assam: Society, Polity,Economy*, Calcutta: K. P. Bagchi & Co.

Gurdon, P. R. T., 1987, *The Khasis*, (Reprint), New Delhi: Cosmo Publications.

Imperial Gazetteer of India (Eastern Bengal and Assam), 1908, Calcutta: Clarendon Press.

Jenks, L. M., 1963, *The Migration of British Capital to 1875*, London: Nelson.

Kar, P. C., 1970, *British Annexation of Garo Hills*, Calcutta: Navabharat Publishers.

Knowles, L. C. A., 2006, *The Industrial and Commercial Revolutions in Great Britain during the Nineteenth Century*, (Reprint), Oxon: Routledge.

Lahiri, R. M., 1954, *The Annexation of Assam*, Calcutta: General Printers and Publishers.

Lamb, A., 1960, *Britain and Chinese Central Asia: A Road to Lhasa*, London: Routledge & Paul.

Mackenzie, A., 1884, *A History of the Relations of the Government with the Hill Tribes of the North East Frontier of Bengal*, Calcutta: Home Department Press.

Majumdar, R. C., 1963, *History of the Freedom Movement in India*, Vol. III, Calcutta: Firma KLM.

Majumdar, R. C., (ed.), 1963, British Paramountcy and Indian Renaissance, Part I, Bombay: Bhartiya Vidya Bhavan.

Medhi, S. B., 1978, *Transport System and Economic Development in Assam*, Guwahati: Assam Publication Board.

Menon,V. P, 1999, *The Transfer of Power in India*, (Reprint) Chennai: Orient Longman.

Misra, T., 1987, *Literature and Society in Assam*, Guwahati: Omsons Publications.

Myrdal, G., 1972, *Asian Drama*, London: Pantheon Books.

Neog, Mahesswar, 1977, *Anandaram Dhekial Phukan: Plea for Assam and Assamese*, Jorhat: Assam Sahitya Sabha.

Neog, Maheswar, 1983, (compiled and re-edited) *Orunodoi*, Guwahati: Assam Publication Board.

Phillips, C. H., 1940, *The East India Company 1784–1934*, Manchester; The University Press.

Reid, Robert, 1983, *History of the Frontier Areas Bordering on Assam from 1883–1941*, (Reprint), Guwahati: Eastern Publishing House.

Robinson, W., 1975, *A Descriptive Account of Assam*, (Reprint), Calcutta: Sanskrit Prakashak.

Roy, J., 1973, *History of Manipur*, Manipur: East Light Bookhouse.

Roychoudhury, N. R., 1983, *Tripura through the Ages*, New Delhi: Sterling Publishers.

Saikia, Arupjyoti, 2002, compiled and re-edited, *Orunodoi*, Nagaon.

Sarma, A. K.(ed), *Benudhar Sharma Rachanawali*, Vol. .IV, 'Tokora Bahor Koota', Guwahati, 1987.

Sema, Piketo, 1992, *British Policy and Administration in Nagaland: 1881–1947*, Delhi: Scholar Publishing House.

Shakespear, L. W., 1980, *History of the Assam Rifles*, (Reprint), Guwahati: Spectrum Publishers.

Sharma, Dipti, 1993, *Assamese Women in the Freedom Struggle*, Calcutta: Punthi-Pustak.

Singh, J. P., 1989, *Monetary Development in Early Assam*, Jorhat:

Singh, R. K., 1966, *A Short History of Manipur*, Imphal:

Sinha, N. K., 1970, *The Economic History of Bengal, 1773–1848*, Vol. II, Calcutta: Firma KLM.

Syiemlieh, D. R., 1986, 'British Policy Towards the Khasis' in J. B. Bhattacharjee (ed.), *Studies in the History of North East India*, Shillong.

———, 1989, *British Administration in Meghalaya*, New Delhi: Heritage Publishers.

Tarachand, 1972, *History of the Freedom Movement in India*, Vol. IV, Delhi: Government of India.

Tarachand, 1972, *History of the Freedom Movement in India*, Vol. III, Delhi: Government of India.

Tendulkar, D. G., 1969, *Mahatma, Life of Mohandas Karamchand Gandhi*, New Delhi: Publications Dision, Ministry of I & B.

Vinacke, H. M., 1971, *A History of the Far East in Modern Times*, (Reprint), London: G. Allen & Unwin.

Woodman, Dorothy, 1969, *Himalayan Frontiers: A Political Review of British, Chinese, Indian and Russian Rivalries*, London: Praeger.

Woodthorpe, R. G., 1978, *The Lushai Expedition 1871–72*, (Reprint) Calcutta: Firma KLM.

ARTICLES

Barpujari, H. K., ' The History of Higher Education in Assam (1826–1900)', *The Golden Jubilee Volume*, Cotton College, Guwahati, 1952.

Bhattacharjee, J. B., 'The Genesis and the Pattern of British Administration in the Hill Areas of North East India', *Proceedings of the Indian History Congress*, Aligarh, 1975

Goswami, Priyam, 'Question of Subletting: Henry Cotton and Public Associations of Assam', *Proceedings of North East India History Association*, 22nd session, Tezpur, 2002.

Rogers, T. E., 'Coal Beds on Namsang Naga Hills', *J.A.S.B.*, June 1848, Vol. XVII.

Wilcox, R., 'Memoir of a Survey of Assam and the Neighbouring Countries Executed in 1825–26–27–28', *Asiatic Researches*, 1832, Vol. XVII.

Index